Reflections on a Politically Skeptical Era

Reflections on a Politically Skeptical Era

Dennis H. Wrong

Transaction Publishers
New Brunswick (U.S.A.) and London (U.K.)

This book is printed on acid-free paper that meets the American National Standard for Permanence of Paper for Printed Library Materials.

Library of Congress Catalog Number: 2003054134
ISBN: 0-7658-0195-7
Printed in the United States of America

Library of Congress Cataloging-in-Publication Data

Wrong, Dennis Hume, 1923-
Reflections on a politically skeptical era / Dennis H. Wrong.
p. cm.
Includes bibliographical references and index.
ISBN 0-7658-0195-7 (alk. paper)
1. Political sociology. 2. Political science. I. Title.

JA76.W76 2003
306.2—dc21 2003054134

Contents

Acknowledgements

Chapter 1. "Reflections on the Death of Socialism: Changing Perceptions of State and Society," *Theory and Society,* 29 (April 2000), 175-185.

Chapter 2. "Is Capitalism Eternal?" forthcoming in *Critical Review,* 15/3 (Fall 2003).

Chapter 3. "Inequality and the Division of Labor: the Davis-Moore Theory Re-examined," *European Journal of Sociology,* 40 (1999), 233-256.

Chapter 4. "Economy and Society: The Future," *American Journal of Economics and Sociology,* 59 (January 2000), 57-60.

Chapter 5. "What is Left of the Left?" *Sociological Forum,* 17 (September 2002), 537-543.

Chapter 6. "Adversarial identities and Multiculturalism," *Society, 37* (January/February 2000), 10-14.

Chapter 7. "Diversity: Catchword and Reality," *Hedgehog Review,* (Spring 2001), 7-23.

Chapter 8. "Conscience and Culture: the 'Moral Sense' and Cultural Relativism," expanded version of "Conscience and Culture," *Dissent,* 42 (Winter 1999), 127-130, including unpublished paragraphs.

Chapter 9. "Communitarianism, Human Nature, and the Spirit of the Times," in Edward W. Lehman, editor, *Autonomy and Order,* Lanham, MD: Rowman and Littlefield, 2000, 23-36.

Chapter 10. "The Apolitics of Community (in an Era Without Politics)," The *Responsive Community*, 9 (Winter 1998/1999), 32-37.

Chapter 11. "Putting Putnam's Thesis in its Place," *The Responsive Community,* 11 (Winter2000/2001), 69-72.

Chapter 13. "The Postmodernist Shuffle," *American Sociologist,* 27 (Fall 1996), 98-102.

Chapter 14. "Raymond Aron," *Contemporary Sociology,* 24 (March 1995), 162-164.

Chapter 15. "C. Wright Mills Recalled," *Society,* 32 (September/ October 2001), 61-64.

Chapter 16. "Digby Baltzell: Sociologist and Critical Celebrant of the Upper Class," *Sociological Theory,* 17 (March 1999), 112-116.

Chapter 17. "Etzioni, Socio-Economics, and Human Nature," forthcoming in volume on Etzioni's work, edited by Edward W. Lehman, (2003).

Chapter 20. "Fated to be a Professor?" *American Sociologist,* 29 (Spring 1998), 7-15.

Introduction

All of the essays included in the present collection, my third, were written between 1995 and 2001. I originally thought of borrowing the title of one of them for the whole book, calling it "reflections on an apolitical era." However, I eventually decided that that title seemed to downgrade the reality and importance of the "normal" political differences that still divide political parties and citizens in democratic nations that I had no wish to appear to minimize. My generation, reaching adolescence before the Second World War, was doubtless too disposed to believe that politics fundamentally consisted of clashes between totalistic worldviews—communism or socialism versus capitalism, fascism or communism versus democracy, even nationalism versus internationalism. The two opening essays here on "the death of socialism" and the likely "eternal" survival of capitalism certainly reflect this disposition as do several others included in the book. But the era when political ideologies amounted virtually to "secular religions" may well have been a historically transitory one, or so one today has reason to hope. Hence my eventual preference for "politically skeptical" over "apolitical," which, while still suggestive of the decline of political faith, is less categorical in emphasis. The collapse of the Soviet bloc in 1989-91 marks a useful chronological dividing line between the old and new eras of thinking about political differences.

"Multiculturalism and identity politics" as well as the "communitarianism" countering them were all perspectives possessing some, not necessarily primary, political implications that emerged and flourished in the 1990s. I have therefore grouped under these headings those essays of mine that directly or indirectly deal with these themes. The fourth section is more heterogeneous since with the exception of its first chapter (12 in the book) it discusses five quite different individual thinkers. Two of them, Aron and Mills, clearly belong to the earlier age of ideological conflict. Both of them were major influences on me, though, as the title of my first essay collection *Skeptical Sociology* suggests, my outlook was closer to Aron's despite not having known him personally. Charles Lemert, my major exemplar of "postmodernism" in the second essay in this section, and Amitai Etzioni clearly write on themes resonant of the more recent period. Digby Baltzell, unlike the others, was less a theorist than a chronicler, critic, and defender of the Eastern American upper class into which he had been born; I place the treatment of him here only because it deals with an individual writer.

The fifth and last section consists of autobiographical reports. The piece on the Rosenbergs and McCarthyism was presented last year on a panel at the New School for Social Research in New York City whose other members were the authors of the three recent books it discusses. Since Communism viewed in retrospect is its major topic, it might have been included in the first section, but I placed it here because it deals mainly with my ownremembered experiences of the subject and the time. A few paragraphs from "Fated to be a Professor?" were included in the autobiographical memoir in my second essay collection, *The Modern Condition.* This is the only duplicated material in the present volume.

As was true of my two earlier collections, not quite half of the present essays were published in academic sociological journals, one in a journal of philosophy. I should at least like to think that these were as readily accessible to potential readers as the essays that appeared in periodicals aimed at a more general readership, most of them mainly concerned with politics and public affairs. The longest essay here, the third in the book, is the most "academic" in tone, approach, and citations: its subject has always been a primary one for sociology. Yet analysis of class and social inequality has also been *par excellence* a sociological topic of wide general interest. Two of the essays here are from anthologies edited by my friend and former NYU colleague, Edward W. Lehman, and were originally presented at conferences he had organized.

My recollection in the autobiographical section of a racial episode is previously unpublished; the essay on cultural relativism (chapter 8) includes unpublished material that was cut by editors who chose to print it as a shorter book review of the major author discussed in it. All of my writings except for an early brief text on demography and my reprinted demographic doctoral dissertation have drawn on fairly wide political, sociological, and literary sources, including my two books *Power: Its Forms, Bases and Uses (1979)* and *The Problem of Order: What Unites and Divides Society* (1994). They reflect, or so at least I should like to think, the influence on me of the so-called New York intellectuals and their journals, which was at least as great as that of my academic education at the University of Toronto and Columbia.

Note

1. As early as 1957 Judith N. Shklar used "The Decline of Political Faith" as the subtitle of her book *After Utopia* (Princeton, NJ: Princeton University Press, 1957).

Part 1

Capitalism: Inequalities and Alternatives

1

Reflections on the Death of Socialism: Changing Perceptions of the State/Society Line

The separate social sciences emerged in the nineteenth century out of a recognition of the distinction between the state and society. This distinction has never been an absolute one and has always been phrased in a number of different ways; public/private, politics/economics, state/market, law-legal order/mores-moral or normative order, and most sweepingly collectivist/individualist in the contrast between socialism and capitalism. Conceptually, it has provided the basis for the differentiation of the social sciences as academic disciplines. Economics, primarily concerned with the workings of the market, was originally called "political economy." "Political science," "public law and government," "politics," and simply "government" are different departmental names in American universities for the same discipline studying the state as an institutional complex and politics as competing efforts to control or influence it, the first being much the most common. "Sociology" has often been defined as the study of "civil society," identified since the early nineteenth century with those areas of social life distinct and separate from the state. Sociology has also been described more invidiously as "the science of leftovers," consisting of areas that had not been preempted by economics, political science, and law. Civil society includes in its scope the market economy, but by the end of the last century "sociology" had become identified with social life apart from both the economy and the state, particularly by Durkheim and his followers in France.

Through the greater part of the twentieth century, the state/society distinction has been more than merely conceptual, for efforts to limit and even eliminate the dominance of the market by state intervention have been a major theme of the politics of democracies, the very source of the "left/right" division itself. At the opposite pole from anarchism as a doctrine and ideology but also projecting the nearly total dissolution of the division between state and society, has been the notion of "totalitarianism"—more important as a concept than as a political goal, [1] let alone a fully achieved reality—defined as the absorption of the traditional state and the penetration of the whole of social life by a hierarchically organized political-ideological movement claiming to represent "the masses." [2] Both major forms of totalitarianism called themselves "socialist," but socialism in its original nineteenth-century form was conceived of as the subordination of the state and politics to the "social question," that is, to the conflicts and sufferings arising out of the class inequalities produced by laissez-faire capitalism. In a different, less determinate way, democracy based on universal suffrage has also represented the subordination of the state to the collective aims and interests of society as composed of the underlying enfranchised population.

The Death of Socialism

The collapse of Communism at the beginning of the last decade of the present century has capped the perception of a reversal in the increasing interpenetration of state and society so long considered the major direction of social change in the advanced societies, although the process of reversal began earlier with policies of economic "privatization" and restriction if not reduction in the scope of the welfare state. Most socialists in the Western capitalist democracies at least since the 1950s disavowed the Soviet model as a true embodiment of socialism because of its authoritarian, not to say totalitarian, character. Accordingly, a few Western socialists have argued that the collapse of Communism should actually strengthen socialism by finally ridding it of identification with the Soviet model and its replicas. But this view savors of wish fulfillment and is not free of disingenuousness. Although most socialists in the West indeed rejected the Soviet Union after Nikita Khrushchev's speech denouncing Stalin and Soviet armed suppression of revolts in Hungary and Czechoslovakia, some of them subsequently cherished illusions about Third World revolutionary socialist regimes such as Mao's China, Castro's Cuba, Vietnam, and Nicaragua. Although the first three of these, and North Korea as well, remain under Communist rule, they too have disillusioned their erstwhile foreign supporters by suppressing or driving into exile all opposition, failing to match the economic performance of capitalist countries including the Far Eastern nations that have achieved successful transitions to advanced capitalism, and introducing major features of capitalist market economies into their own societies in response to this failure.

History is cruel. Despite the authentically democratic and egalitarian credentials of most Western socialists, the economic failures of the Communist states that not long ago included a third of the world's population are likely to prove permanently devastating to the future of socialism as an ideal. For socialism was always first and foremost a proposal for the economic reorganization of society, a new "mode of production" promising greater equality in conjunction with material abundance while maintaining a steady pace of economic growth and technical progress. The collapse of Communism and the full revelation of its sorry and brutal record have destroyed the credibility of this aspiration. In 1919 Max Weber predicted to Joseph Schumpeter that the Bolshevik Revolution would produce "a mound of corpses" and wrote to Gyorgy Lukàcs that it would discredit socialism for a hundred years. These may well be the most accurate specific historical predictions ever made by a major sociologist, although Weber misjudged future Russian history in predicting, as did the later followers of Leon Trotsky, that Bolshevism would be replaced by military dictatorship, or what the Trotskyists chose to call "Bonapartism."

Socialism as an ideal "alternative society" standing in sharp contrast to the image of capitalism as a bleak unchanging order of exploitation, inequality, and meretricious glitter has probably been irreparably damaged. It may be that utopian dreams of a perfect society cleansed of all evil and suffering are ineradicably rooted in human consciousness, although so are anti-utopian sentiments as we were memorably reminded by Dostoevsky in *Notes from Underground.* But socialism purported to be more than a mere universal dream of eternal peace, prosperity, and freedom: it was represented as a concretely definable and attainable way of organizing society toward which history itself was moving. Today not only has the notion of socialism as the progressive direction of history lost credibility, but so has the viability of such an order itself under contemporary conditions of technical progress and economic globalization.

The loss of belief in socialism is comparable to the "death of God" to the many secular intellectuals for whom it had often served for a century and a half as a surrogate for religious beliefs. It was seen in the words of Agnes Heller and Ferenc Feher as "a brand-new society which was to be the absolute negation of everything that had existed, the total transcendence of the modern world." [3] In the absence of faith in this ultimate utopian destination, politics now assumes for old socialists a flat one-dimensional character just as for former religious believers dispossessed of their faith the world became a lesser and drearier place, as expressed in Matthew Arnold's great poem "Dover Beach." Yet whatever the utopian expectations aroused by the prospect of a socialist future, socialist movements have also favored limited specific reforms demanded for their own sake quite apart from whether or not they were envisaged as steps toward a glorious transformed future. Despite its considerable material progress, capitalism continues to display much of the instability and inequality that originally gave rise to socialism in protest. Parties of the left will continue to advocate social democratic reforms and will doubtless register successes in the future. Pressures for such reforms directed toward the alleviation of poverty, the reduction of gross inequalities, and rectification of the failure of the market to protect large numbers of citizens from its sudden unforeseen gyrations remain. They will doubtless survive as political demands though dissociated from the idea of socialism as the name for an ultimate ideal goal. The death of socialism also spells the end of regarding "capitalism" as the sole or major defining feature of advanced or postindustrial societies from which the other major features of their culture and social structure are held to derive. Yet its death by no means implies the end of tension between political demands for state action and the degree of autonomy granted to "market forces."

Capitalism and the Market

There was always an asymmetry between "socialism" as an ideal or goal and "capitalism" as what we've got, the established order of things imperfect and unjust though it may be. Capitalism has been primarily a condition, not a theory or a historical project. It came into being over a long period of time as a complex of "unintended consequences:" The "invisible hand" of the market then institutionalized it as a permanent realm of unintended and unforeseeable consequences, which is both its strength and the cause of its vulnerability to sudden change and crisis. In this sense, a market economy is like a game: a game is defined and governed by a fixed set of rules, but the outcome of each and every playing of the game, who wins and loses as well as its unique sequence of events or moves, are indeterminate. This is precisely what accounts for the fascination of recreational games and, of course, for the emergence of "game theory" as a field of economics. That market outcomes are unintended and unforeseen is what constitutes the "planlessness" and "anarchy" of capitalism denounced by Marx. Yet the rules under which the market operates, enacted statutory laws or Durkheim's "noncontractual conditions of contract," are subject to change by human decision well short of the total substitution of plan for market projected by socialism.

I had the fortune, or perhaps misfortune, to be exposed way back in the 1950s to the forceful arguments of a number of young followers of Milton Friedman before his views became so influential among so-called "conservatives." Those of us who more or less took for granted the enlightenment of the social democratic intervention by the state that prevailed in the wake of the Depression and the immediate postwar era of reform, the Keynesian-welfare state consensus as it has been called, were taken aback by the near-anarchism of Friedmanite readiness to assign nearly all social tasks to the market. We spluttered with indignation at the very idea that Algonquin Park (this was in Canada) should be carved up and sold to private cottagers, and rhetorically queried "how reactionary can you get?" to the suggestion of reliance on "condottieri" by contracting national defense out to mercenaries. Little did we think that such views would become as resonant as they have in recent decades.

I did grasp from these exchanges, and partly learn to respect, the fascinated admiration that academic economists and their epigoni have for the workings of the "market mechanism." A free pricing system is indeed, as Adam Smith was the first clearly to recognize, a remarkably ingenious way of adjusting to the inevitable uncertainties of production and consumer demand. In addition to its game-like character in producing beneficial unintended and unforeseen consequences to which I have already referred, the free market by decentralizing economic decision-making eliminates a hierarchical chain of command and to that extent is potentially "democratic." My adversaries in those arguments of over forty years ago were always, a bit demagogically one thought, trumping arguments for state planning and regulation by triumphantly invoking "consumer sovereignty." The old socialist answer, still entirely relevant, is that under existing conditions it is a sovereignty of money, of the basic units of currency not of individual human beings, and that income composed of these units is unequally distributed. Moreover, since the market itself produces winners and losers and under capitalism presupposes the existence both of powerful private decision-makers and relatively powerless individual employees and consumers, inequality is built into a market economy.

It was a mistake on the part of the socialist movement and, certainly, of Soviet-style communist regimes with their rigid centralized command economies, to hate and fear market forces. The Communist states produced even greater inequalities, notably in political power. The conclusion is that while the possibility of a totally egalitarian society possessing advanced technology, the complex division of labor that goes with it, and a relatively free labor market is indeed utopian—on this Kingsley Davis and Wilbert Moore were right in their famous, or infamous, article, if too sweeping and abstract [4]—the state can and should set the noncontractual limits within which the market operates, including the reduction of the extreme inequalities it is prone to generate.

"Capitalism" is a term that has always tended to be pejoratively used, most notably, of course, by Marxists. The substitution for it of "market economy" is not merely a euphemism like the "free enterprise system," but a tacit recognition that "the market" is a superior "mechanism," as it is often called, for economic production and distribution. But such recognition need not imply that all necessary collective tasks can be carried out through markets, or that even economic production and distribution in the narrow sense preclude intervention by the state in the market situation, starting modestly with but going beyond Durkheim's famous "noncontractual element in contract." Politics and political divisions over how and where the state/market line should be drawn continue and remain the main content of political division in democratic countries including the United States.

The Concept of Civil Society

The affirmation of a "civil society" independent of the state stressed by dissenters from Communism has had a resonance in politics and social science beyond Eastern Europe, but it need not be identified primarily with the autonomy of the market. The superiority of the market over centralized command economies in producing economic growth is now universally acknowledged. But there remain real questions as to whether ceaseless economic growth is desirable, whether there may not be such a thing as the saturation of consumer demand, and whether there is not a need for what one writer has called the "reinvention of politics"[5] to cope with both the underemployment resulting from limited demand and still unresolved social problems that lend themselves to possible political solution. There was a certain pathos in the disposition in Russia and Eastern Europe, now waning, to believe that market economies could be introduced from the top down and would quickly produce standards of living comparable to the capitalist democracies of the West. Despite the element of paradox in believing it possible to create a functioning decentralized economy from the state as center, the Marxism-Leninism imposed on these nations in the past appears to have promoted the kind of totalist ideological thinking that expects enormous consequences for better or worse from the adoption of what is regarded as a different "social system."

The recent fashionable invocation of the concept of civil society by sociologists shows insufficient confidence in their own tradition, granting that Eastern European dissidents had good reason to use it to turn against itself the overall Marxist orthodoxy in which they had been compulsorily indoctrinated. "Society," assumed to be independent of the state, sufficiently identifies the very subject matter of sociology and the prefix "civil" adds nothing to conventional sociological conceptualization. The later sociology of the "classics" also differentiated society from economy. Civil society need not be equated with the market, as in the Marxist usage borrowed from Hegel. The concept of society *tout court* in traditional sociology has been invoked against excessive economism, neoclassical or Marxist, as much as against primary emphasis on the state, as by Durkheim and Parsons in search of a disciplinary mandate for sociology. More recently, Alvin Gouldner in *The Two Marxisms* equated civil society with "a form of human 'connectedness,' something quite apart from the differentiated political or economic specialization this connectedness may develop." He went on to identify the study of it as "sociology's object and historical mission."[6]

Recent uses of the concept are associated with the distinction from the state that dates back to Hegel and took a different form in the emerging sociological perspective that eschewed any "Prussian" conception of the state's normative superiority. I have long favored a formulation of the original sociological outlook that defines it as asserting the historical, causal, and normative priority of society over the state. But earlier uses of the concept "civil society" by Hobbes, Locke, Montesquieu, and Rousseau, as well as by the philosophers of the Scottish Enlightenment, identified it with a stable and peaceful society subject to the rule of law. As this suggests, they did not see society as something entirely independent of the state. There is, however, a strong continuity between the earlier uses that contrasted civil society with tyranny or despotism, the Hegel-Marx usage that treats civil society as "base" and the state as "superstructure," and the later sociological conception. Even Hobbes, for whom the creation of a supreme political authority necessarily preceded and made possible the very existence of social relations not reducible to the "command of the sovereign," thought that all sorts of autonomous cooperative human projects came into being once the creation of the state removed the constant fear of violent death at the hands of others.[7]

The Politics of Democracy

Recognition of the state/society distinction is inherent in political democracy based on universal suffrage coexisting with persistent social and economic inequalities. With equality of voting power—one person-one vote—and governments chosen by aggregated votes, majorities or pluralities, organization into political parties competing electorally, including the organization of less privileged groups, becomes more or less inevitable. The less privileged groups are bound to seek help from the state to redress the inequalities and insecurities from which they suffer. Their political demands, therefore, are likely to be for institutional reforms reducing inequality and insecurity. Privileged groups also, of course, use government to protect and preserve their privileges, but since they already possess them in partial independence from government, chiefly through the operation of the market, they are less likely to favor state action initiating far-reaching changes. This distinction between parties and movements appealing to the relatively less privileged and to the relatively privileged, the former seeking reforms in the direction of greater equality, the latter resisting such reforms, is the basis of the "left-right" dichotomy dating back to the French Revolution.

The old Sombart question "Why is there no socialism in the United States?" no longer has much relevance, though I feel I have been listening to efforts to answer it for most of my life and to suggestions as to how the conditions described in the answer might be overcome. The question never seemed to me to have the significance it was widely thought to have had in focusing on the absence in the U.S. of a nominally "socialist" major political party drawing its support primarily from the working class. The American system of government based on an obsolete but idealized eighteenth-century constitution seemed to me a much greater obstacle to the achievement of a European-style welfare state, let alone "socialism" as a new alternative society, than whether or not there was a political party unambiguously espousing such goals. Even if there had been, if Debs's Socialist party had supplanted the Democratic party in the 1920s as Labour did the Liberals in Britain, I doubt that it would have made much difference in practical politics. Yet anti-statism as a deeply ingrained American attitude remains a staple of the party representing the relative beneficiaries of inequality and has received a new breath of life from the fiscal difficulties plaguing the welfare state, difficulties that are not confined to the U.S. and are independent of the collapse of Communism and the end of the Cold War. Perhaps a more important question than Sombart's would be "why is there no strong tradition of Tory or Bismarckian paternalism in the United States?" The need to overcome the current fiscal difficulties and, most of all, to modify the political outlook that wins supporters by exaggerating them, is certainly the main obstacle faced today by liberals or "progressives" in the Democratic party who do not want to abandon the heritage of the New Deal and the Great Society.

Management of the economy has become the major content of political contestation in the capitalist democracies, the more conservative party often winning support by claiming to promote greater economic growth: The notion that economic growth is the key to alleviating inequality because in the cliché "a rising tide raises all boats" is subject to challenge on the grounds that present economic circumstances are quite different from those of the 1950s and 1960s when growth rates unlikely to ever be matched were achieved. Not only is such economic growth improbable, a strong case can be made that it would be undesirable. Do we really want ceaseless economic growth? The case made for it is usually that it would create jobs at good wages and dissolve the unemployed underclass and the insecurities of the employed working and middle classes. But this is putting the cart of jobs before the horse of the consumer demand the jobs presumably serve. That modern hi-tech technology does not necessarily sustain a full employment economy is a prospect we are going to have to face: in the long-run, dependence on what is now stigmatized as "welfare" may be the future for most of us in modern societies. But that prospect is still remote, especially with mass attitudes still valuing work over dependence and leisure. In the meantime, there is ample opportunity for the state to become the "employer of last resort" and plenty of work for idle hands in rebuilding the country's decaying material infrastructure, a revival of New Deal programs like WPA, CCC, and TVA. Alas, the prospect of this looks in the present political climate almost as remote and utopian as abolition of the need for gainful employment. Predictions of a massive left populist revolt have been around since the 1970s without materializing.

For the foreseeable future, the tension between state and market is likely to remain the central content of politics along with the left-right division of the "body politic" that gives rise to most issues and to the parties and movements promoting them. The most credible case I have seen for what he calls the "reinvention of politics" has been made by Ulrich Beck, envisaging permanent demilitarization with the end of the Cold War, an end to high economic growth as a result of the crisis of the environment, the dissolution of classes combined with the persistence of considerable inequality (something I discerned as a trend way back in 1964),[8] the decline of the nation-state under economic and cultural globalization, and the emergence of a politics "beyond left and right," as these poles have been traditionally been understood. Anthony Giddens has speculated along the same lines in several recent books. Beck also, however, takes note of the end of the Cold War permitting a revival of what he calls, inappropriately I think, forces of "countermodernization:" the resurgence of ethnic, nationalist, and religious fundamentalist movements and fratricidal conflicts between them.[9] But he thinks these will prove transitory. We shall see.

In the meantime, a politics based on dispute over the boundaries between state and market remains central, if many of the terms in which it has been fought out in the past now seem obsolete.

Acknowledgements

This article was originally presented as a paper at the tenth annual meeting of the Society for the Advancement of Socio-Economics (SASE), Vienna, Austria, July, 1998.

Notes

1. Though it was stated as a goal by Mussolini's court philosopher, Giovanni Gentile.
2. The first thoroughgoing description of totalitarianism thus conceived was Emil Lederer, *The State of the Masses*, (New York: W.W. Norton, 1940).
3. Agnes Heller and Ferenc Feher, "Does Socialism Have a Future?" *Dissent,* 36 (Summer 1989), 373.
4. See my article "Inequality and the Division of Labor: The Davis-Moore Theory Reexamined," *European Journal of Sociology,* 40 (1999): 233-256. (Chapter 3).
5. Ulrich Beck in Beck, Anthony Giddens, and Scott Lash, *Reflexive Modernization: Politics, Tradition, and Aesthetics in the Modern Social Order* (Stanford, CA: Stanford University Press, 1994), 3-55.
6. Alvin W. Gouldner, *The Two Marxisms* (New York: The Seabury Press, 1980), 357.
7. In the most famous paragraph of *Leviathan,* Hobbes begins by listing the things that are absent "where every man is Enemy to every man," including "Industry...Culture of the Earth...commodious Building...Knowledge of the face of the Earth...Arts...Letters..." all of them activities that contemporary social scientists would include under the general rubrics of "culture" and "social structure." (Harmondsworth, Middlesex, UK: Penguin Books, 1968), 186.
8. "Social Inequality without Social Stratification," *Canadian Review of Sociology and Anthropology,* 1 (February 1964), 5-16. Reprinted in Dennis H. Wrong, *Skeptical* Sociology, New York: Columbia University Press, 1976, reissued as *The Oversocialized Conception of Man* (New Brunswick, NJ: Transaction Publishers, 1999), 12 1-134.
9. Beck, 43-44.

2

Is Capitalism Eternal?

On several recent occasions when speaking to largely intellectual and academic audiences, I have cited Ernest Gellner who wrote that "Capitalism differs from God in one important respect: where it does not exist, no one will bother to invent it." The quotation has invariably been greeted with appreciative laughter. It was evident to me that the laughter essentially stemmed from the assumption that capitalism was so flawed and undesirable that no one could possibly have wished for it, let alone intentionally brought it into existence. But this assumption was neither mine nor Gellner's, so to make that clear I have several times since added to Gellner's a remark of Fernand Braudel's to the effect that "The great thing about capitalism is that no one invented it." Capitalism, both scholars maintain, emerged "spontaneously" under a set of special historical conditions. It was not imposed by elites at the top of the social hierarchy to realize their articulated collective interests or ideological worldview despite ultimately producing a social hierarchy of its own, nor was it the creation of a social movement mobilizing people from below.

Braudel goes to considerable length to distinguish a market economy from capitalism, seeing the former as a much broader and virtually universal phenomenon in societies with populations larger than a few hundred persons living above subsistence level that have achieved a stable division of labor in production. If I had asked "are markets eternal?" the question would appear to have been framed to receive an affirmative answer. Adam Smith, after all, regarded "the propensity to truck, barter, and exchange one thing for another" as a universal human disposition and he was surely right to have done so in identifying the disposition with the distinctively human capacities for "reason and speech." The passage from *The Wealth of Nations* is often cited dismissively as evidence of Smith's supposed equation of capitalism with human nature as such, but he does no such thing, merely observing after the famous passage that uniquely human capacities make exchange possible whereas dogs do not exchange bones. The "free market," the "free" standing for relatively uncontrolled prices and unrestricted entry for both producers and consumers, Braudel argues, cannot be equated with "capitalism, " as is done both euphemistically by eulogists of capitalism and by anti-capitalists on occasion. Yet he argues in opposition to Karl Polanyi that even where prices are traditionally fixed or controlled by authorities the forces of supply and demand give them at least some variability.[1]

The use of "free market" and "market economy" with positive connotations, particularly common since the collapse of Communism, has led to it being favored even more widely than that old favorite "free enterprise," reflecting the fact that, as Braudel has remarked, the word "capitalism" has to the contrary always carried negative implications. The people who laughed at my quotation from Gellner evidently took this for granted. If market exchange has been a less than universal practice only because there have been small technologically primitive societies that have failed to produce a surplus over the means of subsistence sufficient to achieve even a modest degree of division of labor in production, it is scarcely hyperbolic or grossly ethnocentric to contend that markets at least are eternal. And clearly, even in today's world, as Robert Conquest has maintained with the frequently unfortunate post-Communist experience of Eastern Europe in mind, "The 'creation' of a market economy is…to a great extent a misleading context. Market economies have emerged rather than been decreed." [2] Sometimes it is precisely this fact that is deplored by critics: that markets are decentralized and produce unintended and unforeseen consequences rather than being creations of a unified collective will.

However, as I have already suggested in citing Gellner and Braudel, nor is capitalism a matter of invention or decree even though it connotes something more specific than the general human disposition to barter, the widespread existence of markets as institutions, or the universal, if often partial, influence of supply and demand insisted on by Braudel. Capitalism presupposes the existence of a market economy in which money is the major medium of exchange and goods are produced for sale by a plurality of individuals or groups owning their own means of production. Capitalism can properly be said to exist only when ownership is restricted to a minority and the non-owners survive by selling their labor, or rather labor power, to the owners who also own the proceeds of the sale of whatever the laborers produce. The existence of a market for labor and the sharp separation of the wages earned by the laborers from the proceeds or profits accruing to the owners from the sale of the product of labor is the definitive criterion of capitalism.

The response to the fall of the Berlin Wall of the magazine the *Nation*, which might unkindly be characterized as the foremost rearguard American journal of the sentimental left, was typical of many responses before and since in those circles. The collapse of the "actually existing socialisms" in Europe and the Soviet Union was not, an editorial insisted, "the funeral of socialism;" it should not be concluded that "this death of an epoch heralds a capitalist eternity." One continues just over a decade later to hear such faintly rueful defensive remarks even from people who never invested much hope in Soviet-style state socialism, sometimes rejecting it in the apparently oxymoronic description of it as "state capitalism," a term still invoked today to deny the relevance to any possible future socialism of the Soviet model's sorry past. No new version of a socialism that might amount to a genuine "alternative society" to capitalism has been promulgated, however, and affirmations that a socialist protest is still relevant or is bound yet to emerge amount to little more than complaints about the undeniable inequalities and insecurities that continue to exist in any and all capitalist societies. Socialism becomes no more than a label for an egalitarian utopia rather than standing for as it once did a more centralized and collectivist "mode of production" involving the abolition of "private" ownership and control of the means of production.

Political protests against the poverty, inequality, and cyclical instability apparently endemic to capitalism will certainly persist and even continue to play a central role in the politics of democratic capitalist countries. But the notion of a radically and totally distinct social order fundamentally shaped by some form of collective consensus on economic decisions is unlikely to be revived even if it makes a point of not advocating that the decision-making be centralized in the state as in the defunct state socialisms of the Soviet bloc and its Third World replicas. If capitalism is minimally defined as any economy in which many agents, whether individuals or groups, make independent decisions to produce particular goods and services for sale by means of the purchased labor of others, then in the absence of some total disaster returning humanity to the Stone Age capitalism is likely to last for a relative eternity.

This broad definition, it should be noted, does not clearly exclude what has been called "market socialism" in which the workers in addition to receiving wages participate through established assemblies or councils in the decision-making of the producing organization and receive a share of its profits. Such a version of socialism, eliminating the division between owners and non-owners while keeping economic decisions in a decentralized "private sector" may be both desirable and "feasible," as argued by the late Alec Nove in his *The Economics of Feasible Socialism.* [3] Under contemporary conditions, however, worker participation in management is likely to amount to little more than the ratification, subject to occasional debates and challenges, of the decisions made by a techno-bureaucratic hierarchy not all that different from those of existing capitalist enterprises. Moreover, the distinction between wages and distributed profits will remain, profits continuing to serve as the main criterion of a firm's efficiency.

The term "capitalism" was not widely used before modern times. "Capital" and "capitalist" had a much longer history, always referring to money, wealth, or their possessors, but they acquired their more specific modern meanings as, respectively, productive money and investor or entrepreneur only in the nineteenth century. Even Marx did not until late in his career use the term "capitalism" and then rarely. "In fact, it was not until the beginning of this century [the 20th], " Braudel writes, " that it fully burst upon political debate as the natural opposite of socialism."[4] This political ambience endowed it with negative overtones to a degree that it almost became what the Germans call a *Schimpfwort* ; as a result, scholars sometimes urged its abandonment, although no really adequate alternative has ever found its way into scholarly or common discourse. Yet it was critics of Marxism, namely, Sombart and Weber, who were primarily responsible for the diffusion of the term to describe an economic system with a marked impact on other spheres of social and cultural life transcending the narrowly economic.

The addition of "ism" to the previous use of "capital" to refer to money undoubtedly contributed to misleading connotations that still cling to the term capitalism. "Ism" is a suffix most commonly used to refer to comprehensive systems of belief or ideologies—socialism, communism, fascism—sometimes to more limited policies such as imperialism, isolationism, or pacifism. Critics of the rigidity and dogmatism with which they may be held and propounded often react by roundly repudiating and depreciating the very notion of "isms." To be sure, the "ism" suffix has also been applied to established socioeconomic systems, as in pastoralism, feudalism, or urbanism, and the idea of capitalism is entirely consistent with this usage. But its emergence as the "natural opposite" (Braudel) of socialism, which had at least until 1917 always been an ideal in the form of an unrealized historical project or political goal elaborated into a full-fledged ideology, encouraged the conception of capitalism as a rival ideology, or as an established order founded on an achieved ideological goal. This would imply that a "capital-*ist*" is a true believer in capitalism rather than an investor or entrepreneur. A lesser contribution to this equation of capitalism with a set of beliefs or designs may have been the works of Sombart and Weber which attributed at least the origins of capitalism to a distinctive spirit or *Geist* rooted in religious beliefs. This despite Weber's closing peroration in his most famous work where he clearly distinguished the putative origins of capitalism in the Protestant ethic from its self-reproducing existence once it had fully come into being several centuries later: "The Puritan wanted to work in a calling; we are forced to do so."

But it is the Cold War more than anything else that has in recent decades encouraged the identification of capitalism as an ideology in opposition to the official Marxist-Leninist creed of the Communist states. That the Cold War represented an inevitable ideological confrontation between "socialism" and "capitalism" was, of course, the official view promoted by the Soviet Union, echoed by its partisans in the West and by some segments of the wider left. According to Marxism-Leninism, both Nazi Germany and the United States as its successor were driven by the imperatives of capitalism to undertake a worldwide imperialist quest for markets and investment opportunities with the Soviet bloc alone standing in their way. Revisionist historians in the West adopted a qualified version of this view in explaining at least the origins of the Cold War as the result of an American interest in Central and Eastern Europe as a site for markets, investment, and the extraction of raw materials. These views have never been very credible. As Raymond Aron once observed, it is highly unlikely that the United States as the dominant power of the alliance that defeated Hitler would or could simply have turned its back once again on Europe acquiescing in the Soviet takeover of the very region in which Hitler's aggressions had precipitated the Second World War.

That the Cold War was primarily a conflict between "communism" and "anticommunism" has probably been the most common view of it. Yet the political definition of the conflict as pitting "democracy" against "totalitarianism" was the ideological version favored from the beginning by American governments, continuous with the conception of the Second World War as a crusade against fascism. Interpreters of international relations have tended to polarize between "Wilsonian idealists" for whom the Cold War was a defense of American and Western democratic principles and "realists" who saw it as simply a geopolitical struggle between great powers. The latter group included both conservatives who supported America in those terms and left-wing debunkers of so-called "Cold War ideology."

The policy of "containing" the expansion of the Soviet Union was indeed continuous with Western resistance in the 1930s and 1940s to the military aggressions of Germany, Italy, and Japan, all nations with capitalist economies. Supporters of the West in the Cold War were usually firm anti-Communists though not necessarily celebrants of capitalism since their number included socialists and social democrats; there were also anti-Communists, and certainly non-Communists, who opposed some or all American Cold War policies. Left-wing critics of the Cold War condemned American support for anti-Communist authoritarian regimes abroad, insisting at times on the "moral equivalence" of the United States and the Soviet Union, although they tended to remain silent about the earlier American alliance with the latter against Hitler in the Second World War. If such alliances refute any simplistic understanding of both conflicts as consistently ideological, the hard-headed, sometimes cynical view that *Realpolitik* is the whole story overlooks that resistance both to Hitler and the Soviet Union stemmed from opposition to suppression of the Wilsonian right to national "self-determination" by the threat or reality of military action and the need for international "collective security" to protect it. This amounted to a moral principle transcending mere great power geopolitical interests. Regarding the Soviet Union, the prime historian of the Cold War, John Lewis Gaddis, has noted of earlier claims that its leaders no longer truly believed in Marxism-Leninism except for propaganda purposes that "new sources suggest the need to reconsider, for they seem to suggest that ideology often *determined* the behavior of Marxist-Leninist regimes: it was not simply a justification for actions already decided upon."[5] His "new sources" are, of course, the now partially available Soviet archives.

Increased Russian power at the end of the Second World War inspired resistance by the United States and its European allies to its further expansion. This was clearly seen and stated at the time by such major architects of American foreign policy as Dean Acheson and George Kennan, neither of whom laid primary stress on the threat of Communism *per se.* That the expansionist drive of Soviet power was continuous with that of Czarist Russia was widely recognized. Marxist-Leninist ideology, to be sure, provided the Soviet Union with a worldwide international façade and appeal that made it seem to be an especially formidable adversary, an advantage not possessed by the Czars. At the same time, the values underlying the political systems of the United States and its European allies were hostile to militarism and the subordination of other peoples; to that extent democratic principle contributed to the resistance to both Fascist and Communist expansion at the expense of independent nations. Indeed democratic principle encouraged the final relinquishing after the Second World War of Western colonies originally established by military ascendancy. Yet the enormous superiority of American power in the non-Communist world often endowed it with at least the appearance of imperial domination, although, as Gaddis has argued, American involvements and interventions were always by the invitation of independent governments.[6] This was even true of the misbegotten intervention in Vietnam.

I have engaged in this brief, seemingly digressive, and arguably banal survey of views of the Cold War in order to underline that "capitalism versus socialism" or even anti-communism in and of itself distinct from the actions beyond their borders of Communist regimes made at most very minor contributions to the Cold War and its origins. Apart from Marxist-Leninists and a few Marxist and revisionist scholars in the West, none of the variant conceptions I have reviewed, including those attaching major importance to ideological differences, have accorded great causal significance either to the ideological defense or promotion of capitalism as such or to the advancement of particular capitalist interests. Quite sophisticated Marxists continue to reify capitalism as a world-historical actor capable of becoming the subject of active verbs and "globalization" has given them something of a new lease on life. A full decade "before the fall" in 1989-91 so radical a Marxist thinker as Herbert Marcuse foresaw the survival of capitalism for "a few centuries yet" as a result of its eventual expansion into Russia and China. One of his interviewers found this sufficiently depressing to exclaim "That is a justification for hitting the bottle."[7] "A few centuries" doubtless struck him as equivalent to an eternity though Marcuse also expressed his steadfast faith that capitalism was ultimately doomed by its internal contradictions without specifying at all what might replace it or what form future movements against it might take.

As one writer has concluded, "capitalism has been primarily a condition, not a theory or a historical project."[8] This is not to be understood as suggesting that capitalism is some sort of inescapable fatality like the weather or human mortality, nor the product of an historical evolutionary law that humans are incapable of modifying, nor that it is inexorably determined by its own historically specific "iron laws" as described by Marx.[9] Capitalism does possess a certain fatality inherent in its being first and foremost an economic system, the prevailing means of providing for the insistent recurrent material needs of human beings. This fatality is succinctly expressed in Marx's phrase "the dull compulsion of economic relationships."[10] If Marx's economics purporting to show that capitalism was doomed by its internal contradictions are today totally obsolete and his historical predictions have been falsified, he was nevertheless right to suggest that only the total collapse of capitalism as a result of the accumulation of its contradictions would result in its being supplanted through revolution by either a different system or by historical regression, by "socialism or barbarism" in his words. Marx was also prescient in foreseeing that the politics of capitalist societies would come to center on the demands of the new working class, although he mistakenly believed that these demands would assume a revolutionary rather than a moderately reformist character. As Michael Burawoy, a "late Marxist," aptly contends: "By struggling for immediate concessions, by compelling the state to limit exploitation, by improving its lot, however unevenly, the working class transforms itself from the *gravedigger* of the bourgeoisie [in Marx's forecast] into its *savior*."[11] Social democracy accordingly becomes the highest or at least latest form of capitalism.

Capitalism as a market economy in which goods and services are produced for sale by a plurality of individuals and groups owning their own means of production and employing the labor of others is at the very least a highly *probable* form of economy where there is a sizeable surplus of the means of subsistence, some concentration of the population in towns and cities, and the absence of centralized political power capable of penetrating and profoundly influencing economy and society. By the eighteenth century, these conditions may have fully existed only in Western Europe. Once the enormous productivity and technological creativity of capitalism had become manifest, it was bound to exercise a power of attraction on more static, politically controlled societies in Europe and Asia. Perhaps one should add the decentralization not only of production but of research and development promoting technological dynamism to the preconditions for capitalism. This would constitute what Bendix has called "intellectual mobilization," the creation of a periodical press, publishing houses, and, most importantly, universities as centers of research and education. Bendix sees intellectual mobilization as an autonomous process not reducible to the articulation of bourgeois class interests and as the main medium for influencing foreign societies.[12]

This account in no way precludes wide variation in the forms of capitalism, specifically in the mores and laws that ensure its peaceful functioning and in the kinds and degree of political intervention that limit, redirect, or complement it. If capitalism, short of some enormous historical disaster such as a nuclear war, is eternal in the sense that nothing is likely to replace it, this in no way implies the "end of history" or the survival forever of the major social problems and the grosser inequities it generates. All it precludes is the transition to some unimaginably different society in which economic life will be controlled by the collective consensus of the entire population.

Notes

1. Fernand Braudel, *The Wheels of Commerce: Civilization & Capitalism 15th-18th Century,* Volume3 (New York: Harper & Row), 1982, pp. 225-230.
2. Robert Conquest, *Reflections on a Ravaged Century* (New York: W.W. Norton, 2000), p. 190.
3. London: Allen & Unwin, 1979.
4. Braudel, p. 237.
5. John Lewis Gaddis, *What We Now Know: Rethinking Cold War History* (Oxford: Clarendon Press, 1997), p. 290.
6. Gaddis, pp. 284-289.
7. "Theory and Politics: A Discussion with Herbert Marcuse, Juergen Habermas, Heinz Lubasz, and Telman Spengler," *Telos,* 38, Winter 1978-79, p. 152.

8. Dennis H. Wrong, "Reflections on the Death of Socialism: Changing Perceptions of the State/Society Line," *Theory and Society,* 29/2, April 2000, p.178. (Chapter 1).
9. Alvin Gouldner argued that Marx was not a firm believer in universal unilinear evolutionary laws though thoroughly convinced that capitalism was subject to historically specific "iron laws." *The Two Marxisms* (New York: Seabury Press, 1979), pp. 228-229.
10. Nicholas Abercrombie, Stephen Hill, and Bryan S. Turner make much use of this phrase in their critique *The Dominant Ideology Thesis* (London: Allen & Unwin, 1980).
11. "Marxism after Communism," *Theory and Society*, 29/2, April 2000, p. 161.
12. Reinhard Bendix, *Kings or People: Power and the Mandate to Rule* (Berkeley and Los Angeles: University of California Press, 1978).

3

Inequality and the Division of Labor: The Davis-Moore Theory Reexamined

Moral and political contestation over social inequality has been a major issue since the French Revolution. It has also been a concern of social theory at least since Plato's *Republic* and most saliently since the publication of Rousseau's *Discourse on the Origins and Foundations of Inequality Among Men* (1755). The fullest general discussion of social inequality in recent sociological theory has been the debate of several decades ago over the Davis-Moore functional theory of stratification. Recent events in the world as well as developments within sociological theory have changed the context for assessing inequality in human society, its nature, causes, consequences, and whether, how, and how much it might be limited.

The historical event of major consequence has been the collapse in 1989-1991 of Communism, which claimed to have established a more egalitarian "classless" society. The collapse came as the culminating point of a gradual decline of belief in the feasibility of a markedly more egalitarian society traditionally labeled "socialist." That Communist societies had not achieved significantly greater levels of equality of condition or opportunity than existed under Western capitalism had become increasingly evident since the 1950s.[1] The gap between realities and proclaimed ideals played little part in their final collapse when contrasted with the aspirations to create "socialism with a human face" at the time of the Czechoslovakian revolt twenty years earlier. The failures and abandonment of state-directed economic development plans and the success of the East Asian "four tigers" in the Third World have also contributed to disenchantment with socialism (Berger 1986). Recognition that market economies are more productive than command economies and that they both presuppose and generate inequalities has become general, although there are still sharp political differences over the degree to which markets should be subject to regulation including measures aiming to moderate the inequalities they produce (Wrong 1998).

In social theory what has come to be known as "rational choice theory" has become influential in the social sciences. Essentially, it generalizes the utilitarian assumptions about human motivation in classical economics to wider areas of social action. This approach has acquired new credibility as a result of the "death of socialism" and general acknowledgement of free market capitalism as the most successful model for an economy based on advanced technology. The Davis-Moore theory was presented and criticized as a functionalist theory, but, as several of its critics discerned, its view of human conduct as competitive and impelled by self-interested desires for scarce material and psychic satisfactions was consistent with an economistic market model.

Davis and Moore argued for the functional necessity of a hierarchy of unequal occupations, that is, positions in the division of labor, but critics pointed out that they ignored the division of society into classes (see in particular Buckley 1958). Since they wrote, the condition described as "nonegalitarian classlessness" (Ossowski 1963) or "social inequality without social stratification" (Wrong 1964) has been more widely recognized by analysts of stratification who have maintained that "class analysis" is of diminishing value within sociology because of the partial or complete dissolution of classes as major social formations and collective actors (Clark and Lipset 1991; Kingston 1994; Pakulski and Waters 1996). This claim has been contested (Hout, Brooks, and Manza 1993; Marshall 1997), but it has clearly reduced the relevance of a major criticism of the Davis-Moore theory, as has been recognized by the most forceful proponents of the declining significance of classes (Pakulski and Waters: 38-40). The Davis-Moore model appeared to be vulnerable to the charge that it assumed that all societies approximated "meritocracy," a term later coined by Michael Young (1958). But both a fully realized meritocracy and the restriction of individual access to high positions by gender, race, and ethnicity (also ignored by Davis and Moore) might exist independently of well-marked class divisions as they have been usually understood and survive the dissolution of class society.

Over half a century has elapsed since Kingsley Davis and Wilbert Moore first maintained that social inequality was universal, necessary, and beneficial—"functional"—for human societies (Davis and Moore 1945). They reasoned that unequal material and psychic "rewards" were necessary to induce individuals to staff those positions in a social division of labor that required relatively scarce talents and skills to perform their duties and that possessed the greatest "functional importance" to society. Unequal rewards served as incentives to individuals to undergo the period of training and postponed rewards needed to acquire the skills, including in some cases the conversion of innate talents into skills, that would ensure adequate performance of the most important and demanding social roles. Their basic conclusion was that social inequality was "functionally necessary" to maintain a division of labor .

Eight years later Melvin Tumin challenged their argument, charging that they had ignored undesirable or "dysfunctional" effects of social inequality and that a far greater degree of equality than had yet been historically achieved was entirely possible (Tumin 1953). Tumin's article, published with a rejoinder by Davis, initiated a debate over the next decade in which several prominent sociologists participated. The majority were critical, several drawing responses from Davis or Moore. Most of the critics interpreted Davis and Moore's general argument for the inevitability of social inequality as a defense of existing inequalities in contemporary capitalist societies; they proceeded to deny that the theory described how individuals in fact achieved many or most of the more highly rewarded positions. Many of the critics, starting with Tumin, suggested alternative more egalitarian methods of recruiting the most able and conscientious individuals to fill the critical positions. In dwelling on possible substitutes for the Davis-Moore model of positional allocation, several clearly had egalitarian collectivist models in mind. The collapse of Soviet and Eastern European Communism has come as a climax to the decline in the credibility of these models as viable alternatives to a capitalist market economy, including hypothetical "utopian" models bearing little resemblance to Soviet-style state socialism.

The author of an obituary tribute to Kingsley Davis in the April 1997 issue of the ASA newsletter *Footnotes* commented that the "Davis-Moore Theory of Stratification" was both his best-known and his most controversial work (Scott 1997). The same had been said of the late Melvin Tumin's criticism of the theory. It may well have also been said of the late Wilbert Moore, Davis's original co-author, who made independent contributions to the debate. Yet each of these sociologists published well-received books and articles on a variety of subjects. I think they are so well remembered for the debate they initiated primarily because it dealt with the issue of "the origins and foundations of inequality among men" that has been central to social theory since Rousseau.[2] In addition to its obvious moral and political overtones, the debate was framed in substantive sociological terms, mustering evidence from the historical record of nonliterate "folk," traditional agrarian, and industrial societies and raising fundamental psychological questions about human nature. Controversies in sociological theory that so fully combine logical coherence, empirical reference, value significance, and the direct confrontation of opposed points of view are not all that common (Wrong 1976: 10-11).

Rather than citing all the contributions to the debate, I shall list the most common criticisms, including my own (Wrong 1959: 772-782; 1976: 103-120).[3] There are eight of them mentioned by at least two critics.

1. The most common criticism was that the full equality of opportunity, or meritocracy, the theory seemed to assume was an ideal rather than a reality, because most positions in most societies are not filled by competition for unequal rewards but by inheritance through the family of the positions themselves or of advantages favoring some aspirants to them over others.

2. Davis and Moore's theory implied nothing at all about the *range* of inequality, or just how much greater the rewards granted the incumbents of the most important and demanding positions had to be. Would it suffice to fulfill the functional necessity for inequality if they were only fractionally greater, or would a margin of two to one, ten to one, or even more be necessary? Davis and Moore described this as "the magnitude of invidious differences" and characterized it as a "mode of variation" of stratified systems with which they were not concerned.

3. In stressing the functions of stratification, the theory ignored its "dysfunctions." The failure to tap potential talent in the population when, as stated in the first criticism above, positions are inherited rather than filled through individual merit demonstrated in competition with others, was often mentioned. A much more important claimed dysfunction, however, was the actual and potential group conflict threatening the stability of the social order resulting from

conviction of the injustice of existing inequalities on the part of the less privileged groups. This criticism echoed Marxist and neo-Marxist insistence on "class struggle" as the moving force of history. In regarding conflict as primarily stemming from differences in *power*, an unequally distributed capacity ignored by Davis and Moore, Dahrendorf (1959) became the major founder of the "conflict theory" that emerged as the major theoretical challenge to functionalism.

4. The theory ignored motives leading individuals to seek the most highly rewarded positions other than the desire for material or psychological rewards, such as service to humanity, power or authority, "joy in work," and a sense of "calling" or "vocation."

5. The theory also ignored the existence of many highly rewarded roles such as professional athletes and entertainers, courtesans, and well-paid lackeys of the rich that are of no obvious functional importance to society at large or benefit only special groups within it.

6. The theory said nothing about the uniting or aggregating of the incumbents of privileged positions to form collectivities such as the social classes or strata which have traditionally been considered by sociologists to be the unequal units in systems of stratification.

7. Davis and Moore inferred the functional importance of positions from the rewards they received, so they were guilty of circular reasoning in adducing functional importance as a cause of those unequal rewards.

8. In a related tautological fallacy, they equated functional importance with what societies or their ruling elites consider functionally important, uncritically accepting historically relative cultural values favoring some institutions and positions within them over others.

Controversy over the theory, though hardly over the possibility of achieving full social equality in human society, waned after the 1960s when functionalism fell into disfavor. The three original contestants, all of whom died in the past decade, were self-declared functionalists.[4] Although Tumin was by no means the only "left-wing" functionalist, the general rejection of functionalism was that it ignored or minimized the existence of social conflict and social change and too readily accepted as necessary the inequality regarded as the major cause of both. These defects indelibly branded functionalism as a "conservative" legitimation of "actually existing" capitalist societies. The Davis-Moore theory was often cited as exemplifying this judgment, for example by Gouldner (1970: 421).

Although the Davis-Moore theory has been described as "the first major functional theory in sociology" (Turner and Maryanski 1979: 59), five years earlier, Talcott Parsons, the teacher of both Davis and Moore, had advanced an argument for the universality and necessity of stratification that he expanded over a decade later (Parsons 1940: 841-862 and 1954: 386-439). Regarded as the major theorist of functionalism or "structural-functionalism" (his own coinage that he later rejected), Parsons's arguments for the inevitability of inequality are often conflated with those of Davis and Moore as *"the* functional theory of stratification," although they are actually quite different. Parsons's theory was a typical example of normative functionalism (Wrong 1995: 205-219) in defining stratification as "the ranking of units in a social system in accordance with the common value system" (Parsons 1954: 388). This conception was affirmed by another of Parsons's former students in the opening chapter of one of the first textbooks on stratification, which did not become a regularly taught subfield of sociology until the 1950's (Barber 1957: 1-18). The Davis-Moore theory, on the other hand, as Davis's major obituarist has noted, "applies a labor-market supply-and-demand economic analysis though without any use of economists' terminology" (Scott 1997). Their market model does not presuppose a society-wide value consensus—it assumes only that there are universal human needs and desires for material and some nonmaterial gratifications leading to competition for them when the means of gratification are scarce. Nor did they simply borrow the economists' abstract view of market behavior: as one of Davis's obituarists who had known him as a student and colleague for over sixty years remarks, "he knew how free-market economists viewed the social system, but shook his head in amused disbelief at their unwillingness to observe how real markets truly worked" (Goode 1997: 8).

Over a decade after he and Moore had first proposed their theory, Davis himself rejected functionalism in his presidential address to the American Sociological Society (Davis 1959). He argued that all sociological analysis was functionalist in that it investigated the interaction between the parts of a society, that is, its different institutions and social practices. This lent itself to interpretation as an intellectually imperialist effort to claim the entire discipline for functionalism, for Davis did not reject the notion that the interaction was mutually sustaining both for the parts themselves and for the whole society. That, surely, is the major tenet of all brands of functionalism though hardly of all brands of sociology. But in identifying functionalism with the causal interdependence of its parts, Davis took a more multicausal view of society as a self-regulating system than normative functionalists like Parsons who stressed consensus on social norms and values as the primary integrating force on which the identity of any society is founded. (Parsons himself seemingly abandoned normative functionalism in adopting a cybernetic model of society in his later work, but, as I have noted in distinguishing between "normative" and "systemic" functionalism, he continued to insist upon a "cultural" rather than a "social" determinism (Wrong 1995:212-23). A few years later, Davis and Judith Blake sharply criticized "normative determinism" (Blake and Davis 1964: 456-466) in consistency with Davis's sociology both before and after his rejection of functionalism. Davis's conception of human motivation as early as the original theory has been accurately described as "cynical realism" at odds with the assumption that human beings smoothly internalize the values of their society and thereby achieve its harmonious integration centered on those values (Collins 1975: 423).[5]

Davis's co-author Moore accepted the criticism that their theory implied nothing about the existence of social classes, that is, of unequally ranked or rewarded *groups* or *strata* rather than just positions (Moore 1963: 13-14). It is therefore a "theory of inequality" rather than "the functional theory of stratification" it is still widely thought to be. The family was the authors' chosen unit of stratification and they excluded inequalities based on age and gender that coexist within it; writing long before the revival of feminism and the influx of married women into the labor market, Davis and Moore did not so much as consider the possibility of a dual career family in which husband and wife had jobs differing in income and prestige. Race and ethnicity are also implicitly ruled out on the same grounds. The theory, accordingly, is a limited theory of the inequality of positions in a complex division of labor. An additional limitation is that the theory is relevant only to societies in which there *is* a complex division of labor or system of social differentiation containing positions varying in their requirements for talents converted through training into skills and in their putative importance to the society. This clearly excludes, apart from a few specialized roles, most of the "folk" or "primitive" societies studied by anthropologists. Yet Davis and Moore insist in their opening paragraph that "no society is 'classless,' or unstratified" and go on to refer to the "universal necessity which calls forth stratification in any social system" (Davis and Moore 1945).[6]

Moore and Tumin agreed with the sixth criticism above that the theory does not deal with classes or stratified social aggregates. Of the remaining criticisms, two are warranted. The second was acknowledged by Davis and Moore from the beginning. The theory indeed failed to address conflict, as contended in the third criticism above. The theory in general failed to acknowledge that large inequalities of condition set limits to equality of opportunity ensuring that, in the current phrase, there is never a "level playing field" and some potential talents and skills are always lost to society as a result. The theory as a theory of inequality needs further specification fully to demonstrate these conclusions.

The Causal Argument: Three attributes of social inequality are conflated or insufficiently distinguished by most of the debaters: *universality, necessity,* and *inevitability.* Davis and Moore are charged with inferring the necessity of inequality from its universality, of being guilty, in effect, of *post hoc, ergo propter hoc* reasoning. The charge is not justified, for they presented a full explanation for the universality of inequality that demands assessment in its own right. They distinguished at the outset as separate problems "why different positions carry different degrees of prestige… and how certain individuals get into those positions." In his restatement of the theory four years later, Davis reiterated this distinction under the heading "An Apparent Criticism," noting that he had revised the theory to take into account that many positions in many societies were filled by status ascription through the family which, he conceded, "raises a crucial problem and forces an addition to the theory" (Davis 1949: 369-370). He then maintained that the functional need for family unity conflicts with the functional need for competition to fill the most important and demanding positions, reviewing in some detail the Hindu caste system as an example of a society relying primarily—though not, he pointed out, exclusively—on inheritance though the family to staff its occupational system. He insisted that "the low estate of sweeper as compared with priestly castes cannot be explained by saying that the sons of sweepers become sweepers and the sons of Brahmins become Brahmins. There is a tendency for sweepers to have a low status and for priests to have a high status in every society" (Davis 1953: 395). In addition to responding to informal criticism, Davis had undoubtedly become more sensitized to status ascription by his research on India that led to the publication a few years later of his masterful *The Population of India and Pakistan* (1951). Nevertheless, critics, starting with Tumin, repeatedly accused Davis of assuming the universality of equality of opportunity with individuals achieving their positions as a result of competition in which success went to the more talented, educable, and conscientious.

Davis concluded from his Indian example: "Thus the functional necessity behind stratification seems to be operative at all times, despite the concurrent operation of other functions." But this is a non sequitur. His concession on the inheritance of positions denies that the openness of major positions to competition is "operative at all times," with the limited exception of new positions based on technical innovations that occur on occasion in all societies. Thus Davis's explanation for the universality of inequality breaks down. It might at least be seen as an explanation of how unequally rewarded positions were first established in the past even if they were afterwards filled by ascription, although like most functionalists Davis was concerned with the self-equilibrating maintenance of a society rather than with the historical origins of its institutions.. Privileged positions might have been created by elites who attained sufficient power to shape the institutional structure according to their own interests and values, perhaps by military conquest as in the case of the caste system imposed by the Aryan conquerors of India. The Davis-Moore theory crucially ignores not only the formation of social classes but also that of less comprehensive groups capable of exercising collective power.

Ascendant elites of "new men" —armed knights, grain monopolists, successful revolutionaries, health care professionals—may create new privileged positions on which others became dependent, and, once created, the incumbents of these positions may organize to choose their successors by a variety of means of which family inheritance is only one. Monopoly control over entry excluding categories of persons defined by gender, race, religion, ethnicity, or individual attributes, and the imposition of educational requirements or other credentials, are alternative means. All are forms of *social closure* (Parkin 1979: 44-116) whether at the level of the individual family, the occupational or professional group, or a larger social class or caste.[7] In addition, the unequal material and prestige rewards in themselves give their recipients, if organized, collective power to preserve and even increase their rewards beyond any hypothetical minimum that might have been necessary to recruit individuals to the positions in the first place. Moreover, since incumbents of highly rewarded roles are by definition few in number, it is relatively easy for them to achieve organization and solidarity, although the occupants of less privileged positions and lower classes also may have recourse to organization and solidarity in order to protect and advance their interests.

Collective organization to achieve social closure and to secure and augment rewards perpetuates and increases positional inequality. But might not unequal rewards themselves be inevitable *consequences* rather than *causes* of, or *necessary conditions for*, the emergence of a stable complex division of labor? Celia Heller argues to this effect, suggesting in addition that there might be mechanisms to avert this result. Her conclusion that "it is a logical fallacy to deduce, as many do, inevitability from universality" (Heller 1987: 4) is unquestionably sound, although this applies more unambiguously to necessity than to inevitability. However, if comparisons of performances of the same task by different individuals inevitably lead to unequal judgments of *esteem,* as Davis and Moore recognize, it is hard to see why comparisons of performances of different tasks varying in skill and necessary prior training should not inevitably result in unequal judgments of *prestige*.[8] I think it can be plausibly maintained that in any society containing both brain surgeons and street cleaners, the former will be more highly respected than the latter, that is, receive the differential reward of greater prestige. Visibly inadequate performance in a high position may, to be sure, lead to such loss of esteem that the prestige linked to the position is also lost, as in the case of Fitzgerald's Dick Diver who, we learn in the poignant closing paragraphs of *Tender is the Night,* wore out his welcome as a practicing doctor in a series of small towns in upstate New York. But individual performance, especially that of prominent professionals, is highly visible and subject to collective evaluation in small towns.

In conclusion, if people do not aspire to undergo training for some positions solely in order to earn the high rewards attached to them, positional inequality may nevertheless be both universal and inevitable in complex societies even though not a necessary causal precondition for the creation and subsequent maintenance of a complex division of labor.

Motives and Numbers: A mixture of motives underlies most human decisions and actions. Davis and Moore, in contrast to narrow versions of rational choice theory, need only assume that *some* interest in the rewards attached to positions is usually part of the motivation of *some* individuals for aspiring to them. Nor need they deny that altruistic desire to serve humanity, a sense of a "calling," or the appeal of the intrinsic qualities of positions may often motivate in whole or in part individual aspirants. There are even religious positions that demand renunciation of worldly rewards by vows of poverty, celibacy, silence, and withdrawal from society. The romantic view of the artist starving in a garret is another case in point, although Freud famously remarked that artists renounce wealth, fame, and the love of beautiful women for the sake of their art in the hope that their art will eventually win them wealth, fame, and the love of beautiful women. But monks and artists are relatively few in number. Consideration of the *numbers* of needed role incumbents lends strong support to the Davis-Moore theory, although the authors surprisingly fail to say so explicitly—surprisingly, because both of them published demographic studies within a few years of the article on stratification and Davis's entire later career was in the field of social demography where the basic subject matter is human numbers.

That in the absence of material and prestige incentives other motives would not suffice to attract adequate numbers to important and demanding positions, is all that the Davis-Moore theory needs to contend. Material and prestige rewards serve as "common coin of the realm," so to speak (literally in the case of money), ensuring that there will be more candidates for key positions than a dedicated or altruistic handful responding to duty or a "calling." Tumin invoked the "unrewarded" motivation of parents to care for their children in criticism of the Davis-Moore theory (Tumin 1955) but he overlooked the prior problem of the motivation to procreate for there to be children to care for and socialize in the first place (and a collective birth rate sufficient to achieve population replacement).[9] Davis's later influential demographic argument that providing people with the contraceptive means to choose the number of children they have in no way guarantees that they will have the aggregate number optimal for the welfare of the society (Davis 1967: 730-739) represents a relevant analogy to the problem of motivating sufficient numbers of aspirants to fill the key slots in the division of labor.

The Davis-Moore article appeared before Weber's triad of income, status, and power became widely accepted by sociologists as the major bases, variables, or dimensions of stratification.[10] Weber was actually concerned with collectivities, namely, "classes, status groups, and parties," rather than with individuals or positions and regarded all three as "phenomena of the distribution of power within a community" (Gerth and Mills 1946: 181). Davis and Moore listed three kinds of reward: "things that contribute to sustenance and comfort," "to humor and diversion," and "to self-respect and ego expansion." These are readily grouped into the binary categories of material and nonmaterial prestige or status rewards. Since Davis and Moore recognized more than a single kind of reward, they allow for the possibility that a generous amount of one kind may compensate as an incentive for a deficiency in another kind. This might be called the "crying-all-the-way-to-the-bank" syndrome. One thinks of such positions as call girl, pornographer, financial speculator, racketeer, and a host of other depreciated but well-paying occupations. Then there are positions that are high on prestige but low on income such as religious official (Zelizer 1997: A17), schoolteacher, poet, college professor and scientist at least a generation or two ago.[11] Tumin noted the possibility of the substitution of one kind of reward for another, but other critics overlooked it whether by assimilating the Davis-Moore theory to the normative functionalism of Parsons and Barber in which prestige is the sole reward with money primarily regarded as a status symbol, or by assuming (indignantly) that the theory amounted to a legitimation of the unequal distribution of income in capitalist societies.[12]

Power, which Davis and Moore have been justly charged with overlooking and which Weber viewed broadly in seeing income and prestige as special forms of it, remains to be considered. A theory of inequality might deal with power and authority in several different ways. Most obviously, power or authority might be viewed as a reward to individuals comparable to material comforts and prestige, as by Wlodzimierz Wesolowski (Heller 1987: 430-438).[13] Celia Heller thinks Wesolowski's point is "well taken," but shrewdly remarks "one may wonder whether a stratification system that recruited into positions of power solely people who enjoyed power would not prove more oppressive and rigid than the systems where material rewards attract people into such positions" (Heller 1987:409). The desire for power as an intrinsic satisfaction may indeed draw bullying sadists or more subtle calculating personality types attracted to "grey eminence" positions in which they can covertly influence the public wielders of power. But neither sadists nor would-be "hidden hand" manipulators are likely to be widely distributed in the population. Power over others, therefore, is usually sought as a means to obtain other desiderata, especially income and status but also the implementation of social values, rather than as a reward sought for its own sake.[14] If power is defined, as it often is, as the total resources or generalized capacity possessed by individuals or groups enabling them to realize their goals, then obviously it is universally desired, for people want to get what they want. But the power over others exercised in a position, often seen as "responsibility," may be experienced as a burden rather than a fulfillment. Moreover, the power vested in positions, even in top positions in constitutional democracies, is severely limited in scope. Since Davis and Moore were concerned with rewards as intrinsic incentives, they were right not to treat power as a reward.

Sociologists have often argued that inequalities of power are inherent in complex societies that require positions of authority exercised by the few over the many. This inequality is both distributive in that only a minority possesses power and relational in that a power relation is by definition hierarchical. W.L. Warner, the functionalist anthropologist who was Davis's dissertation supervisor at Harvard, argued that specialized societies required "superordinate and subordinate levels...to order and coordinate their diverse activities" (Warner, Meeker, and Eels 1949: 274-275). Parsons advanced a cognate view in his well-known argument that power is a "collective resource" for the achievement of common goals affirmed by the society's value system. Tumin conceded that "graded authority" is a minimal form of unavoidable inequality in a complex society (Tumin 1963: 13-28). Marx and Engels maintained in opposition to the anarchists that even after the revolution, though before the transition to full communism, authority would be necessary in large-scale industry (Wrong 1995: 248). Since an economy of abundance would have been achieved in the communist utopia that Marx notoriously failed to describe in detail, there would be no economic inequality. Moreover, communism would not only be classless and stateless but would also dispense with any division of labor, thus eliminating inequalities of prestige and power attached to different positions. The Israeli kibbutzim were primarily agricultural and were part of a larger more differentiated national society on which they depended for various services such as medical care. These examples are not only consistent with the Davis-Moore theory but appear to presuppose it.

In contrast to these views that assume power differences to be both functional and consensual, Ralf Dahrendorf argued that, though inevitable in complex societies, hierarchies of power are also a ubiquitous source of conflict between dominant and subordinate groups (1959). In a later statement, he reiterated the Parsons-Barber argument that the existence of a normative order entails the unequal valuation of performances and positions (1968: 151-178). He then pointed out that because norms imply sanctions to enforce them, there must be a sanctioning authority, so a power structure buttresses the normative order with the result that "the system of inequality we call social stratification is only a secondary consequence of the social structure of power." Since there has to be a specific enforcing authority, that is, some semblance of legal and political institutions, it is a "fantasy" to believe that the diffuse power of the Many over the One ever suffices to ensure general conformity to norms. Dahendorf even doubts the claims of anthropologists that there are stateless societies in which "informal" or "diffuse" sanctions uphold the mores. The norms enforced, he asserts, are those of a ruling class of enforcers and arouse the resistance of the powerless. Thus social inequality breeds conflict that is a universal source of change and progress. In writing of a single ruling class, Dahrendorf reverts to a Marxist view he had previously denied in contending that there were as many ruling classes in a society as there were "imperatively coordinated associations" (Dahrendorf 1959). He also acknowledged in a footnote that "Norm has to be understood as anterior to power," implying that consensus precedes coercion in society in opposition to his general stance that coercion and conflict are the primary social realities. His answer to Rousseau's question about the origin and foundation of inequality from which he starts is therefore flawed.

Davis and Moore were right to refuse to treat power as an intrinsic reward and their theory encompasses positions requiring the exercise of power over others since such positions may be presumed to be functionally important if doubtfully dependent on talents that are scarce in the population. What their theory lacks is consideration of the power that accrues to the occupants of the more rewarded positions *after* they have been duly filled. The rewards of income and prestige themselves confer power on individual occupants that they may use to augment their income and prestige even if their positions involve no direct exercise of power. Much more important is the failure of the Davis-Moore theory to take into account social closure: the collective power of the incumbents when organized both to preserve and increase their rewards and to select their successors. Status ascription through the family is itself a microsocial form of social closure in which individual incumbents transmit their positions or the rewards attached to them to their children. The family has been recognized at least since Plato as a major, even the major, cause of social inequality. When Davis conceded the importance of status ascription in his response to criticism of the theory, he failed to define it as a form of power possessed by the incumbents of rewarded positions. The control of professional organizations and trade unions over access to their ranks is an instance of social closure involving groups larger than individual families. Finally, there is the *class* power exercised by the many incumbents of ranges or clusters of rewarded positions. There can be no doubt that the Davis-Moore theory did not adequately acknowledge social closure as an exercise of collective power. The critics correctly sensed this even if they were often guilty of the fallacy of misplaced concreteness in ignoring the abstract level of the theory. That very abstractness reduced the theory's usefulness in accounting for the concrete social inequalities of real societies. The collective power to effect social closure, however, is a result of social organization rather than of universal human motives; fuller discussion of it belongs therefore in the next section.

The Meaning of Functional Importance: Davis and Moore conclude the argument of their opening section headed "the functional necessity of stratification" with the statement "Social inequality is thus an unconsciously evolved device by which societies insure that the most important positions are conscientiously filled by the most qualified persons." This statement more than any other aroused the greatest dissent and moral indignation and is indeed vulnerable on the face of it. To begin with, it seems to "reify" societies as supra-individual actors. By "unconsciously," Davis and Moore meant no more than unknowingly, or outside the awareness of individuals in the form of an unintended—and one might add "unanticipated" (Giddens 1977: 106-109; Wrong 1995: x-xl, 4-5)—consequence of their actions, a use, or misuse, of the word still common among sociologists. But "unconsciously" as opposed to "unknowingly" carries Freudian implications of a psychic process seeming here to impute to society a mind of its own, a justly much criticized view held by some early theorists that in the Davis-Moore usage suggests at the very least the covert teleology with which functionalism has frequently been charged.

Davis and Moore were really claiming that social inequality, whatever its causes, had what Merton later called the "latent function" of contributing to the survival of a complex division of labor. Societies lacking social inequality would be doomed to remain simpler in structure and more technically backward. Davis's main obituarist remarks of his presidential address repudiating functionalism that "he artfully avoided the thesis of 'evolutionary functionalism' of which he had made so much use, the claim that institutions and forms of social organization are shaped over time by a process of competitive selection" (Scott 1997). The theory of inequality certainly exemplified such an approach. Evolutionary survival, however, whatever its inadequacies as a criterion, is not at all equivalent to accepting simply as necessary or "functionally important" what is thought to be so by the members or elites of society themselves as critics of the Davis-Moore theory have contended. [15] Davis and Moore held that some practices and institutions really *were,* objectively, that is, rather than subjectively, crucial to the survival of a society or a particular form of social structure such as the division of labor.

Rather than inferring the importance of positions from the rewards they receive in actual societies as charged by their critics, Davis and Moore put forward independent arguments as to why some institutions are more important for the maintenance of society than others. They raise, for example, the question as to why, if the world is controlled by unseen supernatural forces, the religious personnel who claim privileged access to and control over those forces are not the most highly rewarded and powerful in all societies. Why, in effect, are all societies not theocracies? Davis and Moore's negative answer adduced the relative lack of technical competence involved in performing religious activities and the palpable absence of empirical proof or disproof of claims of access to the supernatural often giving rise to competitive claims. Priests may meet the unequal rewards criterion of functional importance, but they fall short on the criterion of scarcity of talent. A further implication is that all societies must to some degree take into account empirical realities distinct from religious or magical beliefs. Davis and Moore go on to assess more briefly the relative importance of political, economic, and technical roles and institutions. Their entire discussion presupposes a conception of general "functional prerequisites" that must be met by any society, a notion that was more explicitly elaborated in lists of such prerequisites by later writers including Davis himself (1949).[16] The most famous and abstract version, applied to any group or "social system" rather than just to societies, was Parsons's AGIL scheme (Parsons, Bales, and Shils 1953; Parsons and Smelser 1956).

That religion was the first and most thoroughly discussed of the institutions Davis and Moore considered was perhaps a trace of the Parsonsian normative functionalism they largely avoided. Merton criticized Davis and Moore for considering only "the integrative functions of religion" while ignoring that different religious groups within a single society were often a source of conflict (Merton [1949] 1957: 28-29).[17] Moore replied loftily that religion had been "analytically defined" by Davis and himself and that Merton was guilty of "the fallacy of misplaced concreteness" (Moore 1950: 356). This exchange anticipated the later one over stratification, Davis and Moore's major topic. Their critics complained in tones of moral outrage that they were justifying the inequalities present in existing societies; Davis and Moore replied that their argument was on a more abstract and "analytical" level.

This brings us back to the high level of abstraction of the theory that limits what it tells us about actual societies. This applies also to the notion of functional prerequisites presupposed by Davis and Moore in their attributions of functional importance to the various universal institutions. It may be worth saying that it is necessary for the existence and perpetuation of societies that material means of subsistence be produced and distributed, that infants be cared for and children socialized, that deadly interpersonal and intergroup conflicts be avoided, and that some shared beliefs and values ensure cooperation, but it tells us little about actual societies other than that they are likely to have economic systems, agencies to care for infants and socialize children, controls over violent conflict, and some preferred rules of social conduct. It is scarcely meaningful to assert that in the absence of such institutions societies would not "survive" in the sheer biological sense, for existing societies by definition meet these prerequisites. To be sure, populations have been completely wiped out as a result of famine, epidemic disease, or genocide, and the inefficiency of their economic, health care, and military institutions may have contributed to this result (Edgerton 1994). Yet the vast majority of societies have met their prerequisites most of the time though with widely varying degrees of efficiency. Measures of life expectancy, infant mortality, morbidity, death by homicide and suicide, and fertility contributing to population replacement are also partial measures of efficiency relied on by Edgerton. Competition with other societies, or the appeal of their example,[18] may lead to change in a society's basic institutions, but since most societies undergo change all of the time and all societies some of the time it contributes little or nothing to understanding the processes of social and historical causation to claim that they are constrained by the necessity of meeting universal functional prerequisites. Davis grasped this in his later rejection of functionalism.

One must, I think, discard the whole notion of functional importance as contributing to "societal survival" for being too general to illuminate particular cases and for often verging on the tautological. But one need not conclude that the claim that some roles are more consequential for more people than other roles is acquiescence in a value-judgment made by the powerful to legitimate the greater rewards received by their own roles or by the value-consensus of members of the society. The performance or nonperformance of some activities, for example, food production or garbage collection, has a greater effect on more people than the performance or nonperformance of other activities, e.g. writing articles on sociological theory or making pornographic movies. The first named activities are directly related to health and biological survival, although their performance requires no scarce talents or skills. Although their link to biological survival may be doubtful or highly indirect, relatively unskilled activities that are essential to achieving collective goals by means of large-scale complex organizational structures may also be more "important" than some more autonomous activities performed by individuals or small unspecialized groups. Davis and Moore indeed mentioned—in a footnote—the dependence of some roles on others as a criterion of the functional importance of the latter. In response to Tumin, Davis did not deny that unskilled roles may be just as necessary as skilled roles to the overall success of an enterprise, but insisted that the other criterion of "scarcity of qualified personnel" accounted for the higher rewards accruing to the more skilled (Davis 1953: 395). Once again, however, he completely ignored the possibility of the mobilization of collective power by, in this case, the incumbents of the more important if less skilled roles to moderate the inequality. As Gerth and Mills stated with exemplary clarity:

> New York harbor pilots or Manhattan elevator boys—not to mention miners, steel workers, and railroad workers—hold in hand more crucial links in the multiple chains of interdependent functions that constitute modern society than do musicians, barbers, textile workers, or small-scale farmers. Obviously, the functional place of workers is not simply a question of skill; to push the button of an elevator and count the floors requires less skill than to play the violin or operate a barbershop. The question is: What links in the interlocking chains of activity are broken by the group's withdrawal of effort?[19]

The withdrawal of effort by relatively unskilled incumbents of positions controlling major "links in the interlocking chains of activity" defines the strike as the ultimate basis of trade union power. Frank Parkin characterizes it as "disruptive potential" and contends that "those occupations that caused great disorganization by suspending their activities could, by this token, be said to be of especial functional importance to the community and should be rewarded accordingly; while those whose absence would scarcely cause a ripple on the surface of social life would be deemed to be of least functional importance and should have a correspondingly weak claim on the common purse" (1979:76).[20]

Parkin's "functional importance" differs from Davis-Moore's: it is more empirical and lacks both the consensual and universally necessary implications suggested by all versions of functionalism in sociology. Nor does it carry dubious suggestions of "evolutionary survival," but rather points directly towards the sociology of politics and the conditions favoring organization, solidarity, and mobilization in the exercise of collective power. It is worth noting, however, that Parkin, writing in the 1970's, was less than prescient—though he was hardly alone in this—in stressing the newly acquired disruptive potential of the British working class resulting from increases in the capital intensity of industry and foreign competition. The public dissatisfaction resulting precisely from the disruption caused by strikes in the famous "winter of discontent" of 1978-79 led to the electoral victory in the spring of Margaret Thatcher's Tories and her subsequent success in limiting the power of British unions, a limit accepted by "New Labour" returned to office in 1997 under Tony Blair after eighteen years in opposition. Deeper social forces reducing the power of organized labor were clearly also at work, as the success of the Republicans led by Ronald Reagan in the United States attests.

In short, the dependence of some roles, and of the general public, on other roles, whether autonomous or part of a larger organizational structure, is not merely a "measure or index" of something independently identifiable as "functional importance;" it *is* functional importance itself in the only sense in which that contested term can meaningfully be understood and measured. The Davis-Moore theory's claim that some roles are more functionally important than others and therefore command greater rewards is too loosely defined, although not inherently tautological or ideological as critics of the theory have alleged.

Summary and Conclusions: The Davis-Moore theory offended the egalitarian sentiments of many, even most, sociologists in the immediate post-war period. The sheer insistence on the inevitability and desirability of social inequality was in itself almost sufficient to achieve this result. Some of the theory's detailed arguments were indeed vulnerable to the criticism they received. Subsequent historical events and trends in social theory have nevertheless increased the credibility of the theory's overall general claim about social inequality as well as of some of the particular arguments supporting it. This appears to be at least tacitly accepted even by left-wing activists who have shifted the focus of egalitarian ideals and demands from class struggle and economic redistribution to persisting racial, gender, and ethnic inequalities. The Davis-Moore theory had nothing to say about these since it was expressly confined to inequality arising from the division of labor. Marxism, too, centered on the economy, emphasizing private ownership of the means of production as the major source of inequality. The shift to inequalities based on race, gender, and ethnicity has the political advantage of mobilizing groups that already possess some solidarity rooted in ascribed social identities that are not, in contrast to income and prestige, divisible. On the other hand, identity politics is fragmenting (Gitlin 1995; Wrong 1997) and, as Parkin succinctly puts it, "ethnic minorities and women do not typically occupy strategic positions in the division of labor that would endow them with the ability to bring things to a halt" (Parkin 1979: 85).

Davis and Moore were certainly right to regard a complex division of labor as inevitably producing material and status inequalities, although they failed to distinguish between the extent to which this is a consequence of, or a precondition for, the existence of such a division of labor. Their emphasis on rewards as *incentives* for individuals' self-recruitment to occupational roles was also right with respect to the supply of adequate numbers of people to fill the relevant roles, although they failed to mention that motives other than the desire for rewards may influence individual choice. Material incentives have always been stressed by economists and increasing acceptance of the superior performance of relatively "free" market economies has enhanced the plausibility of the Davis-Moore market model. Economists have qualified their materialism by uneasily conceding the existence of "psychic income," the equivalent of the prestige or status habitually stressed by sociologists, including Davis, Moore, and their critics. Despite rightly rejecting power as a consummatory reward, Davis and Moore failed to consider power as a result of social organization enabling privileged individuals and groups to achieve social closure by controlling succession to their positions. Power also enables some groups to win greater rewards in conflict with others as a result of more favorable opportunities to organize, achieve solidarity, and mobilize for economic and political conflict.

If Davis and Moore were right to regard inequality as inevitable in societies with a highly developed division of labor, they had nothing to say about the range or degree of inequality. Yet rather than the inevitability of *some* inequality, this may be "the real question," as one critic has observed (Turner 1986: 42). How much inequality, how great a margin between the privileged and the unprivileged, is regarded as just and legitimate? Where the margin is seen as excessive the group and class conflicts notoriously not mentioned by Davis and Moore that became the defining preoccupation of "conflict theory" may result.

Davis and Moore also failed to distinguish between the possibly different conditions necessary for the origin and favoring the perpetuation of a complex division of labor.

The enumeration of universal functional prerequisites tells us little about the varying ways in which they are met by different societies. It is less than revelatory to be informed that societies must engage in activities that can be classified as economic, political, familial, legal, and moral. The Davis-Moore theory goes further than this in specifying social inequality as a functionally necessary condition for maintaining a particular, broadly defined social structure: the complex and highly organized division of labor or system of occupational social differentiation found in relatively large-scale, technically advanced societies. While not obvious or tautological, the theory remains too abstract to tell us much about the actual inequalities in concrete societies. Yet if all the inequalities based on race, gender, and ethnicity that receive so much attention today were improbably to disappear in short order, the inequalities stemming from the division of labor limned by Davis and Moore would remain.

Since equality and inequality are morally and politically contested issues, the Davis-Moore theory therefore possesses a degree of "relevance" exceeding that of most generalizations invoking the notion of universal functional prerequisites which must be met by any and all human societies. For that reason, it is still a useful starting-point for asking what limits there might be to the general social equality that remains a salient ideal in modern democratic societies and how those limits might conceivably be broadened.

Notes

1. The most thorough and comprehensive survey of the evidence is still Walter D. Connor's study of 1979. See also earlier surveys by David Lane (1971) and Frank Parkin (1971
2. Dahrendorf (1968) to the contrary notwithstanding, Rousseau primarily attributed the origin of inequality to the division of labor rather than to the institution of private property, which is why he deplored the division of labor in celebrating an earlier "primitive communism." This is the case despite the famous sentence that opens Part Two of the *Discourse on Inequality*: " The first man who, having enclosed a piece of land, thought of saying 'This is mine' and found people simple enough to believe him, was the true founder of civil society" (Rousseau 1755: 109). Most of the themes of later interpretations of inequality are present in Rousseau's brilliant essay.
3. I vainly—in both senses of the word—thought I had resolved the debate in rejecting the errors and exaggerations of both Davis-Moore and their critics, citing the major features of social inequality they had neglected, and synthesizing what was valid in their arguments. Shortly after the publication of my article, I asked Kingsley Davis, who had been my dissertation supervisor at Columbia, what he thought of it and he replied with a genial grin that he took it as yet another attack on his theory. Actually, I had intended to provoke both the creators and the critics of the theory. My argument essentially was that the theory was so abstract and "analytical"—in the Parsonsian sense the authors invoked in countering their critics—that it was at best trivially true whereas the critics made the opposite error of assuming that the theory was a defense of that old reprobate the status quo, *any* status quo.
4. They had been colleagues at Princeton in the late 1940s and for several years at that time the Princeton sociology department (then a sub-department) was the most functionalist in the country.
5. Collins fully recognized that Davis and Moore employed a market model. As I had (Wrong 1959), he compared their theory to Schumpeter's (1951), which he, like me, thought superior.
6. One suspects that this statement at the very beginning of the article was meant to be provocative. In denying the possibility of a "classless" communist society, it ob-

liquely affirms the famous opening sentence of *The Communist Manifesto* that "the history of all hitherto existing societies is the history of class struggle" (Marx and Engels n.d.: 9) while denying that the future might differ. Yet Marx and Engels had themselves postulated the earlier existence of societies based on "primitive communism," but the *Manifesto* was an agitational pamphlet. Engels added a footnote qualification to the English edition "That is, all *written* history" (his emphasis) and proceeded to discuss "primitive communistic society" as described by the anthropologist Lewis Morgan assigning it to the "prehistory" of society before it became "differentiated into antagonistic classes." Davis and Moore certainly knew of the existence of the relatively undifferentiated tribal societies studied by anthropologists. Apart from their having possibly overgeneralized for polemical reasons, their theory was sufficiently abstract to fail to rule out as unrealistically utopian most of the egalitarian goals sought by past and present left-wing parties and movements including those inspired by Marx and Engels (see Wrong 1959: 775-776).

7. Parkin follows Weber in defining social closure as "the process by which social collectivities seek to maximise rewards by restricting access to resources and opportunities to a limited circle of eligibles" (44).
8. The distinction between esteem and prestige was developed in an earlier article by Davis (1942).
9. Tumin's suggestion that the unrewarded motivation of parents might be extended to nonfamilial roles in the wider society is vulnerable to the charge of implausible utopianism in suggesting that any large-scale society could come to resemble one big happy family.
10. The title *Class, Status, and Power* and the organization of this first reader in social stratification (Bendix and Lipset 1953) did much to diffuse the idea of a triad underlying social stratification.
11. As an example of high prestige and low income, Gerald Zelizer, a rabbi, maintains that "ministers, priests, and rabbis may be perceived as high-status occupations...[but] the median salary for all clergy in the United States in 1994 was $26,000, the same for car salesmen who rated low in prestige, and nutritionists, flight attendants, graphic artists, machinists, plumbers, and retail buyers, who all ranked average in prestige."

    High income and low prestige are exemplified by Alexander Gershenkron in disputing the claim of economic historians influenced by Talcott Parsons that the high evaluation of entrepreneurial roles was a crucial neglected factor explaining differential economic development: Gershenkron adduced the much-despised tax farmers of eighteenth-century France, who nevertheless became rich and were major "primitive accumulators" as Marxists would call them (1962: 59-60).
12. Even Jonathan Turner, who praises the theory more than he criticizes it, erroneously describes it as confined to "the distribution of prestige" (Turner 1986: 58).
13. Wesolowski also mentions skill, knowledge, and educational requirements as attributes of positions that attract individuals to them. But obviously not just any skill or knowledge would fill this bill: for example, skill in inscribing the Lord's Prayer on the head of a pin, or my knowledge of the full lineup of the Washington Senators baseball team in the late 1930s. This alleged motive is reducible to a special case of service or intrinsic pleasure in work as motives rather than as a reward sought for its own sake (Wrong 1995: 218-227).
14. I mention here the covert exercise of power because when power is exercised openly as a requirement of a position it is difficult to separate the intrinsic satisfaction derived from possessing and exercising it from the prestige that almost invariably accrues to powerful roles.

15. Jonathan Turner, though not primarily a critic of the theory, also makes the mistake of equating functional importance with "the positions in a social system that are defined by the members of that population as functionally important (1984: 49).
16. A highly influential early statement was by a group of Parsons's former students (Aberle, et al. 1950) including A.K. Davis, whom Turner and Maryanski (1979: 60-61) confuse with Kingsley Davis.
17. In a revision in 1968 of his earlier criticism of Davis and Moore on religion, Merton eliminated the reference to inter-religious conflicts within some societies but added that Davis and Moore assume certain *functional prerequisites* without taking into account the possibility of *functional alternatives* (Merton 1996: 78, his emphasis). The same claim was made with regard to stratification rather than religion by the critics who proposed egalitarian alternatives to unequal rewards and Merton himself had first introduced the concept of functional alternatives.
18. The collapse of Communism in Eastern Europe and the Soviet Union would not have occurred in the absence of general awareness of its economic lagging behind the West.
19. Gerth and Mills 1953: 329. Their general point holds despite the fact that they were writing in the 1950s and their examples have been made obsolete by technological change. Nearly all elevators nowadays are automated and the decline in importance of miners, steel workers, and railroad workers is the most salient result of the transition to a service economy marked by deindustrialization. Today one might list in place of their examples electronic engineers, computer programmers, and air traffic controllers.
20. Parkin goes on to advance a similar but much more specific and credible version of the Davis-Moore dual criteria for unequal rewards: "...a distinction should be made between the ability to command resources on the basis of skill and market scarcity, and the ability to command resources on the basis of 'disruptive potential"' (80).

References

Aberle, D. F., A.K. Cohen, A.K. Davis, M.J. Levy, and F. Y. Sutton, 1950. "The Functional Prerequisites of a Society." *Ethics,* 60: 100-111.

Barber, Bernard. 1957. *Social Stratification* (New York: Harcourt, Brace).

Bendix Reinhard and S. M. Lipset (eds.) 1953. *Class, Status, and Power: Social Stratification in Comparative Perspective* (New York: The Free Press).

Berger, Peter L. 1986. *The Capitalist Revolution* (New York: Basic Books).

Blake, Judith and Kingsley Davis. 1964. "Norms, Values, and Sanctions." Pp. 456-466 in *Handbook of Modern Sociology,* edited by R.E.L. Faris (Chicago: Rand McNally).

Buckley, Walter. 1958. "Social Stratification and the Functional Theory of Social Differentiation," *American Sociological Review*, 23: 369-375.

Clark, T.S. and S.M. Lipset, 1991."Are Social Classes Dying?" *International Sociology*, 6:397-410.

Collins, Randall. 1975. *Conflict Sociology* (New York: Academic Press).

Connor, Walter D. 1979. *Socialism,Politics, and Equality* (New York: Columbia University Press).

Dahrendorf, Ralf 1959. *Class and Class Conflict in Industrial Society* (Stanford, CA: Stanford University Press).

—.1968. *Essays in The Theory of* Society (Stanford, CA: Stanford University Press).

Davis, Kingsley. 1942. "A Conceptual Analysis of Stratification." *American SociologicalReview,* 7.309-321.

—. 1949. *Human Society* (New York: Macmillan).

—. 1951. *The Population of India and Pakistan* (Princeton, NJ: Princeton University Press).
—.1953 "Reply." *American Sociological Review,* 18:394-397.
—.1959. "The Myth of Functional Analysis as a Special Method in Sociology and Anthropology." *American Sociological Review.* 24:757-772.
—.1967. "Population Policy: Will Current Programs Succeed?" *Science,* November 10: 730-739.
—. and Wilbert E. Moore. 1945. "Some Principles of Stratification." *American Sociological Review,* 10: 242-249.
Edgerton, Robert B. 1992. *Sick Societies: Challenging the Myth of Primitive Harmony* (New York: The Free Press).
Gershenkron, Alexander. 1962. *Economic Backwardness in Historical Perspective* (Cambridge, MA: Harvard University Press).
Gerth, H. H. and C. Wright Mills (eds.). 1946. *From Max Weber: Essays in Sociology* (New York: Oxford University Press).
—.1953. *Character and Social Structure* (New York: Harcourt, Brace).
Giddens, Anthony. 1977. *Studies in Social and Political Theory.* (London: Hutchinson).
Gitlin, Todd. 1995. *The Twilight of Common Dreams* (New York: Metropolitan Books).
Goode, William J. 1997. "Remembering Kingsley Davis (1908-1997)." *Footnotes.* 25: 4,8.
Gouldner, Alvin W., 1970. *The Coming Crisis of American Sociology* (New York: Basic Books).
Heller, Celia S. (ed.). 1987. *Structured Social Inequality: A Reader in Comparative Social Sratification.* Second Edition (New York: Macmillan).
Hout, M., C. Brooks, and J. Manza. 1993."The Persistence of Classes in Post-Industrial Societies," *International Sociology*. 8: 259-278.
Kingston, Paul W. 1994. "Are There Classes in the United States?" *Research in Social Stratification and Mobility*. 13: 3-41.
Lane, David. 1971. *The End of Inequality? Stratification under State Socialism* (Harmondsworth, Middlesex, UK: Penguin Books).
Marshall, Gordon. 1997. *Repositioning Class: Social Inequality in Industrial Societies* (London: Sage Publications).
Marx, Karl and Friedrich Engels. [1848] n.d. *Manifesto of the Communist Party* (New York: International Publishers).
Merton, Robert K. [1949] 1957. *Social Theory and Social Structure* (New York: The Free Press).
—. [1968] 1996. *On Social Structure and Science* (Chicago; University of Chicago Press).
Moore, Wilbert E. 1950. Review of Merton's *Social Theory and Social Structure, Public Opinion Quarterly.* 14: 3 54-357.
—. 1963. "But Some Are More Equal Than Others." *American Sociological Review.* 28: 13-28.
Ossowski, Stanislaw. 1963. *Class Structure in the Social* Consciousness (New York: The Free Press).
Pakulski, Jan and Malcolm Waters. 1996. *The Death of Class* (London: Sage Publications).
Parkin, Frank. 1971. *Class, Inequality, and Political Order* (London MacGibbon and Kee).
—.1979. *Marxism and Class Theory: A Bourgeois Critique* (New York: Columbia University Press).
Parsons, Talcott. 1940. "An Analytical Approach to the Theory of Social Stratification." *American Journal of Sociology.* 45: 841-862.

—. 1949 and 1954. *Essays in Sociological Theory.* Revised Edition (New York: The Free Press).
—. Robert F. Bales, and Edward A. Shils. 1953. *Working Papers in the Theory of Action* (New York: The Free Press).
—. and Neil J. Smelser. 1956. *Economy and Society* (New York: The Free Press).
Rousseau, Jean-Jacques. [1755] 1984. *A Discourse on Inequality* (Harmondsworth, Middlesex, UK: Penguin Books
Schumpeter, Joseph. [1923] 1951. *Imperialism and Social Classes* (New York: Meridian Books).
Scott, John Finley. 1997. "Remembering Kingsley Davis (1908-1997)." *Footnotes.* 25:4.
Tumin, Melvin M. 1953. "Some Principles of Stratification: A Critical Analysis." *American* Sociological *Review.* 18: 397-394.
—. 1955. "Rewards and Task-Orientations."*American Sociological Review.* 20: 419-423.
—.1963. "On Inequality." *American Sociological Review. 20:*19-28.
—. 1967. *Social Stratification: The Forms and Functions of Inequality.* Englewood Cliffs, NJ: Prentice-Hall.
Turner, Bryan S. 1986. *Equality* (London: Tavistock Publications).
Turner, Jonathan H. 1984. *Societal Stratification: A Theoretical Analysis* (New York: Columbia University Press).
— and Alexandra Maryanski. 1979. *Functionalism* (Menlo Park, CA: The Benjamin/ Cummings Publishing Company).
Warner, W. Lloyd, Marcia Meeker, and Kenneth Eels. [1949] 1960. *Social Class in America* (New York: Harper & Bros).
Wesolowski, Wlodziemierz. 1987. "Some Notes on the Functional Theory of Stratification." Pp. 430-438 in *Structured Social Inequality: A Reader in Comparative Social Stratification.* Second Edition. Edited by Celia S. Heller.
Wrong, Dennis H. 1959. "The Functional Theory of Stratification: Some Neglected Considerations." *American Sociological Review* .24: 772-782.
—. 1964. "Social Inequality Without Social Stratification," *Canadian Review of Sociology and Anthropology.* 1: 5-16.
—. 1976. *Skeptical Sociology* (New York: Columbia University Press).
—. [1994] 1995a. *The Problem of Order: What Unites and Divides Society* (Cambridge, MA: Harvard University Press.
—. [1979] 1995b. *Power: Its Forms, Bases and Uses* (New Brunswick, NJ: Transaction Publishers).
—. 1997. "Cultural Relativism as Ideology," *Critical Review.* 10: 291-300.
—. 1998. "Reflections on the Death of Socialism: Changing Perceptions of the State/ Society Line," Paper presented at the 10th annual meeting of the Society for the Advancement of Socio-Economics, Vienna, Austria, July 14, 1998. (Chapter 1).
Young, Michael, 1959. *The Rise of the Meritocracy 1870-2033* (New York: Random House).
Zelizer, Gerald L. 1997. "And Now for a Few Words..." *New York Times,* Op-Ed, May 27: A17.

4

Economy and Society: The Future

In trying to foresee future trends, the surest approach is simply to project present trends forward assuming the future will resemble the past and present. This approach has not always worked well in the twentieth century. Two world wars interrupted a number of secular trends and the Great Depression of the 1930s reversed nearly all measures of economic progress. Ups and downs of the business cycle were anticipated on empirical and theoretical grounds, but the severity of the Depression and its effects, including political upheavals, were not. The early postwar period witnessed an utterly unexpected rise in fertility, the "baby boom," which ended equally unexpectedly in the 1960s. The postwar economic boom exceeded expectations, its end in the early 1970s combining rising unemployment and inflation was not foreseen, nor was the recovery leading to the long continuing boom of the 1990s. Major technological inventions and their effects are almost by definition unforeseen.

The forecasts of the economists surveyed by Professor Pryor are unremarkable: they do not anticipate any great cataclysms of war, revolution, depression, technological breakthroughs, or ecological collapse. Should such explosive critical events occur, the American people would certainly once again turn to, even run to, the arms of Mama in the shape of the federal government, bringing to an end current depreciation of "the nanny state" and proclamations that "the era of big government is over." Nor do the economists consider more gradual processes of change with uncertain effects on the economy such as changes in cultural values that might affect the market preferences of consumers, a major variable for the economist. What might some of these changes be, presuming that a sociologist is likely to have some sense of their possibility?

A large majority of Pryor's economists foresee rates of American per capita economic growth until 2050 of slightly over 1 percent.

Although they believe this predicted trend will have "a major impact on the economic system or major institutions," they evidently do not anticipate any significant revolt against "consumerism" that might negatively affect the trend. In the past, minorities composed of bohemians, intellectuals, radical students, religious sectarians, and some upper middle-class groups have denounced materialistic consumerism: "zero-economic growth" even became a slogan and goal in the prosperous, rebellious 1960s. Today's mockery of sports utility vehicles is reminiscent of the animus nearly half a century ago against the bulky tail-finned automobiles of the 1950s. Is it not possible that such attitudes might be adopted by a larger segment of the population now that memories of the Depression have dimmed and the satisfactions of relative affluence have become both more widespread and apparently more permanent? The pervasive commercialism of the 1990s has already induced in many a mood of cynicism and resistance, including organized political opposition in several states to the development of remaining open spaces. One form of anti-consumerism that might emerge could be a demand for elimination of commercial low bulk mailing rates that have inundated private homes with an unprecedented volume of catalogues, "special offers," and advertising throwaways. If enough people spent their time perusing this mail instead of instantly consigning it unopened to the wastebasket economic productivity would fall to new lows! Economic growth ultimately depends on consumer demand, both for new goods and services and of new consumers wanting goods and services previously available only to a few. One can conceive of technological innovations generating new consumer demands on the scale of the expanding markets for PCs and VCRs in the past two decades. New telecommunication devices, costly new drug and medical treatments adapted to individual genomes, even small private planes come to mind as possibilities. Yet might not some saturation of consumer demand manifest itself in the twenty-first century with a negative impact on economic growth?

I am certainly not imagining any mass outbreak of asceticism. However, the consolidation of a standard of living at a level of comfort meeting needs for food, clothing, shelter, and leisure amenities for a large majority of the population hardly seems out of reach. A few economists sensitive to the ecological concerns that became prominent in the late 1960s argued that damage to the environment would in itself necessitate an end to economic growth. This has not happened; moreover, some major threats to the environment have been reduced. Yet the environment sets limits that may become tighter.

As the economists acknowledge, low population growth resulting in an aging population will also restrict rates of economic growth. The Census Bureau for years has published three population projections labeled "high," "medium," and "low." The Bureau usually has suggested that its "medium" projections are the most likely to be realized, which turned out to be way off for the 1940s and 50s when birth rates exceeded even the high projections. Today the high fertility of the 1950s is widely seen as the historical norm from which there has been an unprecedented departure since the 1960s. This is utterly wrong: the postwar baby boom was a deviation from nearly a century or more of declining fertility in the major industrial countries, including the United States. Whatever impetus the cultural innovations of the 1960s may have provided, the lower fertility prevailing since represents the resumption of a longstanding trend suggesting that social analysts who once argued that modern society was inherently inimical not only to large families but to parenthood itself may have been right in the long run. Fertility and, obviously, immigration remain hard to predict, but saturation of consumer demand is more likely to become more salient in an aging population.

There are already indications that the private sector in postindustrial capitalist economies is becoming incapable of sustaining full employment for all who want to engage in remunerative work. Stable levels of consumer demand in the future will enhance this condition. A resurgence of the now dormant expectation that the federal government should become "the employer of last resort," as in the depression years of the 1930s, may well result. Repair of communication and transportation infrastructures and conservation efforts to improve and preserve the environment present ample employment opportunities, as in the 1930s. The prospective need to support many more people not in the labor market has even more politically controversial implications, although a term avoiding the invidious connotations that have become attached to "welfare" could doubtless be found. Back in the 1970s some American sociologists, among them Peter and Brigitte Berger, anticipated that politics might eventually center on conflicts between workers and nonworkers. I think this will indeed happen. The European capitalist democracies presently suffering high rates of unemployment while still maintaining heavy taxation to support welfare states much more generous than that of the United States may provide a mirror of the American future. This prospect, whether approved or deplored, goes beyond the careful limited forecasts of the economists surveyed.

5

What is Left of the Left?

Both these long books are *fin de siècle* summations of the related but certainly far from identical "socialist" ideologies, movements, and states that loomed so large in the embattled twentieth century. Since the late François Furet's subject is the totalitarian Soviet version while Norman Birnbaum treats the reformist social democratic versions in the Western democracies, the authors, unsurprisingly, evaluate their subjects differently. Moreover, Birnbaum dislikes historians of onetime communist sympathizers in the West such as Furet, predictably dismissing them as likely to be "ex-Communists, engaged in compulsive efforts to expiate their earlier sins." He mentions Furet's book as "the best of the genre" but makes the baffling complaint that it is "the less complex and masterful, the more closer [*sic*] it comes to Stalinism itself" (79). I am unable to figure out just what he means by this. Like so many French intellectuals at the time, Furet joined the French Communist Party in the immediate postwar years and left it in protest against the Soviet invasion of Hungary in 1956. My NYU colleague Tony Judt was never a communist, but Birnbaum mentions in a footnote to his critique Judt's first-rate *Past Imperfect, French Intellectuals, 1944-1956.* At the time of Furet's death in 1997, Judt wrote an eloquent obituary tribute to him in the *New York Review of Books.*

Furet and Birnbaum nevertheless agree substantially on the present situation. In the wake of the collapse of Soviet communism and its satellites, Furet concludes that "The idea of *another* society has become almost impossible to conceive of, and no one in the world today is offering any advice on the subject or even trying to formu-

Review of François Furet, *The Passing of an Illusion: The Idea of Communism in the Twentieth Century,* translated by Deborah Furet (Chicago: University of Chicago Press, 1999) and Norman Birnbaum, *After Progress: American Social Reform and European Socialism in the Twentieth Century* (New York: Oxford University Press, 2001).

late a new concept. Here we are, condemned to live in the world as it is" (his italics, 502). Birnbaum observes in his final chapter that "Not a world remade but a world slightly improved is what they [parties of the left in the West] now promise. Their modesty seems justified" (371). Both authors doubt whether this situation will endure indefinitely. Furet thinks that "This condition is too austere and contrary to the spirit of modern societies to last." The end of communism "does not," his closing sentence avers, "spell the end of the democratic repertory" (503). Birnbaum writes in his last sentence, "Not a promised land, but a terrain of dialogue and experiment is what remains to be cultivated to replace the immensely fragile and profoundly spurious order of our societies" (382). Though by no means a celebrant of existing societies, Furet hardly regards them as fragile and spurious in tracing the shifts of emphasis in and what he welcomes as the eventual extinction of communist ideology. Birnbaum regards the "American social reform and European socialism" of his subtitle as having achieved much "progress" before their decline with the passing of their "Golden Age" from the 1930s through the 1970s. He rightly sees the New Deal as a rough American equivalent of European and British Socialism.

I doubt that a better book will be, or has been, written on Furet's subject. He has not written a history of communism as such, of which there are many, but of the "idea of Communism" and its vicissitudes. From a historically significant standpoint, the twentieth century began in 1914 and closed with the dissolution of Eurasian communism in 1989-91. Born of the Russian October Revolution in 1917, the communist idea diffused, was redefined, and contracted in response to the major historical events of the century, finally dying in the wake of the collapse of the Soviet Union and its satellites as the century drew to a close. After an opening chapter on the sources of "the revolutionary passion" that animated both communism and fascism, Furet traces the ups and downs of "the Communist idea" in ten historically periodized chapters from its birth in the 1914-18 war to a long "epilogue" on its death in Russia and Central and Eastern Europe just over a decade ago. As the major contemporary historian of the French Revolution, Furet sees the two ideas of "revolution" and "nation" as virtually originating in 1789-93, dominating the politics of the nineteenth century, and then combining in extreme and novel forms under the two totalitarian regimes of the twentieth, the Nazis giving precedence to a racial version of nationalism, and the Soviet Union turning after its initial identification with Marxist-Leninist revolutionary internationalism to a militant de facto nationalism after Stalin had exiled Trotsky and embraced the doctrine of "socialism in one country."

Furet defends the concept of "totalitarianism" as accurately descriptive of the Nazi and Soviet regimes, drawing on such master thinkers and writers as Hannah Arendt, whose great book he summarizes, Raymond Aron, "the political writer with the greatest analytic capacity for understanding his time, " George Orwell, and the early Frankfurt School members Franz Neumann and Franz Borkenau, the author of the first book with "totalitarian" in its title. Having discovered Orwell, Arthur Koestler, and *Partisan Review* while still an undergraduate in Canada in the last year of the war, I recall being rebuked after having used the term "totalitarian" by a friend who said it was a word invented by those who wanted "to conceal the differences between Nazi Germany and Soviet Russia." The reverse was the case: it concisely encapsulated the far more important similarities between them. Furet fully reports on Hitler's conscious imitations of Bolshevism, the denunciation of which had helped him come to power, and on the Stalin-Hitler pact that precipitated the Second World War following the interwar culture of "Anti-Fascism," reborn after Hitler's invasion of the USSR, in the era of Communism's maximum influence. One might object that Furet is too Franco-centric and too prone to detailed comparisons between the French and Russian revolutions, but that is to be expected in light of his intellectual biography.

The main weakness of Birnbaum's otherwise valuable book on the fate of the left in the major Western nations is his attribution to the United States of "proprietorship" of the Cold War and "liberal imperialism" in a quest for "global hegemony." Furet writes that in 1945 "Even in Europe, Stalin encountered only American power. Bolstered by universal anti-Fascism, he had made a political investment, via 'National Fronts' and local Communist parties, in every country in which his army had the last word. The coerced rejection by these parties of the Marshall Plan in July 1947, the subjugation of Poland, and the Czech coup d'état of February 1948 capped off the formation of a territorial empire bordering ravaged Western Europe, where American troops stood guard in guilty Germany" (396). It is inconceivable to me that the major American policymakers of the Truman administration, most of whom had been active "interventionists" in the long debate preceding American involvement in the war that began with the German invasion of Poland, would or could simply have stood by and accepted this new situation, although Birnbaum writes as if strictly domestic factors motivated the emerging American resistance to further Soviet expansion. Birnbaum is no partisan of the Soviet Union or the communist idea, but he relies on the challenged revisionist historians of the Cold War, thereby illustrating Furet's view that during the Soviet Union's last two decades, "By a curious reversal, American professors came to hate the concept of totalitarianism after having studied it and written about it, whereas French intellectuals, at just about the same time, were beginning to study it after having ignored it" (496).

Furet is refreshingly unsociological, not to put too fine a point on it, in refusing to impute in neo-Marxist fashion the communist idea to underlying "social forces" reflecting class interests and conflicts. He recognizes in full not just the autonomy of politics but the autonomy of the ideas embodied in political ideologies. Tony Judt noted that Furet began his histories of the French Revolution as a typical *Annales* historian concerned with deep, enduring "structural" trends in the French economy and society, but, without denying the reality and autonomy of these trends, at a certain point, Judt observes, he abruptly abandoned this approach to focus directly on the political ideas and on individuals, recognizing them as crucially consequential.

I met Norman Birnbaum right after the war when he was still an undergraduate and I was a first-year graduate student. We eventually became good friends. His bibliography in the present book attests to the remarkable extent to which we read and were influenced over the years by the same books, both as academic sociologists and as "New York intellectuals" in the ambience of the post-Trotskyist Left. We have also been associated, though not simultaneously, with the same institutions: the Graduate Faculty of the New School for Social Research, Nuffield College of Oxford, and the editorial board of *Partisan Review*. I recall arguing with Norman after he had moved to Europe and later to Britain over his inclinations to what came to be called "anti-anti-Communism" and his negative view of the Cold War, which still in the present book he has never treated as continuous with the Second World War against an expansionist totalitarian power on the European continent. I was from its start what my teacher C. Wright Mills labeled with invidious intent a "Cold War liberal, " and my major criticisms of Birnbaum's new book still derive from that position, although I opposed as fully as any *bien-pensant* liberal the misdeeds and excesses of American anti-communism, especially though not exclusively McCarthyism at home and overcommitment to the Vietnam War abroad. Nearly half a century provided ample time, after all, for many abuses, missteps, and outright errors in what remained a constant policy though subject to the politics of democratic competition; it would, I believe, have continued in some form for as long as the Soviet Union retained control over its European satellites even if the "détente" and "peaceful coexistence" affirmed by Birnbaum had been more fully implemented.

My differences with Birnbaum are nuanced: essentially, I miss the outrage some of us felt over the discovery that people of an insufferable self-righteousness and doctrinaire certainty refused to recognize and even apologized for mass murders, suppressions of democracy, and territorial aggrandizements at the expense of other nations, all equaling or exceeding Hitler's, carried out by a tyrannical dictator and to a lesser extent his successors. Birnbaum rightly deprecates the *idée fixe* of avoiding another Munich as a rationale for the Vietnam War, but he never mentions the relevance of the analogy in the immediate postwar period. I recall strolling beside Lake Carnegie in Princeton on a lovely June day in 1950 and feeling a burst of sheer euphoria on hearing over someone else's portable radio that the United States in the person of President Truman had decided to resist militarily the invasion of South Korea by North Korea. I knew my response was the same as that of the policymakers and diplomats in Washington, including my father, most of whom (except for George Kennan and a few others) knew little about Communism but had begun their careers as opponents of appeasing Hitler. The "containment" and "deterrence" they favored ultimately succeeded in averting a third world war.

Birnbaum draws amply on his informal conversations with leading politicians of the European and British Left, even dedicating his book to the memory of his "departed friends" Enrico Berlinguer and Willy Brandt (also Michael Harrington). Without wishing to lay claim to "insider" knowledge, this induces me to mention that in my youth I often heard Dean Acheson, an old family friend; Kennan, by whom I was employed as a research assistant during his first year out of government service; Lester Pearson, the original choice of the United States and its allies to be secretary-general of the UN vetoed by the

Russians (later both foreign minister and prime minister of Canada); as well as several other less prominent figures, including the British representatives in Washington, discourse informally on what they thought they were doing in the early years of the Cold War. I have to say that I experience a shock of nonrecognition in reading Birnbaum on the origins of the American policy of "containment " (Kennan's term), although by the time I worked for Kennan in 1951 he was already criticizing its overextension despite his support for the Marshall Plan, NATO, the Berlin airlift, and the Korean intervention.

I also question Birnbaum's contention that Furet, Judt, and others exaggerate retrospectively the extent of pro-Soviet sentiment on the Western left including in the United States. Birnbaum may be reflecting his youthful experience in New York City and Cambridge, where there was, atypically, a visible anti-Stalinist left presence. While I cannot come close to matching his intimate knowledge of the postwar left in France, Germany, and Britain, in all of which he lived for a time, nor of Italy and Spain, which makes his book an excellent report on the whole subject, I did attend a "progressive," cosmopolitan school in Geneva just before the war. This was the period when Maxim Litvinoff was the major advocate of "collective security" against Hitler and Mussolini; my classmates included the sons of the president, foreign minister, and ambassador to London of embattled Republican Spain, and many Jewish refugees from Nazi Germany who ended up in Britain or the United States. There was general outrage over the Munich conference, which excluded Russia and was called by the *Journal de Genéve "un club de charcutiers"* —a gathering of pork butchers. Spending the summer of 1948 in Paris, I sought out old schoolmates and found that nearly all of them had become communists or fellow travelers. Two brothers, nephews of my French Geneva principal, were Communists, one of them the chief adviser on nuclear physics to the French Communist Party. When first told this by another old friend, she remarked that they would disapprove of my anti-Stalinist left associations more strongly than of my general support for American foreign policy. This was a few years before Birnbaum's European sojourn, which perhaps accounts for our different impressions of the extent of pro-Sovietism on the Western Left for events moved very quickly at that time.

Birnbaum like Furet is admirably free of neo-Marxist reductionism in reporting and crediting the *sui generis* impact of political struggles rooted in ideological differences though he is guilty of a few lapses. He commits a colossal and truly amazing blooper quite in line with his bias in stating that a 60 percent majority of the U.S. Senate is required to enact *any* legislation, evidently confusing this with the majority required to end the rare filibusters by minorities against proposed statutes, which has precisely the opposite effect of enabling ultimate majority rule. He too often invokes "capital" and "the market" as collective historical actors, perhaps out of a wish to avoid the cliches of "the bourgeoisie," "Big Business," or "the corporations" but as a result reifying economic abstractions. Birnbaum certainly fully understands why a full-fledged "socialism" is no longer credible, but his tone is, as Peter Gay notes in his jacket endorsement, "melancholy" in recalling abandoned visions of "the emergence of a new society," "a world remade," "total social reconstruction," "larger social changes of a purposeful sort," "alternatives to market capitalism," and like phrases that he regularly deploys. He also deprecates Sir Karl Popper's "piecemeal social engineering," ascribes a "contentless liberalism" to Isaiah Berlin, and is cool towards the Blair-Clinton-Schroeder Third Way for allegedly acceding to "the domination of capital."

Yet Birnbaum's definition of "socialism" is so abstract as to reflect its decline to little more than a noble sentiment, for he identifies it solely with the realization of the French revolutionary ideals of *"liberté, egalité, fraternité,"* especially and repeatedly with the "values of solidarity," synonymous with the third of these. He describes it as a "secular religion," which has usually been intended as criticism, but the waning of which he regrets, although one would suppose that any secular model of a possible reformed new social order is subject to the test of history. Socialism, after all, originally stood not just for high ideals but for particular means of achieving them, namely, public "ownership" of the economy and central economic planning, which have now been rejected as projects, considerably but not exclusively as a result of the Communist experience. (The socialist program of the one political party I ever joined was entitled "Social Planning for Canada.") Also, as Birnbaum indeed fully recognizes, the projected "social base" for socialist movements, the proletariat that Marx expected to become a huge majority of the population, has proportionately declined. Both the utopian socialists and the Marxists envisioned a transition to an entirely new kind of society that would parallel the transition from feudalism to what Marx called "bourgeois society" and what came to be called "capitalism" at the beginning of the twentieth century, largely owing to Sombart and Weber. But nothing comparable to that transition from a predominantly agrarian to an urban-industrial order such as a change that would achieve the total fulfillment of liberal and egalitarian ideals, now appears credible.

These books complement each other in providing a valuable record of a major feature of the history of the previous century unlikely to have any sequels in the present century.

Part 2

Multiculturalism and Identity Politics

6

Adversarial Identities and Multiculturalism

One has the impression that "identity" is the most widely used concept these days in the social sciences and humanities from which it has passed into popular discourse. In academic sociology, where it is probably most ubiquitous, entire sessions at the annual meetings carry titles like "Identity Construction and Representation" or "Culture and Identity: Selves in Western Culture-History," both real examples. A sociology editor at a leading university press told me the other day that she was swamped with manuscripts entitled the "social construction of…" this or that, from which one readily concludes that "The Social Construction of Identity" serves as an all-purpose title in current sociology, closely approximated indeed by the first session title cited above. If one could work in a reference to "culture," as in the second example above, one would have covered just about all of the major catchwords that pervade the discourse of social science and social criticism today. "Culture" is, of course, of more ancient provenance than "identity" and "social construction," but it has recently been revived as an all-encompassing label for nearly anything and everything human beings do in association, although half a century ago when I first encountered sociology as a student the field's most advanced practitioners were severe critics of its use as a blanket monocausal term borrowed from anthropology.

Though it has a long history in philosophy, the term "identity" first became widely used in social criticism and commentary in the 1950s. Its origins were in the writings of psychoanalysts as its obvious relation to the important psychoanalytic concept of "identification" suggests. As the more or less stable product of the plural identifications that shape individual character, or at least that segment of it called the "ego" by Freud and his followers, it had a special appeal to those psychoanalysts concerned, in contrast to more orthodox

Freudians, with the social and cultural determinants of personality. Erik H. Erikson was more than anyone else the theorist responsible for the popularity of the concept. There is a less than accurate tendency among sociologists to treat the identity concept as a product of Chicago symbolic interactionism, understandable in light of its obvious congruence with that school's emphasis on the self as formed through interaction with others. I recall Erving Goffman in the early sixties expressing to me his admiration for Nigel Dennis's 1955 novel *Cards of Identity* and being impressed when I told him I had once spent an evening in Dennis's company. One of Goffman's more influential books, *Stigma* published in 1963, is subtitled "Notes on the Management of Spoiled Identity." Goffman drew heavily in his sociology on satirical novels about contemporary life, but he was not the creator, nor ever claimed to be, of identity as a sociological concept. Harry Stack Sullivan's "significant other" which has also passed into popular discourse (mainly as a euphemism for "lover") is another concept of psychoanalytic origin that is frequently misattributed by sociologists to George Herbert Mead, the father of symbolic interactionism.

Sociological appropriation of the term perhaps accounts for the fact that nowadays identity is mainly used to refer to *social identities,* that is, to identities acquired by membership in organized groups or recognized social categories. The relevant groups or categories are most commonly those of race, gender, or ethnicity to which individuals are initially and more or less permanently ascribed at birth. Erikson regarded identity as an individual's not necessarily fully conscious sense of self, reflecting the continuity of her/his life-history and the synthesis of various past identifications with others, especially in the family. Erikson's concept is social in the sense of giving primacy to the impact of others without, however, equating this impact simply with the fact and imputed influence of group or category membership as such, or with the adoption of established cultural self-definitions. Several sociologists have so defined *social* as contrasted with *personal* identity in the Eriksonian sense. Both conceptions refer to attributes of individuals, but Eriksonian personal identity does not treat recognized social groups or roles as the bestowers of identity on individuals, although it in no way denies the existence of broad social and cultural prerequisites for the attainment or failure to attain secure personal identity after coping with what Erikson called "identity crisis."

Erikson essentially equated identity with personal individuality, including not just the qualities actually, that is, objectively, possessed by a person, but her/his subjective awareness of those qualities and the recognition of them by others. Identity corresponds to the uniqueness of individual personality, the particular selection and synthesis the individual has made out of past identifications with significant others, and the perception by self and others of that uniqueness. "It arises," Erikson wrote, "from the selective repudiation and mutual assimilation of childhood identifications and their absorption into a new configuration." The possession of a secure identity resembles the personal "authenticity" extolled by existentialist thinkers. Clearly, such a conception is a far cry from seeing identity as simply the individual's prideful awareness of inclusion in a group or occupancy of a prescribed social role. It even implies a certain distancing from collective identifications and role expectations, a consciousness of one's own inalienable individuality. Most disquisitions on identity assert that "Who am I?" is the basic query individuals pose to themselves in seeking identity. In the Eriksonian view that became popular in the 1950s and 1960s the answer began with a capitalized proper name and a search for the personal correlates of its unique referentiality.

Like most terms that acquire a special meaning in academic social science, "identity" has long been a common English word. I have the impression that before Erikson endowed it with its distinctive psychological connotation, its most common use in social and political commentary was with reference to nations and nationalism, as both achievement and aspiration. As a Canadian I am perhaps unduly sensitive to this use, for Canadians have long been obsessed with the question of whether they truly possess a national identity: books with titles like "The Search for Identity"—an actual title in a major series on Canadian history—regularly pour from Canadian presses. There is a continuity between identity in this sense and its more academic usages by Erikson and contemporary social scientists: identity is *always* problematic, something that is not just given but that has to be sought, striven for, and forged out of fragments, or if attained is constantly subject to "diffusion" and "confusion," in Erikson's terminology, even to outright dissolution.

In the case of Canada, the division between French and English since the country's foundation, the British connection, the presence of a much larger and more powerful English-speaking nation as a southern neighbor, and the regionalism of a small and geographically scattered population have presented obstacles to any strong sense of national identity. For Erikson, identity poses a problem, even a crisis, experienced by the individual at a particular stage in her/his life-history, notably adolescence. For sociologists, identity reflects the freedom and mobility available under conditions of modernity, confronting individuals with a wide array of choices and holding them responsible for those that are made, which inevitably leads to uncertainties, regrets, an illusory sense of achievement, or outright "anomie" and "alienation" on the part of many people. Identity is inescapably a result of the rise of "individualism" as a value-set distinctive of modernity, the heir of the Enlightenment. Locating it in a narrower historical context, another psychoanalyst much influenced by sociology, Allen Wheelis, argued in the 1950s that "the quest for identity" was inherent in the situation of mid-twentieth-century individuals and was experienced much less intensely by their grandparents.

The current popularity of the term refers less to the putative universal plight with which modern life confronts the individual than to the identity-conferring power of particular groups, especially those defined by race, gender, and ethnicity. This is continuous with the older notion of national identity though singling out subnational groups and categories as the major bestowers of identity on the individual person. However, as in the notion of national identity, social identity in this view becomes a collective as much as an individual attribute. The attainment of identity, or "identity formation" as it is commonly called, is seen as a social process involving the interaction and aggregate consciousness of many individuals rather than as a psychological process constituting a phase of personal development. Identity formation becomes equivalent to what used to be called group formation, the recognition of a shared collective identity having long been a major defining criterion of a group in sociology as distinct from a mere "aggregate" of individuals or a social category. A British sociologist, Ken Plummer, has suggested a parallel between identity formation so conceived and the Marxist view of the genesis of class consciousness in the famous transition from a "class-in-itself" to the solidarity of a "class-for-itself" though it is unlikely the influence has been a direct one at least in the United States.

The current notion of a "politics of identity" does in one respect resemble the Marxist view, for politics is a realm of group conflict and the active promotion of collectively affirmed goals. It is no accident that identity *politics* has arisen in the wake of the various protest movements of the 1960s and early 1970s under the banner of "multiculturalism," its "race, gender, class" mantra reflecting black nationalism and feminism, the two most successful and durable of the earlier movements. As has often been noted, the reference to "class" is largely a concession to the dwindling number of Marxists still ensconced in the universities, for aggressive assertions of *class* identity are notably absent, apart from a few minuscule political sects still affirming the ultimate triumph of the proletariat.

Despite the overwhelmingly middle-class origins of the sixties protesters, they have never been, to put mildly, given to affirming proudly their "bourgeois" identities. Some years ago speaking on the teaching of sociology at a neighboring university, I was asked by a young faculty member—who had previously been the center of controversy over academic freedom following her dismissal from another university for an extreme act of radical protest—whether emphasis on race, gender, and class was not a promising new direction. I replied obtusely that the study of gender had now been, though belatedly, incorporated into the sociological curriculum, while race relations and social stratification had long been established as specialties within the field, so where was the novelty in proposing them for study? I completely missed that "race, gender, class" connoted not just areas of study but an activist orientation growing out of the radical ferment of the sixties. A subdisciplinary section bearing that label has since been established within the American Sociological Association presenting its own program of papers and roundtables at the annual meetings.

Yet there is an oddity in the grouping of blacks, women, and gays and lesbians together under the "multicultural" or "diversity" label, for they hardly represent separate cultures rather than at most subcultures shaped by past oppression and discrimination for blacks, sex role differentiation for women, and sexual deviance for gays and lesbians. Multiculturalism more obviously and literally suggests markedly different traditions brought to the country by immigrants past and present. But emphasis on the cultural diversity of the American population resulting from mass immigration is hardly a novelty: it has long been a heavily stressed component of the "pluralism" extolled as an outstanding and even unique feature of American democracy. The New Left of the sixties assailed the claim of pluralism as Cold War propaganda hypocritically masking the rule of the privileged few bent on perpetuating the inequalities at home and imperialist designs abroad of corporate capitalism. I remember the radical caucus in the American Sociological Association actually distributing printed lapel buttons reading "pluralism = fascism" at the 1969 meetings in San Francisco. Today's advocates of multiculturalism and identity politics on the so-called "cultural left" reaffirm pluralism under a new name and in an adversarial spirit insisting that there is too little of it. As Russell Jacoby observes, "The politics that emerges either ratifies familiar (and estimable) sentiments about respecting all groups or pretends to a subversiveness that has no foundation."

The adversarial spirit is a leftover from the sixties in the ferocity of its opposition to what survives of past negative identities based on race, gender, and sexual orientation. There is a sense in which all the protest movements of the sixties were spin-offs from the earlier civil rights movement, adapting and echoing its slogans and tactics. But the sixties also witnessed a revival, probably for the last time, of Marxism and the prospect it projects of a total "socialist" transformation of modern society. Most socialists in the West had long ago ceased to regard Soviet-style communism as a desirable model for their own societies. Nevertheless, its quick total collapse in 1989–91 without arousing any popular resistance either in the Soviet Union or in its European satellites was the culmination of a long retreat from ideology and utopia, regretted and even deplored by Jacoby in his new book, although he documents rather than refutes it. The preoccupation with culture and identity is a fallback position, a last-ditch oppositional stance, in face of the death of socialism that has brought about the "end of utopia." Undoubtedly, "we are all multiculturalists now' but as Nathan Glazer argues in his book of that title it is largely the persistence of black poverty and unemployment, the failure to achieve full racial integration after several decades of trying, that is the main support for the label, which provides a rationale for the proclamations of racial pride and educational efforts to promote black "self-esteem" in the inner-city ghettoes. In the case of women, despite the elimination of legal discrimination, it will be a long time if ever before all traces of informal gender distinctions that can be construed as invidious are entirely eradicated. Gays and lesbians may be accepted as practitioners of an "alternative lifestyle," but it is exceedingly doubtful that it is a lifestyle that will ever be widely recommended in preference to heterosexuality—by, for example, parents to children—or that it will spread beyond a small minority of the population—three to five percent according to the most reliable recent estimates. The persistence of invidious distinctions penalizing these groups in major and minor ways ensures that movements upholding their identities and interests will not soon disappear; yet basing a firmly adversarial attitude towards modem society at large primarily on them is a mirror image in reverse of the well-known disposition of people at the bottom of the status hierarchy to make bedrock claims of racial, religious, or ethnic superiority, a disposition that has always itself been a major source of racism and prejudice.

Advocates of multiculturalism habitually insist that American society is becoming increasingly racially and culturally diverse and this has come to be widely taken for granted. It is regularly invoked by educational administrators committed to increasing the "diversity" of student bodies as well as by other bureaucrats anxious to present an enlightened face to the public. But it is nevertheless a questionable assumption. A number of surveys have shown that both whites and blacks underestimate the size of the white population by roughly a fourth, overestimate the black population as between a quarter and a third, and also overestimate the Hispanic and Asian-American proportions of the total. The belief that "people of color" will by the third decade of the twenty-first century constitute a majority of the population is wish-fulfillment cultivated by the more ardent multiculturalists, for Census Bureau projections indicate that the white population will at most then have declined by only a few percentage points and will still amount to nearly three-quarters of the total. Future fertility more than immigration is the most hypothetical factor in these population projections. It is also wishful to think that all nonwhite groups are likely to come together in a liberal-left political coalition organized on the basis of common interests not shared by whites. Moreover, intermarriage rates between all groups except blacks have been high and black-white intermarriages have recently increased.

Recent immigration has, to be sure, brought to these shores larger numbers of Asians and nonwhite Hispanics including Buddhists, Hindus, and Muslims as well as Hispanic Catholics outside of the Protestant American tradition. Yet there have not been widespread complaints of racial or religious discrimination against these groups.

"Angry white males" and Christian "moral majorities" have formed a dissenting nativist faction in American politics, but their outlook has been defensive and they are hardly as formidable as nativists earlier in the century who imposed "Americanization" requirements on immigrants and succeeded in the 1920s in restricting immigration not only from Asia but from parts of Europe regarded as culturally and even racially alien to the American majority. One may doubt whether contemporary non-European immigrants despite their different racial and religious composition are more culturally alien to most Americans than the Slav and Latin peasants from Eastern and Southern Europe of the much larger mass immigration earlier in the century when nearly half of the native-born population still lived in relative social and cultural isolation in rural areas.

Globalization has been a cultural as well as an economic process and the equation of it with Americanization is not entirely without foundation. The spread of American popular culture around the globe has meant that most recent immigrants already possess some familiarity with American life that their predecessors a century ago lacked. Adjurations in favor of the "recognition of difference" and understanding "the Other" often seem to suggest that ordinary Americans regularly experience what anthropologists describe as "culture shock" as a result of encountering magical and animistic beliefs involving esoteric rituals, or alien practices such as infanticide, polygamous marriage, genital mutilation, foot-binding, and the like. That this is clearly not the case underlines the extent to which the case for multiculturalism rests primarily on the persisting problems of the largest minority, American blacks, who, in contrast even to West Indian immigrants of the same racial origin, were brought here as slaves and later endured a century of legal segregation in the region of the country where they were most numerous.

The adversarial political thrust of multiculturalism stems from its fixation on groups that have suffered victimization in the past in which membership is involuntary. The less politicized preoccupation with cultural identity reflects resistance to the featureless uniformity and impersonality of a technological mass society dominated by strictly instrumental routines and the shallow ephemera of a commercially produced popular culture. The wish for a distinctive cultural identity reflects the quests for identity and community that were first widely expressed in the 1950s representing the desire for a sense of belonging to smaller and more cohesive groups than the large, sprawling, inescapably diverse total society. Though their stance is marked by political anger, this may also apply to white males mobilized in support of "traditional values." Not the increasing diversity of American society, but its growing homogenization underlies the preoccupation with identity. Russell Jacoby is one of the very few social analysts who has fully perceived this in face of the widespread claims to the opposite effect. Paradoxically, fear that mass society and mass culture were imposing a banal conformity that suppressed both individual identity and genuine community was a major theme of social criticism in the 1950s, the period seen nowadays as the heyday of "traditional values." Long before the rise of industrial and/or post-industrial society, Tocqueville famously interpreted the American tendency to create voluntary associations as a response to the isolation inherent in democratic individualism.

The pluralism and multiculturalism of American society create multiple social identities for individuals to acquire and cherish. The emphasis on social as distinct from personal identity, however, suggests that individuals have a single identity based on a dominant group or category to which they belong. Yet it has long been a sociological commonplace that individuals in modern society belong to many different groups and networks and play many different social roles within them. Leon Wieseltier notes that "the American achievement is not the multicultural society, it is the multicultural individual....Many things are possible in America, but the singleness of identity is not one of them." As Todd Gitlin, whose discussion of this point is especially valuable, states, "By none of my identities am I 'determined' in the sense of 'compelled.'" Whether or not personal identity successfully synthesizes the individual's multiple social identities, or even whether there is any "core" personal identity merging or underlying plural social identities, is a separate question. Erikson thought there was even if often hard to attain, to win its recognition by others, and subject to the identity crisis and diffusion he diagnosed. Postmodernists deny the very existence of a stable single subject, seeing individuals as no more than sites where diverse cultural "discourses" intersect. Yet the very debunking tone and spirit in which they make such declarations testify to the reality of the aspiration to a unique biography worth recounting and remembering if not necessarily emulating. The enormous popularity of memoirs, biographies, and autobiographies, genres distinctive of modernity, is convincing testimony, along with the pervasive fascination with journalistic accounts of the lives of celebrities. The much-touted "decline of the novel," also a modern invention originally centering on the representation of fictional individual "characters," has—if it is indeed a reality—not been matched by any decline in these non-fictional genres. Their popularity is, to be sure, often adduced as a cause of the novel's alleged decline. But this may be interpreted as evidence of the prevalence of Erikson's "identity crisis" leading to a reduced interest in imagined as distinct from real characters rather than to the effacement of personal identity by social identity.

7

Diversity: Catchword and Reality

"Diversity" is one of those ordinary words that on passing into public discourse become freighted with meanings and overtones conflating the descriptive and the normative. Not more than a decade or two old as a catchword, it has become, in the United States at least, what my friend Nathan Glazer once called "a semantic beacon of our time." Glazer was referring to the term "alienation" way back in the late 1940s when its use was still confined to intellectuals, although over a decade later it became a negative rallying cry for the rebellious youth of the 1960s. Unlike alienation, diversity is represented as a social condition deemed desirable, to be encouraged to the extent of promoting policies extending it throughout American society. While its literal meaning is purely descriptive, "cultural pluralism" and, more ambiguously and uncertainly, "cultural relativism," both of them ideas with a long history of favorable connotations in the intellectual world, have been invoked to justify it. "Diversity" in this respect resembles other words, whether referring to approved or deplored phenomena, that have diffused from academic and intellectual parlance to the wider public. This process occurs regularly enough to deserve intensive study in its own right: it is one manifestation of the "reflexivity" that sociological theorists have seen as peculiarly characteristic of modernity, or at least of "late modernity" as Anthony Giddens has described the present era.[1] Each special instance of it, however, requires examination in its own particular social and historical context.

"Diversity" is a fairly common though abstract word, chosen as a favored or "politically correct" term, one surmises, in preference to the faintly frivolous nuances of "variety," or the more academic-pedantic "heterogeneity" which literally mean the same thing. Postmodernist writers have used "difference" as a synonym for it, endowing that innocuous word with the same blend of descriptive and normative implications. *Cultural* diversity is what is indicated and approved, not just any and all of the myriad ways in which individuals differ, though gender and sexual orientation with real or hypothetical foundations in biology have also been prominently included under its rubric. Though having come to mean much the same thing in current rhetorical usage, diversity is a more neutrally descriptive term than "multiculturalism," which has notoriously become an embattled verbal icon in the "culture wars" that administrators and other official spokespersons who employ it understandably wish to bypass. Educational administrators nowadays often defend the admission of larger numbers of minority group members on the grounds that they will increase the diversity of the student body as if that were the only, entirely sufficient and unchallengeable, justification for such policies.

The most obvious reason, though by no means the primary one, for the attention paid since the 1960s to the cultural diversity of American society has been the increase in immigration from Asia, Latin America, and the Caribbean following the passage in 1965 of new immigration laws abandoning the quotas favoring Europeans that had been in effect since 1924. The term "multiculturalism" was borrowed from Canada in the 1970s, reversing the usual direction of discursive traffic across the border. Canada was created as a union of two distinct European peoples differing in language and religion and concentrated in different regions that became the separate federal provinces of Quebec and Ontario. In order to maintain the often-strained unity of English-speaking and French-speaking Canadians, Canada had always officially proclaimed its *bicultural* and bilingual nature, though largely honoring it in the breach rather than in the observance before the 1960s. Having like the United States experienced mass immigration from Europe in the late nineteenth and early twentieth centuries, the label "New Canadian" was added to the English/French distinction and officially affirmed. Immediately after the Second World War, Canada, unhampered by the restrictive American quota laws, experienced renewed mass immigration, chiefly from Southern Europe, but also from Asia and the Caribbean. In 1971 multiculturalism replaced biculturalism as government policy with the creation of a Department of Multiculturalism in the federal cabinet at Ottawa. Clearly, nothing remotely comparable has occurred in this country.

The Canadian experience a few years before this development illustrates how words can come to carry significant ideological overtones in ways that later seem strange and paradoxical as well as misleading. The resumption of mass immigration to Canada in the 1940s and 1950s when restrictive laws still prevailed in the United States resulted in a major increase in the size and ethnic diversity of the Canadian population, especially in the larger cities. Throughout the postwar period the proportion of foreign-born Canadians has been about 15 to 16 percent, higher than in any other Western nation. The American figure by contrast has been about six percent in the last few decades. In the 1950s the Canadian Department of Citizenship and Immigration in its pronouncements on immigration policy habitually drew a distinction between "assimilation," rejected as coercive and ethnocentric, and "integration," the outcome the Department wished to encourage, defined as tolerant and accepting of cultural differences. Typically for Canadians, always anxious to draw an invidious contrast between themselves and Americans even when little more than a "narcissism of minor differences" in Freud's famous phrase is at issue, "assimilation" and the "melting pot" metaphor associated with it were depicted as representing chauvinistic Americanization policies in contrast to a more enlightened Canadian outlook favoring cultural pluralism with the metaphor of a "mosaic" applied to the population enriched by immigration. The contrast between "bad" assimilation and "good" integration, "bad" melting pot and "good" mosaic, the second terms identified with what today is called diversity or multiculturalism, was, therefore, a familiar rhetorical theme in Canada over forty years ago, long before it achieved its present prominence in the United States. To be sure, it did not become the focus of a heated culture war, Canadians not being given to that sort of thing, although there is some evidence that Francophones disliked the language and, for that matter, the policy of unrestricted immigration itself, since immigrants were more likely to settle in Anglophone Canada.[2] Moreover, more recently, in the 1990s, multiculturalism as a policy has been attacked by some of the federal opposition political parties and even by a few spokespersons for the non-British and non-French ethnic groups themselves with arguments that bear some resemblance to those deployed by the foes of multiculturalism in the United States.[3] Canadian opponents have gone so far as to call for the abolition of the Department of Multiculturalism in Ottawa.

The contrast drawn back in the 1950s between assimilation and integration was precisely the reverse of how the latter term came to be used on this side of the border where to this day the two are treated as virtual synonyms, the latter as a somewhat milder version of the former. I don't think it was the naming of racial integration as the stated goal of the American civil rights movement that led Canadian immigration officials to opt for the word to describe their own preferences, for that movement did not get fully underway until the late 1950s and I recall Canadian invocations of the terms as polar opposites some years earlier. I also remember that several sociologists who later returned to academic life were employed by the Department of Citizenship and Immigration in the early 1950s; they may, I conjecture, have interpreted "integration" as signifying the peaceful incorporation of different groups into a harmoniously functioning larger society in contrast to the enforced conformity suggested by assimilation. Several of them, like most aspiring Canadian sociologists at that time (among them myself), had done graduate work at American universities, including Harvard where Talcott Parsons's theories of the success of modern, and specifically American, society in integrating highly differentiated social parts into a functioning whole were then dominant. I shall pursue this topic no further, but it is an interesting example of how abstract academic jargon may acquire quite contrary ideological resonances in different social and, in this case, national contexts.

It is conventionally assumed that the affirmation of diversity and multiculturalism reflects a democratic aspiration that all ethnic and racial groups in the population should be proportionately represented in the major institutions and organizations of the society and that this has become especially urgent in the wake of the increased volume of Asian and Latin American immigration since 1965. Education, unsurprisingly, was the first sector in which diversity became a declared desideratum, but government agencies at all levels, particularly those dealing directly with the public, and some professional organizations and businesses anxious for wider public patronage and approval, as well as a few larger voluntary associations striving for representativeness, soon followed suit. The celebration of diversity was seen as a response to the alleged increasing diversification of American society the reality of which is still regularly asserted today. Yet America has always been recognized as a large, sprawling, and heterogeneous society and there are good grounds for doubting that it is presently becoming even more diversified in its beliefs and practices than earlier in the century, as I shall argue below. The affirmation of diversity is not therefore simply a reaction to an unambiguous objective situation. The new immigrants themselves have not been in the forefront of demands for greater diversity and multiculturalism in American life, nor is it plausible that the advocates of diversity have been presciently anticipating the raising of such demands in the future. What, then, accounts for the chorus applauding multiculturalism and insisting on the need for greater recognition of it by Americans and their leaders?

If the belief that the population has become more diversified as a result of the new immigration has sometimes supplied a rationale for it, three independent groups have largely contributed to and/or sustained the multiculturalist ideology. African Americans have been by far the most important. This is Glazer's major argument in his recent book *We Are All Multiculturalists Now*. Nor shall I discuss feminism, which has also, though more ambiguously, brought women under the multicultural canopy. The oddity of grouping blacks and women under the label and theme of multiculturalism, which has quite different intellectual and ideological origins from the original civil rights and feminist movements, has not been fully grasped, let alone explored.

It should be noted that the civil rights movement from its beginnings in the late 1950s sparked the entire turn to the left in the following decade and the black movement and feminism have been the most prominent, successful, and durable of all the protest movements that have come to define the ethos of the 1960s. The original black demand was for their full integration into American society; this became the goal of affirmative action policies and of all efforts to increase black participation at higher levels in education and employment, justified as remedial compensation for the handicapping scars still borne by blacks resulting from their heritage of oppression under slavery and legalized segregation and discrimination. Only some years later was greater black participation advocated on multicultural grounds because it contributed to diversity. Among blacks themselves, the spread of black nationalist sentiment in the late 1960s led to their defining themselves as a distinct culture, although there is clearly a sense in which, though certainly constituting what social scientists used to call a "subculture" shaped by their peculiar and painful experiences in America, they are the most quintessentially American of all groups in the American population except for the original inhabitants of the empty continent. William

Raspberry recently observed in one of his newspaper columns that "'assimilated'" [is] a concept many nonwhites find repugnant, because it seems to entail the necessity of giving up one's own culture and accepting the superiority of the dominant American (white) culture." Raspberry mildly demurred from this attitude, supporting the creation of "a truly multiracial, multicultural society in America" not identified with "whiteness."[4] Yet the insistence on black cultural distinctiveness is of recent origin, reflecting the elevation of "culture" into the major source of difference among Americans.

The third group responsible for the ideology of diversity and multiculturalism played the leading role in creating it rather than, like the blacks and feminists, in primarily sustaining it. This is the academic left concentrated in the humanities and to a lesser extent the social sciences, and at present the only left remaining in existence in American politics and society. Far from representing a new direction responding to a new social reality, the promotion of multiculturalism and "identity politics" represents a fallback position, a last-ditch stand in reaction to the death of socialism, the revived prestige of the free market in an increasingly globalized world economy, the decline of labor unions and the reduction in size of the working class, the electoral victories of right-wing politicians eager to trim and even dismantle the welfare state, and the waning of many of the movements and countercultural demands of the 1960s as the combined result of their partial successes in winning general acceptance in the larger society and the rise of popular counter-movements seeking to reverse their achievements. In the academic left's litany of "race, gender, and class," class has obviously played a distinctly subordinate role and has often seemed to be included simply as a bow to the Marxists of yesteryear still entrenched in the university, which has so often in Western history been less the base camp for a vanguard political army than a sanctuary for the followers of lost causes. After all, the preponderantly bourgeois origins of academic leftists does not give them an identity they are bursting to affirm. Bedrock opposition to racism and ethnocentrism oddly mirrors the tendency in the past of whites near the bottom of the class hierarchy to claim status on the basis of their unalterable racial or ethnic identities—a bulwark in itself of racism and ethnocentrism.[5]

By the death of socialism, needless to say, I do not mean the failure of nominally socialist parties to flourish and win elections in major Western nations, but the extinction of the *vision* of socialism as a truly feasible "alternative society" towards which history is steadily progressing, a society that will abolish the obnoxious and unstable features of capitalism and fully realize for everyone the luminous ideals of liberty, equality, and fraternity. The collapse of Communism in 1989-91 was less the cause than the culmination, the final capstone, of a much longer process of the fading of this vision to which the brutalities and economic inefficiencies of Communist regimes on four continents had indeed made a signal contribution. The full meaning has yet to be grasped of the abrupt and nearly total disappearance of what has been the major secular utopian model of a good society in modern history, attracting generations of passionate believers for over a century and a half. For the remaining faithful the world suddenly became a one-dimensional place deprived of any prospect of transcendence.[6] And all this happened less than twenty years after the numbers of declared socialists, especially in the United States, had grown as a result of the ferment of the 1960s with Marxists for the first time winning a substantial place in Western universities, particularly in the English-speaking countries.

Racial and cultural differences are relatively permanent and deeply rooted features of most modern societies, certainly of the United States. They have in the fairly recent past been the source of the ethnocentrism and prejudice of majorities leading to the victimization of minorities and many such attitudes survive. Discrimination against minorities excluding them from some fields of activity thus remains a credible target justifying an adversarial attitude towards existing society. The desire to cling to such an adversarial stance is what motivates the aggressive postures favoring multiculturalism and identity politics that one finds in the academy today. This also accounts for the incorporation of blacks, women, and gays and lesbians into the ranks of the culturally oppressed and the lumping of all white ethnic males into the category of "Europeans," who cannot be convincingly represented as victims of exclusion or even as bearers of the scars of past exclusion. Significantly, the groups most emphasized as the prospective beneficiaries of multiculturalism and identity politics are those entered at birth in which membership is ascribed by real or alleged biological heredity or acquired as the internalized result of early socialization in childhood, differences in short that have the longest history and are least likely to cease being subject to some minimal discrimination in the course of future social and cultural change.

The most deeply rooted feature of commitment to a radical political ideology seems to be less belief in a particular kind of new political or economic system, nor identification with a specific oppressed class or group, but simply an adversarial attitude towards existing society itself, opposition as such regardless of its content. From this perspective, the insistence of so many liberal and radical intellectuals on the deep, utterly ineradicable racism of the American population, regarded as independent of the great if still incomplete improvements in the conditions of blacks in the past half-century, becomes more understandable. It is a substitute for the lost conviction that a final crisis of capitalism is inevitable and imminent, or that the innate revolutionary disposition of the working class will eventually show itself.

Both liberal and conservative critics of the academic left have pointed out that its ideological initiatives involve no risk whatever to "tenured radicals" ensconced in secure positions in the university where their commitment at most involves "marching on the English Department"[7] rather than organizing revolutionary movements to seize state power. Conservatives have nevertheless muttered darkly about the left-wing professoriate's subversive "political agenda." The very notion of a political agenda seems to carry the unspoken suggestion that it is hidden and therefore disreputable, echoing language used in the past against domestic Communists who indeed kept their affiliation secret and concealed their basic allegiance to the Soviet Union. "Politicization" and "politically correct," also terms widely deployed by the right in the culture wars, are similarly of Communist origin. As so often happens in long standing conflicts and controversies, the enemies end up mirroring one another. If the academic left clings to an adversarial stance against that old miscreant the status quo lacking in any substantive political content, their right-wing detractors grossly exaggerate the depth, extent, and power of the multiculturalism, postmodernism, political correctness, and literary deconstructionism they have been assailing now for nearly two decades. Conservatives and neoconservatives go so far as to declaim that the United States is "falling apart" under the impact of these deplored ideological tendencies, and, even more extravagantly, that they pose a threat to the survival of Western Civilization itself—a term, incidentally, that is less than a century old. The academic front in the culture wars centering chiefly on the curricular canon has at last somewhat quieted down with neither side winning a clear victory. The debate has become a tired one with more and more people of diverse political and intellectual persuasions distancing themselves from it. The result, typical of how such controversies are usually resolved in the university, has been the institutionalization of the academic left's preoccupations in new courses and programs side by side with the retention of the older, more traditional curriculum defended by their opponents.

The extra-academic concerns expressed in the conflict have involved a kind of surrogate politics with little actual bearing on divisions in the outside world and at most minor implications for public policy. There may indeed be a sense in which "everything is political," "the personal is the political," and all social relations are permeated by a Foucauldian "micro-politics of power." But if one confines oneself to political power, to "real" politics in the larger "macro" world, the absence of any overmastering political conflicts in the United States today is striking, most recently illustrated, of course, by the inordinate and obsessive importance attached to the essentially trivial Clinton-Lewinsky scandal. In national politics, political deadlock, apathy, symbolic rather than substantive "issues," and a fairly vacuous centrism prevail. "The consensus right now is not to have a consensus about what the country as a whole should be or do," as Nicholas Lemann has perceptively remarked.[8] The decline of the New Deal Democratic majority in the Reagan years, the virtually complete termination of European colonialism, the end of the Cold War with the collapse of Communism, and the debacle of the Republican "counter-revolution" mounted in 1994 are the domestic and foreign developments that have contributed to this outcome. These conditions would quickly change if there were a major war or a severe economic downturn, outcomes hardly to be desired. We live in an apolitical era. In this climate, it is far from surprising to witness both a multiculturalism affirming in angry adversarial tones the supreme value of "identities" based on membership in groups that have suffered victimization in the past, and a new communitarianism that often appears to extol "community" and nation-wide "core values" for their own sake regardless of content. The celebration of diversity as well as the demand for a renewed universalism, or at least communitarianism, transcending it suffer from a certain vacuousness that truly reflects the spirit of the times.

The question remains whether American society is really becoming more culturally diverse than in the past. While the new immigration has obviously brought to these shores more non-Europeans who do not adhere to Judeo-Christian religions —Moslems, Hindus, Buddhists—there is little or no evidence that they have experienced religious discrimination, or are themselves vocal in seeking greater public acknowledgement of their cultural distinctiveness. Although they also differ in skin color, they have not experienced severe racial discrimination and efforts to mobilize "people of color" as a solidary political bloc remain a wishful aspiration rather than an achievement. Multiculturalists lay great stress on the need to avoid anything like the past demands for the Americanization of immigrants at the time of the much greater waves of immigration early in the century. But it seems highly unlikely that there would have been any repetition of those policies, least of all of the nativist sentiments and excesses that attended them, if we had been spared the current multiculturalist dispensation. The earlier immigration was not only much greater, but a mood of intense wartime patriotism followed it that led to harassment of ethnic groups with ties to enemy nations or antagonism toward our allies, something that was not repeated during the Second World War apart from the outrageous and shortly afterwards universally condemned internment of Japanese-Americans. The Bolshevik Revolution gave rise to the Red Scare which was also aimed to a great extent at immigrants from Russia and other Slavic countries from whose ranks most of the early supporters of the American Communist Party were recruited.[9] Notions of racial inferiority applied to different European peoples as well as to African Americans and Asians had by the 1920s yet to be decisively refuted by social and biological scientists. It was in this context that the Ku Klux Klan revived and spread north of the Mason-Dixon line and in 1924 the statutes restricting immigration from regions other than Western and Northern Europe were passed by the Congress. The 1930s, however, witnessed the rise of FDR's New Deal Democratic majority that included urban immigrant groups as a major component. The Second World War was fought against an enemy committed to an ideological racialism that, as was revealed in its aftermath, inspired the utterly unprecedented crime of bureaucratically organized genocide. Throughout this period social scientists challenged the existence of immutable racial mental and moral differences, attributing instead such differences to historically created cultures subject to continual variation and combination. Recognition of cultural differences has become the centerpiece of current affirmations of diversity, yet it antedates by decades the present period. In contrast to the 1920s nativist sentiments have long been on the defensive.

It is also doubtful whether recent Asian immigrants, despite differing from the American majority in race and religion, should be regarded as more culturally alien to the majority of Americans than the East and South European peasants who made up so large a proportion of the earlier immigration. Globalization is a cultural as well as an economic process and the international diffusion of American popular culture, much as it may be deplored on many grounds, has undeniably reduced the unfamiliarity of the ways of the host society to a degree that had no counterpart early in the century. It has led to the adoption by the immigrants even before immigrating of habits of consumption and a variety of Americanized practices. Nor do the Asian immigrants bring with them cultural practices such as polygamy, animal sacrifice, genital mutilation, or female foot-binding, that are strongly at variance with majority American sentiments. At most, a few differences in dress, diet, musical tastes, and some family conventions set them off from other Americans. These differences are neither sharply at odds with the beliefs and habits of most Americans, nor likely to strike them as strange, immoral, or threatening.

The wider resonance of the stress on diversity and distinctive cultural identities may follow not from any increase in their presence in the American population, but rather from uneasiness about a trend in the very opposite direction: the homogenizing pressures of a pervasive popular culture, mass consumption, and the higher educational achievements required for success and advancement in a tightly coordinated high-tech urban economy. Cultural origins are emphasized as identity markers or labels rather than standing for sets of values and ways of life that contrast sharply with those of other Americans. The very insistence on an "otherness" held to reflect deep-rooted cultural difference may register an awareness that the differences are not in fact all that great.[10] Nor are they seen as durable, for they are clearly likely to diminish as a result of high intermarriage rates and wider participation in a thoroughly urbanized and suburbanized society penetrated by the mass media of communication. The actual assimilation, or acculturation, to use a term that has been less subject to depreciation, of new immigrants is likely to be a quicker and less stressful process than in the case of the earlier mass immigration from peasant backgrounds to an America still containing a large and relatively isolated rural population amounting to nearly half of its total population.

Nor is the majority culture, as it still was a century ago, predominantly Anglo-Saxon with roots in England. My friend the late Digby Baltzell documented and in his later years increasingly lamented the decline of the upper-class Protestant Establishment and their WASP culture in postwar America.[11] Insofar as there is a general American culture it is a thin one, consisting largely of common norms and habits, mostly of a utilitarian or instrumental nature, necessary to sustain the system integration—that is, the economic and technical coordination—of a complex, technically advanced urbanized society, but not necessarily implying a deeper social integration rooted in shared traditional values. There are also the commonalties of a consumer culture: brand names, celebrities from the worlds of sports and entertainment, gossip spread by the newspapers and television. When E. D. Hirsch, Jr. a professor at the University of Virginia, listed a dozen years ago "what every American needs to know," the subtitle of his book *Cultural Literacy*, he was vehemently attacked as an ethnocentric traditionalist, even an outright chauvinist, and lumped with Allen Bloom, who had denounced cultural relativism as the cause of "the closing of the American mind." Hirsch's list consisted almost entirely of items drawn from popular culture, the news media, and elementary public school and college courses. "Black hole of Calcutta," "Ghenghis Khan," "Necessity is the mother of invention," "left wing," "William Penn," "peeping Tom," are typical items picked at random.[12] The denunciation of Hirsch's book by some professed multiculturalists seemed thoroughly irrational. The content of this common culture may, as is often claimed, be becoming less standardized with more options in the popular culture for selection by groups and individuals, but it is still disseminated by mass media controlled by large organizations and involves no more than minor variations. As Russell Jacoby observes, "The most radical Afrocentric ideologue in the United States is culturally an American citizen."[13]

I may have confined myself in the previous paragraph to contemporary forces sustaining a common American culture while neglecting historical attitudes first identified by Tocqueville over century and a half ago. The lack of fixed statuses descending from feudalism that made America the "land of opportunity" attracting immigrants was a necessary condition for its surviving deeply entrenched individualism. Egalitarianism in the form of belief in the possibility of economic success for everyone, commitment to cooperation based on voluntary "teamwork," and tolerance of most differences so long as they do not impose themselves on others, especially by means of the powers of the state, are the foundation of the "American Way of Life," although it is worth noting that that phrase is employed nowadays only by people who wish to repudiate or deride it. Nevertheless, there is such a thing, even if the demands it makes on citizens are fairly limited. As Charles Lindholm and John A. Hall observe in a thoughtful article,

> Clearly, despite the plethora of noisy interest groups, in the United States there is little recognition, whether resigned or enthusiastic, of genuinely alternative ways of life, despite the rhetoric about difference. ... The American experience has not been that of a clash of utterly different ways of life—except for the challenge from the South, whose opposition was so completely destroyed. Rather, the differences that exist in American civilization are relatively small, objectively; whilst ideologically "all are different," Americans are in fact remarkably "all the same." The homogenizing powers of this framework have been astonishing, and the dynamics of the culture suggest that this is scarcely likely to change: America will remain a land intolerant of real divergence but simultaneously capable of absorbing differences and turning outsiders into Americans in short order.[14]

That African Americans alone of the major ethnic or racial groups did not come here voluntarily has everything to do with their very special situation. As Lindholm and Hall do not fail to observe, guilt over "the historical memory of slavery" encourages rationalizations (in the Freudian sense) by whites for the continuing poverty and de facto segregation of so large a proportion of the black population.

There have been periods of aroused interest in ethnic diversity before the current vogue of multiculturalism. They have not, however, led to culture wars, for they have lacked the angry, accusatory thrust expressing a political identification with the militant left evident in the focus on African Americans, women, gays and lesbians, and some Hispanic groups, all of whom have suffered discrimination, even victimization, in the past in clear violation of American egalitarian ideals. There was a spurt of interest in "white ethnics," as they were then called, back in the early 1970s, variously described by sociologists at the time as "the resurgence of ethnicity" and "the legitimation of ethnic self-consciousness." It was, however, widely considered to be a reaction to black nationalist militancy, even a veiled apologia for racism, and was viewed as a conservative, even illiberal phenomenon. Michael Novak wrote of the "unmeltable ethnics," certainly indicating a rejection of the melting pot image, yet this was the beginning of his passage from 1960s radicalism to the Right and the American Enterprise Institute.[15] At the same time, Andrew Greeley documented and extolled as "primordial" continuing ethnic differences in American society.[16] I once at the request of the editors of *Dissent* presented a paper at a *Dissent* forum following one by Greeley arguing for the primacy of class over ethnicity in American politics.[17] In the 1930s, the historian Marcus Hansen formulated "Hansen's Law" of the different perspectives of the second and third post-immigration generations: "What the father wants to forget, the grandson wishes to remember."[18] Such an interest in their ethnic "roots" by third generation sons and daughters, however, hardly constitutes the embrace of a traditional way of life distinct from some American norm. As an "ethnic option" it amounts rather to little more than choosing a badge of identity as a form of marginal differentiation. In this vast mass society characterized by so much internal differentiation and social and geographical mobility, the desire for identification with a group larger than everyone's micro-society of family, friends, and neighbors is perennial. Quests for community and social identity are constants in American experience and ethnic groups have often seemed to fill the bill.

The celebrations of diversity and multiculturalism are not therefore unprecedented on the American scene despite the adversarial rhetoric in which they are often phrased. Nor do they portend a dangerous fragmentation and disunity in a period when no overarching national purpose is visible. Neither multiculturalism now increasing as a condition if not an ideology in all major Western nations nor globalization necessarily threatens the survival of the nation-state. They do, however, suggest the decline of nationalism, in the past far the most successful of the "secular religions" that emerged in the wake of the Enlightenment and the French Revolution. But that is a huge subject requiring at the very least another paper to do it justice.

Notes

1. Anthony Giddens, *The Consequences of Modernity* (Stanford, CA: Stanford University Press, 1990), 36-45.
2. As noted in my *American and Canadian Viewpoints* (Washington, DC: American Council on Education, 1955), 46-51.
3. Yasmeen Abu-Laban, "The Politics of Race and Ethnicity: Multiculturalism as a Contested Area," in James P. Bickerton and Alain-G. Gagnon, editors, *Canadian*

Politics (Peterborough, Ontario: Broadview Press, Second Edition, 1994), 242-263.

4. William Raspberry, "Are White Pride, Family Pride All That Different?" *The Times* (of Trenton, N.J.), March 12, 1999, A19.
5. I argue to this effect in "Cultural Relativism as an Ideology," in Dennis H. Wrong, *The Modern Condition: Essays at Century's End* (Stanford, CA: Stanford University Press, 1998), 87-95.
6. See my paper "Reflections on the Death of Socialism: Changing Perceptions of the State/Society Line," *Theory and Society*, 29/2, April, 2000. The significance of the death of socialism has been most fully stated by Russell Jacoby, *The End of Utopia: Politics and Culture in an Age of Apathy* (New York: Basic Books, 1999).
7. Todd Gitlin's term from his *The Twilight of Common Dreams: Why America is Wracked by Culture Wars* (New York: Metropolitan Books, 1995), 126-165.
8. "The New American Consensus," *New York Times Magazine,* November 1, 1998, 70.
9. Nathan Glazer, *The Social Basis of American Communism,* (New York: Harcourt, Brace & World, 1961).
10. One of the very few arguments to recognize this is Russell Jacoby's in *Dogmatic Wisdom: How the Culture Wars Divert Education and Distract America,* (New York: Doubleday, 1994), 120-159. See also chapter 2 of the *End of Utopia*, 29-66.
11. Dennis H. Wrong, "Digby Baltzell: Sociologist and Critical Celebrant of the Upper Class," *Sociological Theory,* March 1999, 112-116. (Chapter 16).
12. E. D. Hirsch, Jr., *Cultural Literacy: What Every American Needs To Know* (Boston: Houghton Mifflin, 1987).
13. Jacoby, *Dogmatic Wisdom*, 158.
14. Charles Lindholm and John A. Hall, "Is the United States Falling Apart?" *Daedalus,* Spring 1997, 202.
15. *The Rise of the Unmeltable Ethnics: Politics and Culture in the Seventies* (New York: Macmillan, 1972).
16. *Why Can't They Be Like Us?* (New York: E.P. Dutton, 1970, 1971).
17. "How Important is Social Class?" in Dennis H. Wrong, *Skeptical Sociology* (New York: Columbia University Press, 1976), 144-162, reissued as *The Oversocialiozed Conception of Man* (New Brunswick, NJ: Transaction Publishers, 1999).
18. Marcus Lee Hansen, "The Problem of the Third Generation Immigrant," in Peter Kvisto and Dag Blanck, editors, *American Immigrants and Their Children* (Urbana: University of Illinois Press, 1990). 194-195.

8

Conscience and Culture: The "Moral Sense" and Cultural Relativism

James Wilson contends that there is a universally human moral sense that makes possible the existence of stable human societies. He divides his moral sense into four parts: sympathy, fairness, self-control, and duty. Wilson thinks that many prevailing doctrines in and around the social sciences deny the existence of such a sense, most notably the cultural relativism propounded by anthropologists and postmodernist philosophers, but also Freudianism, behaviorism, and the egoistic utilitarianism favored by economists. He therefore seeks to ground his moral sense in nature itself, specifically in human biology. Yet most sociologists, including this writer, would find little that is questionable in Wilson's general conception, although they would probably attribute his moral sense to a socialization process that creates human beings out of unformed biological organisms. They would equate sympathy with the formation of an emotional identification sensitizing individuals to "the role of the other," fairness with a universal "norm of reciprocity," and self-control and duty with the "internalization of social norms."

Wilson, however, repeatedly insists that the moral sense is "natural," "inborn," "inherited," "innate" or "instinctive" and is the product of Darwinian natural selection. Mother-child bonding is especially important, for without it children would be neglected and die terminating the species. Wilson does not regard all aspects of the moral sense as genetically based: he concedes that he is not prepared to argue that there is a "sympathy gene," merely "some heritable disposition that helps us explain why sympathy is so common, as a norm if not a motive, among humans." Such a heritable disposition is in his view partly a matter of neurochemicals in the brain and

Review of James Q. Wilson, *The Moral Sense* (New York: The Free Press, 1993).

partly a matter of psychic mechanisms such as an infantile tendency to imitate that both reflects and seems to presuppose an innate emotional attachment to the mother.

Wilson's argument for the necessity of a moral sense is cognate with my own in *The Problem of Order: What Unites and Divides Society,* published a year later by the same publisher in the same format and about the same length. We both believe that there is a common human nature underlying cultural and historical variation and that this nature includes sympathetic identification with others that restrains violence against them and the ruthless pursuit of self-interest at their expense. We draw on some of the same specific evidence: infantile dependency and social bonding, Stanley Milgram's famous experiments on obedience to authority, Edward Banfield's account of what he called "amoral familism" in southern Italy, social psychological research indicating that individuals alone rather than in groups, as in the much-publicized Kitty Genovese case, are more likely to intervene to prevent crimes, psychiatric descriptions of psychopathic or sociopathic personalities who lack the capacity to sympathize with others or to feel remorse after harming them.

Wilson and I differ on a number of more general issues. He thinks that Freud and psychoanalysis have undermined belief in a moral sense by criticizing excessive instinctual repression. I think that they offer the most credible explanation of why human beings possess a moral sense and how they acquire it. We also disagree on cultural relativism, his primary culprit for the allegedly widespread denial of a moral sense. He criticizes Clifford Geertz for maintaining that "there is no such thing as a human nature independent of culture." Wilson seems to think that this statement precludes the existence of cultural universals, equating "culture" exclusively with the particulars distinguishing one society or group from another. He nevertheless observes in a footnote that Geertz "acknowledges" human universals and insists merely that the notion of a person who embodied only them would amount to a "cartoon."

Earlier in the book Wilson quotes George Peter Murdock whom he describes as "an anthropologist who spoke out against his profession's bias toward cultural relativism." In *Sick Societies Challenging the Myth of Primitive Harmony,* another recent Free Press book by a social scientist in the same format as Wilson's and my own, Robert B. Edgerton reports "the strong antirelativistic sentiments" of Alfred Kroeber, Ralph Linton, Clyde Kluckhohn, and

Robert Redfield as well as Murdock in the 1950s and describes these five scholars as "anthropology's equivalent of the 1927 New York Yankees." Edgerton concedes that their views rejecting the presumptive superiority of "primitive" to "civilized" societies "were not accepted by the majority of anthropologists," but this very disagreement implies recognition of a trans-cultural standard for evaluating cultures rather than the moral neutrality imputed to cultural relativism by Wilson and other conservatives.

Four related but distinct questions are at issue in this debate. First, is there a common human nature cutting across or underlying cultural diversity? Second, assuming such a nature, does it include a moral component resembling Freud's "superego" or Wilson's "moral sense"? Third, assuming such a component, what combination of nature and nurture, biology and culture, produces it? Fourth, does not such a component provide a cross-cultural standard for morally evaluating cultures that rules out extreme relativism? Wilson devotes most attention to the third question, seeking biological roots for the moral sense he postulates. His effort to ground morality in biology is clearly animated by the desire to find a pan-human standard that will invalidate extreme relativism.

Ruth Benedict's *Patterns of Culture* is often regarded as the *locus classicus* of cultural relativism and is even blamed for the excesses of contemporary multiculturalism. First published in 1934, it was one of the original books of intellectual quality reprinted in the "paperback revolution" of the late 1940s, becoming the all-time anthropology best-seller. Both Wilson and Edgerton credit Benedict with first using the very phrase "cultural relativism." Wilson remarks that she discussed cannibalism "without explicitly condemning it," whereas Edgerton charges her with having praised it. Benedict came to anthropology from a literary background—Wilson and Edgerton both overlook the Swiftian satirical sense to which Geertz calls attention in *Works and Lives: The Anthropologist as Author* that led her to write an essay "The Uses of Cannibalism," published only posthumously, that was clearly modeled on Swift's "A Modest Proposal."

Wilson, with characteristic fairness, credits Benedict with wishing primarily to reject racism, implicitly discounted by the prefix "cultural," and ethnocentrism, the rigid moral condemnation of another culture by the values of one's own, encoded in the "relativism" of the famous phrase. However, he joins Allen Bloom in *The Closing of the American Mind* in deploring the perversion of cultural relativism into a nihilism that rules out any moral judgments at all. Bloom complained that his students refused to condemn the Hindu practice of suttee, the burning of widows on their husbands' funeral pyres, that was suppressed by the British. Wilson is shocked that his students reserved judgment about Nazi genocide. "What worried me," he explains, " was not that the students were prepared to accept some excuses, but that they began their moral reasoning on the subject by searching for excuses." The notion of cultural relativism, to be sure, was used in questionable ways from the very beginning: I remember arguing in 1947 with a fellow student who reproached me for denying to the Soviet Union the culturally relativist tolerance I was willing to extend to the Trobriand Islanders and the Samoans. (I asked him if it should apply to the Nazis as well—he said that was an altogether different matter.)

The era of Hitler and Stalin indeed cast a shadow over cultural relativism for several decades. Critics were quick to note that Benedict obviously preferred the peaceful and cooperative Zuni to the other two cultures she described. In the context of her final chapter on psychology—essentially psychopathology—and culture, "that last disastrous sentence," as Geertz describes it, in which she refers to "equally valid patterns of life" can be understood as meaning equally genuine representations of the varieties of human nature at least as much as that any and all patterns are equally acceptable morally. Cannibalism, human sacrifice, and slavery are, after all, patterns of culture just as much as the nuclear family, humanitarianism, and democracy. The thrust of Benedict's formulation, and that of her fellow students of Franz Boas including Margaret Mead, was directed against moral judgment of the behavior of *individuals* who were merely conforming to the norms of their culture. Benedict and her colleagues were primarily concerned to oppose the narrow, puritanical moralism of Christian missionaries and often enough colonial officials by calling attention both to the *fact* of great cultural diversity and to the inescapable shaping of individuals by the dictates of their cultures. An individual cannibal cannot be expected to know any better, but refusal to judge him or her in no way precludes condemnation of cannibal*ism* as an undesirable cultural pattern. Such a version of "love the sinner, hate the sin" is altogether defensible.

A half-century ago a much sharper line was drawn between factual or existential statements and moral or normative judgments. Both sides in the current debate over multiculturalism reject the clear-cut fact value distinction upheld earlier in the century. The postmodernist partisans of multiculturalism are epistemological as well as moral or cultural relativists, affirming "equal validity" in both a cognitive and a moral sense. Wilson, on the other hand, wants to conclude from the existence of a universal moral sense validated by science that there is a transcultural standard of moral judgment. It is, to be sure, a highly general one: he does not argue that the moral sense dictates the content or scope of moral propositions. Much to Wilson's credit, he is always careful to note qualifications and possible criticisms of his own tentative generalizations. Conservative publicists like George Will, however, who have used him as ammunition in the "culture wars," have not been so circumspect.

I also have doubts about many of the specifics of Wilson's efforts to ground the moral sense in human biology. Sociology textbooks used regularly to describe reports of abandoned "feral" or completely isolated children "where the social environment approaches zero" who lacked all distinctively human attributes including morality. Wilson never mentions this body of literature that has aroused scientific interest at least since the accounts of Kaspar Hauser and the Wild Boy of Aveyron—the subject of a François Truffaut movie—in the eighteenth century.

Wilson's knowledge of recent research on infantile bonding is much superior to my own, but I wonder about some of the things he reports. Years ago as a graduate student I worked briefly as a research assistant to Dr. René Spitz, one of the pioneers of psychoanalytic research on infancy. Dr. Spitz was trying to establish that smiling in the second or third month of life was the first specifically social response of the infant and that it was evoked solely by the presence of some reasonable facsimile of the mother bending over the child and moving her head. The research showed that anyone at all or even a paper bag on a stick with rough facial features drawn on it sufficed to evoke the response. Spitz argued in a long monograph that the smile could *not* be the result of imitation, for how could the infant identify the perceived mouth movements of the mother with its own similar movements when it could not discriminate between the mother and other people or even a crude representation of them? He concluded that the smile was an expression of pleasure at the mother's apparent presence, a movement of the mouth muscles previously associated with the deep oral satisfactions of feeding (not necessarily breast-feeding).

Yet Wilson constantly invokes "imitation" and "imitative responses" as evidence of "natural sociability." Conceding with his usual honesty that "this is controversial in some quarters," he cites research by Andrew Meltzoff, a psychologist, suggesting that even newborn babies imitate some facial and hand gestures. He argues in favor of imitation against learned or purely reflex explanations of this behavior, but does not mention Spitz's work or interpretation, although he draws heavily or the work of Spitz's psychoanalytic contemporary John Bowlby.

Later on Wilson argues against reinforcement theories of learning in asserting that "children imitate what they see others doing." Early in the century the philosopher and social psychologist George Herbert Mead insisted that language with its duality of reference to self and other made possible much of the acquisition of common habits that psychologists were prone to attribute to inborn psychic mechanisms such as "an instinct to imitate," "suggestibility," or even "sympathy." Wilson avoids much reference to language, the most distinctively and universally human capacity of all, presumably out of a desire not to conceive of his moral sense as language-dependent. Yet although the pre-lingual child may lack any innate tendency to imitate, he/she will learn language even if eventually growing up to be a psychopath totally bereft of any moral sense. The question of whether or not there is an innate disposition to acquire language is, of course, central to the controversies over Noam Chomsky's linguistic theories.

Perhaps the possible analogy between language and the moral sense accounts for Wilson's scant references to the former. For obviously, even if there is an innate "deep structure" of "generative grammar," as Chomsky claims, it in no way predisposes humans to speak any particular language represented in the Tower of Babel of linguistic diversity. Similarly, Wilson's moral sense tells us little about particular moral issues or even about the range of others it embraces: is it confined to the family as in Banfield's "amoral familism," does it stop at the boundaries of the tribe, or does it at least adumbrate the brotherhood of man? Wilson tries rather unconvincingly to argue for a biological bond binding mother to child as well as the reverse, but this does not take us very far. He suggests that natural selection would have eliminated peoples who practiced drastic child neglect or all-out Hobbesian war of all against all, but population genetics is not necessary to produce this result: such cultural practices would have made survival improbable whether genetically based or not and, of course, we would not know much about past societies that had engaged in them precisely because they would not have survived. Edgerton mentions several societies in the historical and ethnographic record that have institutionalized practices threatening their survival. He invokes adaptation in a broad sense that includes but is not confined to moral norms as a criterion for evaluating societies, but he does not identify it with the biological process of Darwinian natural selection.

It is hard to see why Wilson's quest for a biological basis for morality is necessary to the claim that at least most human beings possess a definable moral sense. Moreover, since his moral sense consists of sentiments and impulses rather than definite rules of conduct it does not go very far towards providing a trans-cultural standard for moral judgment beyond suggesting that human beings should be nice to one another, especially to infants and children, and should cooperate on important projects. He attaches almost as much importance to the mother's bonding to the child as to the child's to the mother, but this hardly seems essential if the child manifests a positive social response in the first few months of life. For the mother herself was once a child and "the child is parent to the person," to provide a politically correct paraphrase of Wordsworth. At a few points Wilson seems to suggest that the nuclear family, private property, and prevention of addiction to substances that lessen self-control are desirable, which echoes conservative themes in current debates. But he does not go very far in this direction. Wilson's eminence as a social scientist—much greater than that of the quirky and cantankerous Allen Bloom—accounts more for his being taken up by conservative publicists than the direct bearing of anything he says on the "traditional values" extolled by contemporary conservatives.

Although Wilson is hardly a dogmatic hereditarian, many (though not all) conservatives have in the present century favored nature over nurture, biological over cultural determinism. Wilson wants to refute the suggestion that, in his words, "if culture is everything, then nature is nothing" by stressing the contribution of biological nature to socialized or acculturated human nature. There are indeed cultural universals which have been partially shaped by biological universals just as cultural particulars necessarily depend on potentialities within the broad limits set by biological universals. The capacity to create and acquire culture itself rests on biological endowments common to the species. Attachment and affiliation to others undeniably is rooted in the helplessness and dependency of the infant, a condition peculiar to the human species which biologically resembles "infantilized" or "fetalized" apes in Géza Roheim's suggestive formulation. Why is more than that needed to affirm the existence of Wilson's moral sense?

Many of Wilson's arguments for a moral sense resemble those that liberal sociologists commonly advance against the recent revival of economistic cost-benefit or "rational choice" models in the social sciences, for example, Amital Etzioni in *The Moral Dimension* still another Free Press book of several years ago. Yet sociologists would instantly shy away from Wilson's case for "natural sociability" as the foundation of morality and social order. Wilson recognizes that many factors, including both other innate dispositions, external circumstances, and even the putatively baneful influence of theories like cultural relativism can override the moral sense in determining individual conduct. But his efforts to ground the moral sense as a human universal in biology and natural selection are not as consequential as he thinks given that most human beings are born as helpless infants dependent on others for survival and possessing an enormous capacity to learn an immense if not infinite range of different ideas and practices. That there are deep commonalities in this human experience including some that involve positive and sympathetic orientations towards others is not to be doubted.

Part 3

Communitarianism

9

Communitarianism, Human Nature, and the Spirit of the Times

The communitarians articulate in thoroughly convincing fashion many sociological home truths that have often been ignored in current discussions. In Amitai Etzioni's books, most notably in *The New Golden Rule*,[1] he insists that *society* as a partially independent realm needs to be added to the state and the market in all considerations of social policy and collective goals. Recognition of the autonomy of society as against state and economy, which had become subjects of systematic study a few decades earlier, was a primary mandate for the very birth of sociology as a distinctive academic field in the late nineteenth century. Etzioni's argument for a voluntary moral order independent of state coercion and market exchange is central to his case for communitarianism and makes it both more and less than a political movement in the conventional sense. Communitarian insistence that human nature is a social product through and through is unexceptionable.

Occasionally, however, communitarians, including Etzioni, seem to be attacking a familiar straw man in imputing to liberals a belief in individuals with fully formed attributes that are independent of any social influence or shaping. There are vestiges here of the polemics against psychologism and biologism that were favored by the founders of sociology, especially Durkheim, in addition to their rejection of the too exclusive emphasis on force and self-interest of classical political theory and economics. A "revolt against individualism"[2] whether conceived of in economistic or bio-psychologistic terms, animated both the fathers of the field, such as Comte and Marx, and its founders as an academic discipline. Echoes of this continue to resound in sociology at large: I have been listening to attacks on "atomistic individualism" ever since I first studied sociology half a century ago. Yet I don't believe that even Hobbes, Locke, and Smith, the original targets of this polemic, were really guilty of seeing human beings as asocial or antisocial animals. They rather, out of the normative political and legal concerns with which they were primarily preoccupied, failed to "problematize," to use a fashionable term, the natural and/or social sources and determinants of human nature. Rousseau is a more complicated case: he believed that human beings had once lived in a largely asocial state of nature in which they lacked all the distinctively human qualities of language, foresight, and morality that later social thinkers have regarded as products of socialization.[3] Since under these conditions human beings possessed no moral sense at all, they were not subject to internal conflict between right and wrong, between the beast and angel in their natures. Indeed, they *were* no more than beasts, but amiable, peaceable beasts equipped with natural sympathy for one another's pain rather than the ferociously aggressive and competitive creatures of Hobbes, the Social Darwinists, and Rousseau himself in his negative conception of the stage *after* men had become more dependent on one another in society.

The neoclassical economists' conception of individuals as rational egoists continuously engaged in "utility-maximizing" calculations that dictate their behavior is another matter. In this view, although the very capacity for calculation, or "rational choice," is the result of the acquisition through socialization of language which makes possible action guided by foresight in pursuit of desired ends, objects of desire are simply taken as given "preferences" and moral restraints on the choice of both ends and means, also results of socialization, are ignored.[4] Contemporary neoclassical economists make plain that these are heuristic assumptions: human mental processes are deliberately treated as a "black box" that need not be opened for accurate predictions, the goal of science, to be made. Predictability and the construction of mathematically refined "modeling" of economic behavior are regarded as sufficient justification for the assumptions, incomplete or unrealistic as they may be from a psychological or sociological standpoint. Etzioni's *The Moral Dimension: Toward A New Economics* is a book-length critical examination of this utilitarian paradigm in which "individuals are assumed to be the effective actors, able to act independently and to be psychologically complete unto themselves."[5] It led to his creation of a new academic association, the Society for the Advancement of Social Economics, which has attracted leading scholars from several nations and all of the social sciences—including economics—who are critical of the narrow free-market economism of neoclassical economic theory.

In the debate between liberals and communitarians, the communitarian political theorists have deployed fairly commonplace sociological considerations against their adversaries. I find it quite remarkable how frequently these days writers in other disciplines aggressively reinvent the wheel in propounding ideas, often in oversimplified versions, that are utterly familiar to sociologists. This may reflect the recent decline in influence of sociology, although the field has never ranked high in the university nor come close to matching political science, economics, psychology, or the major fields of the humanities in the numbers of its practitioners.

The communitarian political theorists have insisted that there is no such thing as an "unencumbered self"—the phrase is Michael Sandel's.[6] A fundamental tenet of sociology, primarily based on the work of George Herbert Mead, is that the very existence of the "self" derives from social interaction involving the exchange of symbolic gestures. "Self" here means the reflexive awareness by individuals of their own thoughts, actions, and feelings. Yet it does not necessarily follow from this that one owes a primary moral debt to the "encumbrances" with which one is burdened, as some communitarians seem to imply. The very notion of encumbrances suggests hindrances one might want to rid oneself of, even while admitting that one can never do so completely and that the formation of one's own nature was much influenced by them. We are all, for instance, most powerfully shaped by our parents—without them we would be different people altogether. But it does not follow that we owe an immeasurable lifelong debt to them and should therefore devote much of our lives to serving them and honoring their memory, granting that some societies have engaged in ancestor worship.

The view that we are primarily the products of the social forces that have made us underlies the claim of postmodernists that "socialization goes all the way down."[7] That this imposes on us a moral obligation to celebrate and affirm those forces is plainly implied by the insistence of partisans of identity politics that our essence resides in social identities that we cannot and, accordingly, should not try to transcend nor to subordinate to individual identities forged out of multiple and unique personal social experiences. Etzioni's argument is a more balanced one. His dictum "the me needs the we to be" certainly evokes cloying rhetoric about "togetherness," "belongingness," and "we-feelings." Yet he immediately follows the phrase with the statement "the normative implications of this ontological observation are subject to different interpretations; however, that humans are social is incontestable."[8] Moreover, he explicitly repudiates an oversocialized conception of human nature that treats people simply as mirrors of the social and cultural environment to which they have been exposed.[9] He also fully recognizes a need for and the value of individual autonomy, according it equal status with community as both need and value. Etzioni's title "the new golden rule" suggests, undoubtedly by intention, Aristotle's "golden mean," in this case the balance Etzioni recommends between autonomy and order, the two components of his "spirit of community," the title of an earlier book of his.[10] He roundly rejects libertarianism, on the one hand, and authoritarian traditionalism, on the other, the opposed extreme ideological exemplars of these values.

Communitarianism as a perspective has been assimilated to the longstanding theme in social thought of "loss of community" as a major affliction of modern life. It has, accordingly, been accused of succumbing to the often-exaggerated lamentations of the many sociologists and social critics who have made much of this proclaimed loss. Given the movement's name, it is scarcely surprising that communitarianism should have been subjected to such criticism, but it is nevertheless far from fully warranted. The familiar theme represents "community," the unfulfilled psychological need and ensuing "quest" for it, as the antidote to the "alienation of modern man," "the world we have lost," "the lonely crowd," "the need for roots," "the pursuit of loneliness," "the homeless mind" —all conceived of as constituting the virtual essence of modernity and the titles of well-known books by social scientists and philosophers.[11] Yet far from celebrating "the ecstasy of belonging"[12] and "the pleasures of social cohesion,"[13] the very title of Etzioni's most recent and major communitarian book asserts the *moral obligation* imposed by community rather than the satisfactions it provides. If the title suggests Aristotle, it more directly echoes traditional biblical morality, for "the golden rule" is, of course, "do unto others as thou wouldst thyself be done by." Nor does Etzioni confine himself simply to affirming community and consideration for others as abstract "values:" he is unfailingly concrete in specifying the kinds of actions—actions not just words—he would like to see independently undertaken by individuals or mandated by public policy or law. Examples are: striving to prevent littering and vandalism in public places, police checks on drunk driving, intervening to admonish a mother who is beating her child, protesting queue jumping, praising an adolescent who offers help to a disabled senior citizen, taking legal account of the interests of children before granting a divorce. Most of these and other examples given require some individual gumption, even a minimum of moral courage, to carry out, going well beyond mere rhetorical prating about common values. Many presuppose the efficacy of *shaming* people who engage in antisocial behavior, although one critic oddly claims that Etzioni ignores shame as "a powerful instrument of moral order."[14]

If community has been "lost" under the conditions of modern life, it presumably was present in the past. This belief was dubbed "*Gemeinschaftschmerz*" by the late Christopher Lasch.[15] to connote mourning over the lost world of "organic community" that allegedly prevailed before it was shattered by the great transformations of modernity. Derek Phillips wrote an entire book refuting the idealization of past social orders implied by such a view, complaining that it overlooks or minimizes the frequent oppressive conformism and authoritarianism of premodern societies. Etzioni was one of Phillips's targets and he objected that such criticism was "misdirected" in focusing on "old or total communities, which are neither typical to modern society, nor necessary for, nor even compatible with, a communitarian society."[16] If Etzioni avoids waxing nostalgic for the distant past, he is nevertheless too inclined like a great many others, mostly social conservatives, to invoke America in the 1950s as a recent more communitarian alternative to the present. Yet the 1950s were a decade in which *both* the "quest" for the lost community[17] "eclipsed" under modern conditions[18] *and* stifling conformism imputed to American life in general and suburbia in particular evincing an *ersatz* enforced and unspontaneous version of community, became major themes of social criticism.[19]

In both of his books propounding communitarianism, Etzioni included chapters entitled "the moral voice," underlining his definition of community as morally demanding rather than merely psychologically fulfilling. His insistence on such a voice as universally human (except for sociopaths) also endorses the basic assumption of sociologists that a central feature of the socialization of individuals is their *internalization* of social norms. Etzioni recognizes that this view is derived from Freud's conception of the superego and the process of its formation, although he otherwise does not dwell on psychoanalytic theory. Freud regarded an internal "moral voice" as a universal component of human nature formed out of the young child's emotionally charged identifications with its parents and the eventual self-imposition of their moral directives and prohibitions. The performance of active duties dictated by the moral voice of the superego is largely confined to the individual's microsociety of family, friends, and neighbors. Relations with strangers, on the other hand, are primarily subject to negative prohibitions against theft, violence, fraud, vulgar display, and milder forms of incivility.

Contrary to the alleged "isolation of modern man in mass society," sociologists in the immediate postwar years "rediscovered" primary group relations governed by informal social norms and sentiments of solidarity flourishing even in the interstices of large-scale organizations where impersonal bureaucratic rules and regulations prevailed.[20] More recently, alarmists decrying the nation's alleged moral decline have deplored high rates of crime, sexual abuse, unmarried motherhood, substance addiction, and divorce resulting in child neglect, as well as such lesser derelictions as "road rage" and queue jumping. To his credit, Etzioni takes note of what he calls "curl back," the recent tapering off and even decline in the rates for most of these forms of antisocial behavior that had been rising since the 1960s.[21] He thus refuses to add his voice to the more heated jeremiads of conservatives like William Bennett and Robert Bork. The communitarian movement continues to see its mission as opposition to antisocial behavior both in "private" personal relations and in more public places involving encounters with strangers, although its main concern has been with the latter and with the total society, conceiving of "community" at the macro and the intermediate level sometimes labeled "meso" rather than in micro terms.

A moral sense may be regarded as largely innate, as by some conservatives,[22] or as acquired through early socialization, as by Freudians and sociologists, but it is indeterminate whether its commandments are considered binding beyond the sphere of family and personal relations. Freud recognized this in *Civilization and Its Discontents*.[23] Are the superego's injunctions confined entirely to kin as in the "amoral familism" Edward Banfield[24] attributed to South Italian peasants, do they fail to apply beyond the boundaries of the tribe or local community, do race, gender, ethnicity, and class set important limits to them, or do they at least adumbrate in their reach the brotherhood of man, or humanity at large?[25] Etzioni insists on the need for shared and recognized "core values" underlying the "community of communities" he extols and wishes to see more fully realized. The larger society must itself become a prime object of value reflecting a social bond extending beyond the personal and local levels. This value entails concern for a wider sense of a "common good" or "public interest" to guide "behavior in public places"[26] as well as enlisting support for enlightened public policies. But at this point communitarian rhetoric about "values" becomes abstract and often vacuously hortatory in contrast to the very concrete examples of approved individual actions toward strangers that Etzioni adduced to illustrate a proper spirit of community.

Etzioni lists "patriotism" as a "core value" of Americans in the 1950s that has since faded as part of a general deterioration of "moral order." This leads one to reflect that there is nothing about the spirit of national community that a really big threatening war or even cold war could not revive. A major depression might have the same effect: it has often been observed that the economic crisis of the 1930s created a wider and deeper sense of the American experience. It is commonly noted how at the local level group and individual differences are ignored and conflicts suppressed in response to public disasters such as floods, earthquakes, blizzards, power blackouts, terrorist bombings, mass murders. or even perceived threats to neighborhoods as in NIMBY ("Not in My Backyard") groups. Perhaps there is a trade-off between the avoidance of actual or potential calamities facing communities and their fragmentation into individuals and groups "doing their own thing," including quarreling with each other short of civil war.

Etzioni is much too ready, I think, to accede to the argument of social conservatives that there has been a moral decline originating in the various protest and countercultural movements of the 1960s. Like the conservatives, he overlooks that many of the trends seen as exhibiting this decline had deep roots in the fairly distant past, some of them going back to the closing decades of the previous century. Changes in the status of women, increases in sexual permissiveness including the legalization of homosexuality, abortion, and pornography, as well as greater tolerance for nonmarital sexual relations, liberalization of divorce laws, and concern for the rights and treatment of criminals are cases in point. Some of these changes, to be sure, came about quite abruptly, lending plausibility to the notion of a "sexual revolution" bursting out in the 1960s. Policies and laws, some of which dated back to the eighteenth century, were abandoned or repealed and longstanding taboos on acceptable public discourse vanished, including protections of the "privacy" of politicians and other public figures, as has been remarked on ad nauseam in connection with the Clinton-Lewinsky sexual scandal. Right-wing politicians have made a particular issue of the vastly greater openness in the depiction of sex and violence in the mass media, especially movies and television.

There can be little doubt that the removal of legal restrictions has increased the incidence of speech and behavior that were once illegal, morally tabooed, or, in the case of divorce, subject to restrictions that required often costly subterfuges to overcome. Yet there is still a problem, familiar to researchers of crime and deviance, of the extent to which formerly banned or concealed actions have now become merely more visible rather than more frequent. The honoring of values and norms in the breach rather than in the observance has long been recognized, especially with regard to sexual behavior. Do communitarians wish for, or unrealistically think possible, an actual abandonment of the various "liberations" associated with the 1960s? Do they want no more than to reinstate public professions of values and rules to which lip service is duly paid but which no one is really expected to live up to in conduct? Some conservatives are thoroughly realistic about this: they have no objections to hypocrisy as the tribute vice pays to virtue; they want only to restore it to its past prevalence, never mind how people, including conservatives themselves, may conduct their private lives. Most of us who came of age between the 1920s and the 1960s could not help but be partly aware that the sexual morality publicly affirmed when we were young was a relic of the Victorian past that rarely guided actual behavior (and may not have done so then). The sexual revolution produced greater changes in public expression and visibility than in actual behavior, and came after decades in which private sexual conduct and the norms actually governing it frequently transgressed the standards frozen in the letter of the law and upheld in the ritualized language of "official" public discourse, including the injunctions of parents and teachers. The wider diffusion and greater penetration of the media into everyday life accelerated these changes making them seem more abrupt and far-reaching than they really were.

The notion, shared by social conservatives and communitarians, that traditional "family values" reigned in the 1950s is also contestable. The decade was the first since the 1920s in which both peace and prosperity prevailed. High rates of marriage, decreasing ages at marriage, higher fertility—the "baby boom"—reflecting, however, only modest increases in the number of children per couple as against a larger number of child-bearing couples, and the mass migration to single-family homes in the suburbs that was both cause and effect of these vital trends reversed the demographic profile of the two previous decades. But this conduct to a considerable degree represented a "making up" of postponed family-building and residential choices that had been blocked by depression and war rather than either the continuation of traditional ways or a new family pattern replacing an earlier one.[27] These trends and the values affirmed in conjunction with them may have reflected a kind of "neo-traditionalism" in the wake of a devastating depression, innovative reforms to cope with it, a world war, and the threat of another one involving nuclear weapons. Most of the consensus and stability that marked the 1950s came after Stalin's death in 1953, the censure of Senator McCarthy the following year, the end of the Korean war, and the "spirit of Geneva" that ushered in for the first but not the last time what was called "détente" in relations with the Soviet Union. The baby boom was part of this neo-traditionalism and so was the "feminine mystique" later deplored by Betty Friedan, but they too came after the reversal of previous all-time lows in marriage and fertility. It is therefore questionable that the 1950s, and only the late 50s at that, truly exhibited a stable "moral order" rooted in a national consensus on "core values." As in the specific case of the higher birth rates that produced the baby boom[28] many features of the 1950s now mourned and idealized in retrospect were aberrations reflecting a very particular set of conditions when viewed in the larger context of the preceding half-century or longer.

Nor did the elimination in the 1960s of the gap between operative and publicly proclaimed "official" norms represent merely an outbreak of antinomian hedonism inspired by the "counterculture," although there was certainly much of that. Legal reformers, psychiatrists, intellectuals, and bohemian avant-gardists had long been advocates of greater sexual permissiveness on the morally principled grounds of improving psychological health, increasing personal freedom, and ending cynically deceptive manipulations of the legal code that contributed to disrespect for the law. Opposition to restrictions on abortion, capital punishment, and the harsh treatment of criminals also had a history antedating the 1960s by many decades. Far from manifesting the breakdown into nihilism of an established moral order, the 1960s witnessed the implementation of reforms long favored for moral, largely humanitarian, reasons: the reduction of mental suffering and social stigma, the elimination of hypocrisy, greater tolerance of individual differences, expansion of the range of personal freedoms. It may be that, though advocated on moral grounds, this amounted in the end to a "triumph of the therapeutic"[29] that undermined moral judgment as such. Undoubtedly, the removal of restrictions on formerly proscribed or severely disapproved actions produced at first overindulgence and the testing of remaining limits. In addition to initial excesses, the new practices produced, as changes always do, some unwanted unanticipated effects, such as, most notoriously, AIDS and other epidemics of sexually transmitted diseases, and the problems associated with single-parent families. A stabilizing adjustment to the new order may account for the "curl back" Etzioni recognized in the rates for crime and extremes of hedonistic behavior, which has since become greater than when he wrote. The failure of the American public to be as shocked by the Clinton-Lewinsky affair as conservative moralists think it should be may also reflect a realistic recognition, if not necessarily approval, of sexual practices that before the 1960s were veiled in relative ignorance.

Critics of communitarianism have charged that it focuses almost exclusively on the behavior of individuals. Etzioni's emphasis is indeed on public-spirited individual conduct rather than on the actions of large organizations and the hierarchical power structures they embody. Steven Lukes, reviewing the major communitarian journal, has written, "There is very little...about the moral and cultural consequences of market processes, and virtually nothing about the ramifications of economic inequality."[30] Protests against inequality and the effects of uncontrolled markets have been virtually definitive of socialism. Socialism is "about equality," as a British socialist leader once declared, but it has also been about *fraternity*, the third in the famous French revolutionary triad of "*liberté, egalité, fraternité*." "Community" as an ideal to be pursued and "fraternity" in the slogan clearly amount to much the same thing.

"Communitarianism" belongs to an entire family of words coined since the early nineteenth century to encapsulate social ideals opposed to the egoistic individualism imputed to laissez-faire capitalism and to the suffering caused by it during early industrialization: collectivism, cooperativism, fraternalism, mutualism, solidarism, communalism, communism, socialism. The last two, of course, became the names of the ideologies and political movements that have dominated the politics of so many nations in the present century. Doubtless this verbal kinship to "communitarianism" accounts for the hostility to the present movement of some conservatives despite the similarity of communitarian complaints about moral decline to their own and the—excessive, in my view—efforts of Etzioni to enlist their support.

The United States has notoriously never possessed a major socialist movement. Nevertheless, most of the features of socialist programs and ideals that have been combined in a single party, movement, or ideology in Europe have been present here though espoused at different times by different groups and political actors. Middle-class professionals in both parties supported the Progressives in imposing regulations on big capitalists; Gompers's "business unionism" promoted the interests of workers and defined the character of the American labor movement; the New Deal exhibited "a social democratic tinge," as Michael Harrington once put it, in laying the foundations of an American welfare state; feminist and civil rights movements acted in different periods to extend the electoral franchise. The American creed itself, as has often been pointed out, extolled most of the same egalitarian ideals that have animated socialists elsewhere. Communitarianism can be seen as another example of this parceling out of democratic, egalitarian, and collectivist objectives among a variety of groups and organizations, one that stresses the fraternalism and social responsibility inherent in the socialist appeal. It is a political movement insofar as it presses demands for certain legal restrictions on antisocial behavior such as drunken driving and ignoring the interests of children in divorce; it is both more and less than a political movement in proselytizing for greater sacrifice and subordination of individual interests to the common good in contemporary America. This clearly differentiates communitarianism from libertarianism and free market economism, although what it affirms is widely assented to, at least in the abstract, by partisans of quite different persuasions.

Unsurprisingly, I find myself as a fellow-sociologist in complete agreement with Etzioni's basic assumptions about the relation between society and the individual. I also approve of the communitarian movement's broad summons to greater concern for the common good as well as most of its specific political demands for the curbing of various forms of anti-social behavior. Yet I confess to a certain ambivalence to communitarianism both as a theory and a movement even though I find Etzioni himself innocent of many things I dislike about them. I have had the frequent experience of starting to read in a sympathetic spirit communitarian polemics against the egoistic and narcissistic excesses of individualism only to find my liberal-individualist hackles rising in opposition to aspects of the case being made. This also applies to at least some of Etzioni's strictures against liberals and individualists, although most of the time he recognizes that there are many breeds of these, not all of them guilty of the sins he imputes to some. I am therefore driven to conclude that I stand closer to the liberal-individualist end of the autonomy/order continuum in political and ideological terms. The political and social thinkers I have most admired for the better part of my life have been Max Weber, Raymond Aron, Isaiah Berlin, Ernest Gellner, David Riesman, and Leszek Kolakowski—liberals all, none of them tainted with the libertarianism or extreme free market economism, let alone support for what the late Brough Macpherson called "possessive individualism," that communitarians rightly reject, though Etzioni criticizes Berlin on "negative liberty" at one point.[31] These thinkers, be it noted, are mostly Europeans and it may be, as has often been charged, that the excesses of capitalist individualism in both its acquisitive and hedonistic-narcissistic, or "expressive"[32] forms are particularly pronounced in America. But accusations of superficial conformism and chameleon-like other-direction have also been seen as typically American. Communitarians lack a fully comparative perspective separating what is distinctively American from what may be inherent in modernity, which embeds small groups and communities in a far-flung system of indirect and impersonal connections.

I confess to a sense of identification with Richard Ford's central character in his novel *Independence Day* who reflects that "'Community' is actually one of those words I loathe, since all its hands-on implications are dubious." Earlier he says: "I don't think communities are continuous... I think of them—and I've got a lot of proof—

as isolated, contingent groups trying to improve on an illusion of permanence, which they fully accept as an illusion."[33] Ford's character is talking to a childhood friend who has been describing his not entirely happy experiences living on an Israeli kibbutz. One suspects that Etzioni's enthusiasm for community may go back to his youth on a kibbutz, although in fairness to him he is by no means a supporter of any version of the "goofball utopian ideals of every stripe" that Ford's character finds in "hippie communes, Brook Farms, kibbutzes."[34] In my own case, I am unable to dissociate calls for more community from the denunciations by the authorities in high school of "three-fifteeners," students who went home after classes without participating in sports or other extracurricular activities thereby revealing a deplorable lack of "school spirit." More significantly if rather predictably, Ford's character alludes to Hitler in rejecting model utopian communities; enthusiasm for communitarian appeals is likely to be tempered by anyone with a vivid recollection of the terrible events of the 1940s. Zygmunt Bauman has pointed to a strong similarity between the traditional appeals of extreme nationalism, considerably if not, alas, totally discredited by the Nazi experience, and the communitarian message.[35]

Bauman, however, thinks it paradoxical that communitarians support precisely the "natural communities of origin" based primarily on locality that earlier nationalist ideologues (Maurice Barrés is his major example) wished to transcend to create a supralocal identification with the nation-state. Bauman's argument seems more applicable to proponents of muticulturalism who affirm identity politics than to communitarians, for Etzioni's "community of communities" encompasses both a pluralist appreciation of local communities and a wider loyalty to the larger society in which they are embedded. Yet there are clear affinities as well as differences among communitarians, celebrants of multicultural "diversity," and neo-Tocquevillian[36] advocates of "civil society," all of them reflecting a *Zeitgeist* in which alarm over "the rise of selfishness in America"[37] has become as prevalent a theme of social criticism as complaints over conformism were in the 1950s and over alienation and bureaucracy in the 1960s. Alan Wolfe maintains that community as an ideal "has probably been much more frequently proclaimed in *limited* rather than in expansive form"[38] (his emphasis). Undeniably, there is tension between the two forms, but Wolfe's remarks, like Bauman's, fit multiculturalist identity politics better than the communitarian movement.

Three group or social levels are involved in these debates: primary group relations or the micro level of friends, neighbors, and relatives; the intermediate or meso level of voluntary associations extolled by neo-Tocquevillian theorists of civil society; and the macrosocial level of the most comprehensive unit, usually the nation-state. The ideal relation among levels, adumbrated at least in Etzioni's "community of communities," pictures successively widening loyalties and identifications with the smaller groups "nesting" within the larger ones, or forming a set of concentric circles. Disequilibrium among levels, the overvaluing of one over the others, is the basis of a number of variants of contemporary social criticism. Complaints about the "privatization" of American life, whether in the form of gated residential enclaves of the rich or the political apathy and indifference of the poor, deplore the primacy of the micro level. Attacks on identity politics assail the vesting of ultimate value in the second level seen as dominating the first while repudiating the "universalist" third. Fears of the totalitarian potential in the exaltation of the most inclusive level, whether sacralizing nation, race, or the solidary "toiling masses" as the major object of veneration, have only too often been justified by the terrible events of this century and inspire in some an almost reflex rejection of any appeal to "imagined communities" in Benedict Anderson's resonant phrase.[39] And just about every group beyond the micro level—and even that in one sense[40]— is an imagined community. Only small tribes or isolated villages constitute possible exceptions larger than small face-to-face groups.

There is a parallelism between Horace Kallen's image of the United States as a "nation of nations" in his famous argument for "cultural pluralism" and Etzioni's ideal of a "community of communities." But Kallen was speaking up for the meso level of the diverse cultures immigrants brought with them against an overarching Anglo-conformity, whereas Etzioni's aim in an altogether different period is to insist on obligations to the larger national community that override without superseding the diverse group identities celebrated by the partisans of multiculturalism. The emphasis on the civic duties of individuals and the lack of a substantive national reformist or state-interventionist program that has aroused critics who are descendants of the old socialist tradition, "what is left of the left," also reflects the current political mood. If Etzioni's communitarianism is not, as I have argued, oriented to the past, to what Stephen Holmes calls "deprivation history" bemoaning the world we have lost, neither is it what he calls "promissory history" projecting a vision of a glorious future establishing a new moral consensus that will redeem us all.[41] The "nebulousness" of communitarian politics about which Holmes as well as others have complained attests to its congruence with the present.

In a brilliantly perceptive article subtitled "the smallness of centrism," Nicholas Lemann observes: "The consensus right now is not to have a consensus about what the country as a whole should be or do."[42] No large national projects in domestic or foreign policy are the order of the day, not the ending of poverty, instituting universal health insurance, addressing the widening inequalities of income, intervening except minimally to curb local wars abroad, reconstructing Russia after winning the Cold War, facing up to the Asian economic crisis with more than unsolicited advice.[43] As the Republicans learned after winning control of Congress in 1994, even negative objectives have failed to win public support, such as scaling down the welfare state, reversing most of the cultural changes since the 1960s, or impeaching a president of the other party. The New Deal era of forceful policy initiatives from Washington ended in the 1980s with the success of the Republicans' Southern strategy under Reagan; Clinton's accommodations and small-bore reforms ended the "counter-revolution" misperceived as having triumphed in 1994. The period is truly conservative in its literal meaning of preserving the status quo against any alteration rather than in the ideological sense the label has acquired in political rhetoric and the lucubrations of right-wing intellectuals, many of them defectors from the left. Under these conditions it is hard to see what the communitarian movement would gain by advancing a comprehensive program of reform even were it so inclined. Perhaps communitarianism can be seen as a kind of holding action keeping alive a spirit of commitment to larger goals transcending self-interest and narrow group "special interests" for the day when such a spirit is once again needed to deal with truly national opportunities and crises.

Notes

1. Amitai Etzioni, *The New Golden Rule* (New York: Basic Books, 1996).
2. Robert Nisbet, *The Sociological Tradition* (New York: Basic Books, 1966), 7-9.
3. Jean-Jacques Rousseau, *A Discourse on Inequality* (New York: Penguin Books, 1984).

4. Dennis H. Wrong, *The Modern Condition: Essays at Century's End* (Stanford, CA: Stanford University Press, 1998), 15-25.
5. Amitai Etzioni, *The Moral Dimension* (New York: The Free Press, 1988), 6.
6. Michael Sandel, *Liberalism and the Limits of Justice* (Cambridge, UK: Cambridge University Press, 1983).
7. Richard Rorty, *Contingency, Irony, and Solidarity* (Cambridge, UK: Cambridge University Press, 1988), xiii.
8. *The New Golden Rule,* 166-167.
9. *The New Golden Rule,* 169-171.
10. *The Spirit of Community* (New York: Simon and Schuster, 1993).
11. Dennis H. Wrong, *Skeptical Sociology* (New York: Columbia University Press, 1976), 71-80; *The Modern Condition*, 140-141.
12. Derek Phillips, *Looking Backward* (Princeton, NJ: Princeton University Press, 1993).
13. Richard Sennett, "Drowning in Syrup," *Times Literary Supplement,* February 7, 1997, 3.
14. Sennett, "Drowning in Syrup," 3.
15. Christopner Lasch, *The True and Only Heaven* (New York: W.W. Norton, 1991), 139-143.
16. *The New Golden Rule,* 128
17. Robert Nisbet, *The Quest for Community* (Oxford: Oxford University Press, 1953).
18. Maurice Stein, *The Eclipse of Community* (Princeton, NJ: Princeton University Press, 1960).
19. David Riesman et al., *The Lonely Crowd* (New Haven, CT: Yale University Press, 1950); William H. Whyte, *The Organization Man* (New York: Doubleday, 1956); William J. Newman, *The Futilitarian Society* (New York: George Braziller, 1960); Daniel Bell, *The End of Ideology* (New York: Basic Books, 1960).
20. Edward A. Shils, *The Present State of Sociology* (Glencoe, IL: The Free Press, 1948), 40-52.
21. *The New Golden Rule,* 77-78.
22. James Q. Wilson, *The Moral Sense* (New York: The Free Press, 1993): for my critical discussion of this book, see Dennis H. Wrong, "Conscience and Culture," *Dissent* (Winter 1995): 127-139.
23. Sigmund Freud, *Civilization and Its Discontents* (New York: W.W. Norton, 1961).
24. Edward Banfield, *The Moral Basis of a Backward Society* (Glencoe, IL: The Free Press, 1958).
25. Martha Nussbaum, *Cultivating Humanity* (Cambridge, MA: Harvard University Press, 1997).
26. Erving Goffman, *Behavior in Public Places* (Glencoe, IL: The Free Press, 1963).
27. Dennis H. Wrong, *Population and Society* (New York: Random House, 1977), 67-71; "Discussant" in Wilbur J. Cohen and Charles F. Westoff, *Demographic Dynamics in America* (New York: The Free Press, 1977), 101-110.
28. Charles F. Westoff, in *Demographic Dynamics in America*, 53-88.
29. Philip Rieff, *The Triumph of the Therapeutic* (New York: Harper & Row, 1966).
30. Steven Lukes, "Arguments," *Dissent* (Spring 1998), 87-89.
31. *The New Golden Rule,* 22-23.
32. Robert Bellah, et al., *Habits of the Heart* (New York: Harper & Row, 1985).
33. Richard Ford, *Independence Day* (New York: Random House, 1995), 386.
34. *Independence Day,* 384.
35. Zygman Baumann, "Communitarianism, Freedom, and the Nation-State," *Critical Review,* 9, 1995, 539-553.

36. Sheri Berman, "Civil Society and the Collapse of the Weimar Republic," *World Politics,* 49, 1997, 401-429.
37. James Lincoln Collier, *The Rise of Selfishness in America* (Oxford: Oxford University Press. 1991).
38. Alan Wolfe, "Making Sense of Multiculturalism," *The Responsive Community,* 6, 1995, 65-68.
39. Benedict Anderson, *Imagined Communities* (New York: Verso, 1983).
40. Michael Walzer, "Only Connect," *New Republic,* August 13, 1990, 32-34.
41. Stephen Holmes, *The Anatomy of Antiliberalism* (Cambridge, MA: Harvard University Press, 1995), 177-178.
42. Nicholas Lemann, "The New American Consensus," *New York Times Magazine,* November 1, 1998, 70.
43. Fareed Zakaria, "Our Hollow Hegemony," *New York Times Magazine,* November 1, 1998, 44-47, 74, 80.

10

The Apolitics of Community (in an Era without Politics)

Robert Nisbet ended his review of Amitai Etzioni's 1968 book *The Active Society* with the comment that "like a good major league shortstop, he knows how to go both ways, to his right and to his left." I am delighted by the baseball metaphor, but the remark was not exactly meant as praise. The late Nisbet was just about the only truly classical conservative in sociology at that time (or since) and his *American Sociological Review* piece, laced with heavy irony, described Etzioni's book as a work of eschatology in conformity with the New Left and countercultural spirit of protest so visible in that fateful year of 1968. "For those who prefer *counter*-eschatological sociology," Nisbet wrote, "I recommend going back to one or two of Etzioni's earlier works. He is a talented mind...."

The book was indeed dedicated to "The Active Ones, in particular my students at Columbia and at Berkeley," the two universities that were the sites of the most extreme and publicized student revolts. The dedication page also included a mother-daughter dialogue quoted from the *New York Times* in which the daughter defended "flower children [who] believe in love, beauty, peace, understanding, freedom, sharing and helping each other [and] are trying to change the world with these ideas." The mother stodgily replied that "the flower children and the hippies are not creative persons, are not really doing anything useful." *O tempora, o mores*. How long ago it all seems! Yet Etzioni's book, if shrewdly attuned to the zeitgeist of the moment, was much more than a tract for the times, living up fully to its subtitle "A Theory of Societal and Political Processes." Over 650 pages in length, it summarized, expanded upon, and added to major themes of his earlier work and remains today his major theoretical statement, the subject of positive appraisal by several leading sociological theorists at a session of the American Sociological Association a few years ago.

Like nearly everyone else, Etzioni overestimated the depth and duration of the youthful protest movements of the late sixties. But it is not to his discredit that he tried to link his theorizing—which obviously long predated those movements—to what was dominating the political and cultural worlds at the time. In this respect he was then, and still is today, a "public intellectual," a type whose relative disappearance is regularly bemoaned these days. I confess I dislike the term, thinking it redundant: "intellectual" *tout court*, coined at the time of the Dreyfus Affair, has always connoted persons who went beyond their own fields of specialized knowledge to make pronouncements, often of a prophetic nature, on the state of the world and the direction of politics and history. The anti-Dreyfusards objected that *"les intellectuels"* were presumptuous bystanders who thought that because they were experts in one scientific or cultural field their opinions on any and all public issues had a special weight. Etzioni, having written books on arms control, space exploration, genetic engineering, and economics, as well as articles on a large variety of other subjects, has been accused of such presumption, but, be that as it may, it clearly does not apply to *The Active Society* nor to his contributions to the communitarian movement, whose major themes are obviously congruent with his own academic discipline of sociology.

Grounding a Movement: Part Substance, Part Timing

The communitarian appeal grows out of approaches that have been central to sociology since its foundation as a university discipline in the late nineteenth century. Etzioni has been an activist intellectual in his leadership of the movement, editorship of its journal, and authorship of his most recent books on the movement's major themes. And as in the late sixties, he has displayed a sense of timeliness: founded in the early 1990s, both the Communitarian Network and the *Responsive Community* address an American society in which political deadlock, apathy, and a fairly vacuous centrism prevail in national politics, a condition that has existed since the decline of the New Deal Democratic majority in the Reagan years. Their foundation also coincides with the end of the Cold War, which had provided a national purpose of sorts for over four decades despite having become a somewhat taken-for-granted permanent condition.

Into the resultant ideological vacuum have stepped various theorists of community. That the social transformations of the last two hundred years have led to a "loss of community"—a decline in the close and durable social bonds of small, relatively homogeneous, self-sufficient territorial communities—has been so standard a theme of sociology that its fullest and most direct version, the historical passage from *Gemeinschaft* to *Gesellschaft*, has been taken into English-language sociology without translation from the German. From there it has even diffused to a wider public: there was a disco bar on the upper West Side of Manhattan a few years ago called *"Gemeinschaft."* Predictably, Etzioni and the communitarian movement have drawn criticism for allegedly indulging in the only too familiar lamentations that the late Christopher Lasch dubbed *Gemeinschaftschmerz*.

Communitarians, including Etzioni, occasionally strike this note, but in general they are not guilty of waxing nostalgic over an idealized vanished past. Their major emphasis, no less grounded in sociology, is quite different and realistically conscious of basic conditions of modem life that are unlikely to change. Moreover, far from stressing the security and deep satisfactions of the world we have lost, Etzioni in the very title of his most recent book (*The New Golden Rule: Community and Morality in a Democratic Society*) proclaims his concern with the moral obligations that community imposes on its members. Here too he reflects his sociological heritage. A major emphasis of classical sociology was its identification of normative consensus as the foundation of social solidarity, the social cement that makes society itself possible and holds it together. Paradoxically, Etzioni's earlier work on the sociology of complex organizations and on social power and political mobilization was valuable for its qualification of the widely perceived overemphasis on the normative in the work of Durkheim and Parsons. Etzioni saw normative commitment achieved through moral persuasion as one of three bases for social relations and the exercise of social power, the other two being coercion and utilitarian material or nonmaterial interest. His communitarianism, however, stresses the importance of the normative, of a voluntary moral order based on "core values" that is partially independent of state coercion and market exchange.

Etzioni also repudiates the oversocialized conception of human nature which sociologists have been accused of holding. In *The New Golden Rule,* he not only explicitly rejects this conception, but he accords individual autonomy equal status with community presenting the former as both a need and a value in modern society. But some sociologists who have accepted the oversocialization critique have tended to affirm a radical "creative" individualism that comes close to denying altogether the reality (and necessity) of socialization as the internalization of collective values in individual character. Etzioni, however, recognizes that individuals acquire a "moral voice" that is in part an inner voice corresponding to Freud's conception of the superego and in part "an expression of the community to which they belong." He suggests that there is an autonomy-community continuum on which societies and historical eras can be located and that there is a "golden mean" that gives both their due. The conviction that in the present period we have strayed too far towards the autonomy end of the continuum is clearly the rationale, the very *raison d'être,* for the communitarian movement.

Fellow Plumbers of the Zeitgeist

Unsurprisingly, there is an affinity between communitarianism and several other current intellectual-political tendencies, for they are influenced by the same zeitgeist. Social conservatives bewailing the alleged moral decline of the nation since the sixties strike some of the same notes, although the communitarians have avoided their more rabid jeremiads. Several moderate conservatives have associated themselves with the communitarian movement. Etzioni, to his credit, has noted what he calls the "curl back" in the rates for most forms of social pathology that had been rising since the sixties, a trend that has continued up to the present and that the more extreme conservative moralists (such as Bennett and Bork) have ignored. The neo-Tocquevillian advocates of "civil society" are also plowing much the same furrow as the communitarians in voicing alarm over the decline of civility in America and in the membership of voluntary associations. And on the left the partisans of multiculturalism, in their commitment to a politics of identity, also extol community-albeit at the level of racial, ethnic, and gender subgroups within the larger society.

There is an apolitical flavor to all of these tendencies, although they are commonly regarded as political movements or perspectives. Strident proclamations of "family values" usually are more symbolic and expressive than committed to substantive public policies or legislative programs (apart from minor changes like eliminating the "marriage penalty" in tax law). The upholders of civil society are concerned with the implications for democracy of the presence or absence of a thriving nonpolitical social structure of "intermediate" groups. Unfortunately, as political scientist Sheri Berman has shown, the existence of such a social infrastructure in Weimar Germany was unable to prevent its collapse with the coming to power of Hitler and may even have facilitated it. As for identity politics, its partisans have specifically asserted the primacy of social identities shaped by membership of groups into which one is born, at the expense of "universalist" commitments to the larger heterogeneous society. (One exception to this apolitical nature would be the militant conservatives who wish to recriminalize behavior, most notably abortion, that was decriminalized in the wake of the sixties.)

It is worth noting that generally the above-mentioned political-intellectual "schools" concentrate on a single level of social life: the family in the case of the social conservatives, the intermediate-level institutions in the case of the neo-Tocquevillians and the multiculturalists. In contrast, by affirming a "community of communities" as the goal of the communitarian movement, Etzioni clearly remains sensitive to the different levels of social life and social relations in modern society. In fact, a major contribution of *The Active Society* was its specification of the different levels and social units—micro and macro—that are involved in social and political mobilization. Since that book, other analysts have added a "meso" or middle level to the micro/macro distinction.

Community in the abstract is equivalent to the fraternity extolled in the famous French revolutionary slogan of liberty, equality, fraternity. It is a property of any and all groups, political or nonpolitical, micro, meso, or macro. A few critics have, accordingly, complained of the avoidance of real but divisive political issues by the communitarian movement, arguing that it strives to be all things to all people. In this, however, it is indisputably a child of its times, times that are conservative not in the current ideological sense, but in the literal sense of resisting major politically-directed change of any kind, right or left in orientation. As Nicholas Lemann has observed, "The consensus right now is not to have a consensus about what the country as a whole should be or do." No large national purpose in either domestic or foreign policy animates present-day politics since, the end of the New Deal Democratic majority, the Cold War, and the Republican "counter-revolution" of 1994. It is hard to see under these conditions just what the communitarian movement would gain by committing itself to a comprehensive program of reform that would provoke opposition without overcoming the prevailing apathy and flaccid centrism. Perhaps its major function is that of keeping alive a spirit of commitment to larger goals transcending self and narrow group interests until the day when such a spirit is once again needed to confront real and urgent national opportunities and crises.

11

Putting Putnam's Thesis in its Place

Whether or not one is persuaded by Robert Putnam's major thesis on the decline of social and civic participation in America, *Bowling Alone* is based on an enormous assemblage of relevant and interesting data. There are sixty pages of notes in small print—too small not to place a strain on my aging eyes—and three methodological appendices covering thirty pages on how Putnam utilized his major sources. Nearly a hundred researchers and Harvard colleagues are acknowledged in a closing section entitled "The Story Behind This Book." Needless to say, the project cost several million dollars.

The basic "story behind the book" is that the author published two articles (one of them in this journal) that aroused wide attention, including a conference with the president; they promptly inspired efforts to counter his argument. The striking notion (no pun intended) that people nowadays bowl alone probably accounts for a good deal of the initial interest, although Putnam concedes that it is not literally true: people bowl today in the limited company of family and friends rather than in the organized competitive leagues that once flourished. Putnam contends that since the 1970s though starting a bit earlier there has been a marked decline in the United States in all forms of what he variously calls "civic engagement" or "social capital." This trend includes not only the fully publicized drop off in political participation beginning with voting but extends to reduced memberships in what social scientists have long called "voluntary associations" from veteran's groups, trade unions, and the PTA to sports clubs, and even such "informal" social gatherings as dinner parties at home as well as family activities outside the home. Americans, in short, come together in face-to-face interactions far less frequently than before.

Review of Robert Putnam, *Bowling Alone*: *Collapse and Revival of American Community* (New York: Simon & Schuster, 2000).

Putnam's massive evidence and his refutation of many of the early criticisms are comprehensive and often persuasive. The most salient rebuttals of Putnam's work have suggested that the forms of social interaction have changed with new kinds of association replacing venerable club memberships and local get-togethers. A few such criticisms spring immediately to mind: Putnam attributes the decline of home entertaining and club activities depending heavily on women to the growing entrance of women into the labor market as one cause. But it is hard to believe that women themselves would view this as civic disengagement rather than as evidence of considerably *greater* involvement in the society around them than in the old confining "homemaking" days.

Putnam frequently cites the sociologist Robert Wuthnow, but he fails to mention Wuthnow's 1999 book *Loose Connections* based on his own research. In this book, Wuthnow maintains that new "looser" forms of "connection" such as various ad hoc and single-issue groups now prevail, not the outright disconnection postulated by Putnam. Indeed, Wuthnow explicitly addresses and questions Putnam's early articles.

I read *Loose Connections* for its publisher and, while recommending publication, I was critical of Wuthnow's vagueness about just when he regarded the old order of closer group ties to have been securely in place. At times he seemed to be harking back to early in the century and even to the previous century, at other times to the 1950s as has become altogether conventional in the American social criticism of recent decades. Putnam too refers a few times to the allegedly traditional 1950s as the point of contrast and of departure for the transition he identifies. Yet a welcome feature of his work lacking in Wuthnow is that he identifies the change with specific birth cohorts: those born from 1910 to the 1930s, the baby boomers, and the post-60s so-called X generation. This cements the trend demographically with the 1950s the period when the generation that in its youth experienced world wars and economic depression was in its prime. Accordingly, the 1950s were not some stable American norm; instead, they were years when the disruptions of earlier decades finally abated, thus fostering an era of neo-traditionalism. I remember a friend, a brilliant young sociologist of upper-class origin, exclaiming back then "Why are we trying so hard to live like our grandfathers?"

But often overlooked is that the 1950s also witnessed a proliferation of books like David Riesman's *The Lonely Crowd,* Robert

Nisbet's *The Quest for Community*, Allen Wheelis's *The Quest for Identity*, and Maurice Stein's *The Eclipse of Community*. And many authors since such as Philip Slater, Christopher Lasch, Amitai Etzioni, and Robert Bellah have also bewailed and deplored the excesses of individualism. Their lament is summed up by two titles: Lasch's *The Culture of Narcissism* and the morally unambiguous *The Rise of Selfishness in America* by the jazz historian, James Lincoln Collier. These earlier writers shared Putnam's belief that they had diagnosed a threat to "democracy."

Putnam's theme is actually even more ancient, going back to the origins of sociology in the middle of the nineteenth century. Nisbet once characterized those origins as "the revolt against individualism;" a classical conservative, Nisbet was a rare bird among sociologists, and he provocatively overemphasized that the major ideas of sociology's founding fathers had affinities with Burkean Counter-Enlightenment thought. Yet socialists too, including Nisbet's *bête noire* Marx, clearly also diagnosed as social pathology the individualism they saw as endemic to capitalism. Indeed, Durkheim, the analyst of *anomie,* and Toennies, the theorist of the transition from *Gemeinschaft* to *Gesellschaft*, were both socialists, though not of the Marxian variety. Still earlier, Tocqueville, predictably much quoted by Putnam, reported the disposition of Americans to create new organized groups as a response to the individualism (a term he coined), population mobility, and resulting rootlessness of the new, not yet fully formed nation. I apologize for larding this text with so many names and titles, but it has been insufficiently recognized that Putnam comes at the end of a long line of thinkers, though I grant his fuller empirical evidence.

Complaints about "rampant individualism" have had two distinct emphases: they either express concern over a weak sense of social obligation, of commitment to a larger social purpose, or they stress the undesirable effects of social isolation on individuals in the form of higher rates of suicide and mental and physical illness.The absence of collective purpose and the social isolation of individuals are not, of course, unrelated and Putnam borrows his "social capital" metaphor from economics for what is plainly a means to both collective and individual ends.

My initial response to Putnam's thesis was that there was nothing about the decline he reported that would not be quickly reversed in the event of a major war or a depression. But he not only recognizes this, he identifies the Great Depression and the Second World War as formative of the active engagements of his 1910-1930 cohort dominant in the 1950s; he also observes that many of the fraternal orders and "bonding" associations now in decline were Progressive Era responses to the full-scale urbanization and industrialization of American society. However, "for better *and* for worse, America at the dawn of the new century faces no such galvanizing crisis" (emphasis author's). He notes the overlapping in time of his two major causes, generational succession and the introduction and rapid diffusion of television. (One is pleased to note all the unpleasant personal traits associated with heavy TV watching.) The entrance of women into the labor force and suburban sprawl are seen as having made lesser contributions to the "ebbing of community." The causal analysis is precise and immensely impressive.

Ultimately, one still asks "So What?"—the heading Putnam gives to his section on the consequences, as distinct from the causes, of the trends he reports. Comparing aggregate data for the separate states, he correlates low scores on his "Social Capital Index" with less education and child welfare, more crime-ridden and violence-prone neighborhoods, greater poverty and economic backwardness, poorer health and happiness, and lower political participation. Smaller, more rural states like the Dakotas, Montana, Iowa and Nebraska come off best with all the Deep South states and Nevada, obviously a special case, at the bottom. The heavily populated urban Northeastern and Midwestern states crop up regularly in the middle. I think Putnam might have made more of the regional differences and their historical roots, although he does make a few intriguing observations such as the presence of a strong Scandinavian element in the populations of high-scoring states like Minnesota, Wisconsin, and Oregon.

One remains less than convinced of the dangerous implications of Putnam's trends in light of the long history of such alarms. Putnam's book nevertheless is valuable as an extraordinary compendium of information about the country at the beginning of the new century.

Part 4

Theory and Theorists

12

What Happens but Once Might as Well not Have Happened at All: The Limits of Social Theory

Two well-known contemporary novelists, Iris Murdoch and Milan Kundera, have, each in a single novel, eloquently expressed the view that "theory" is fundamentally useless in illuminating, let alone overcoming, the quandaries of human life when major decisions have to be made. Both of them essentially identify theory with general statements from which practical prescriptions might be inferred to aid in the resolution of the highly contingent problematic situations in which human beings inescapably find themselves. Both writers considered this insight into the irreducible particularities of individual human lives important enough to invoke it allusively in the very titles of the novels in question, *Under the Net* and *The Unbearable Lightness of Being,* and it clearly provides the central rationale or message of the novels.

In what was the first in 1954 of the seemingly innumerable—actually just over twenty-five—novels she subsequently published, Iris Murdoch presented the following imagined dialogue from a text by her central character debating the views of another major character, Hugo, a movie magnate who renounces his exalted position to become a watchmaker. "Annandine" is the character based on Hugo whose views clearly reflect Murdoch's as indicated by the choice for title of the novel of the final phrase ending the part of the dialogue I have reproduced here:

> TAMARUS: But life has to be lived, and to be lived it has to be understood. This process is called civilization. What you say goes against our very nature. We are rational animals in the sense of theory-making animals.
>
> ANNANDINE: When you have been most warmly involved in life, when you've most felt yourself to be a man, has a theory ever helped you? Is it not then that you meet with

> things themselves naked? Has a theory helped you when you were in doubt about what to do? Are not these very simple moments when theories are shilly-shallying? And don't you realize this very clearly at such moments?
>
> TAMARUS: My answer is twofold. Firstly that I may not reflect upon theories, but I may be expressing one all the same. Secondly that there are theories abroad in the world, political ones for instance, and so we have to deal with them in our thoughts, and that at moments of decision too.
>
> ANNANDINE: If by expressing a theory you mean that someone else could make a theory about what you do, of course that is true and uninteresting. What I speak of is the real decision as we experience it; and here the movement away from theory and generality is the movement toward truth. All theorizing is flight. We must be ruled by the situation itself and this is unutterably particular. Indeed it is something to which we can never get close enough, however hard we may try as it were to crawl under the net.[1]

Kundera's "unbearable lightness of being" refers to the absolute uniqueness and contingency of crucial biographical events in human lives. Lives are permanently changed as a result of chance meetings with particular persons, the arbitrary choice of one route rather than another on a journey, learning through hearsay at just the right moment of residential, educational, or occupational opportunities. Kundera applies an old German saying *Einmal ist keinmal,* literally "one time is no time," or "what happens but once might as well not have happened at all" as he renders it, to choices and actions taken under circumstances that will never recur. There is no bridge from the past to the present or from the present to the future: we are totally at the mercy of the particular situation we confront. It usually fades into the past and is forgotten—this is what constitutes its unbearable lightness.[2] Anthony Powell, the author of the remarkable twelve-volume work of fiction *A Dance to the Music of Time* narrating the interlocked lives of a group of well-educated, twentieth-century, upper-class Englishmen described his work as showing an underlying pattern ruled by "the inexorable law of coincidence."[3]

Murdoch and Kundera can both be described as philosophical novelists, at least in these two books. Murdoch was an academic philosopher before abandoning philosophy as a profession for her very successful career as a novelist, if not for the modest occupation of skilled craftsman chosen by her character Hugo. Kundera explicitly presents the unbearable lightness of being as an interpretation of Nietzsche's doctrine of "eternal return" in *Thus Spake Zarathustra.* Nietzsche insisted that a true affirmation of life required embracing the conviction that an individual life will repeat itself an infinite number of times, not just exhibiting a broadly repetitive or cyclical pattern but reenacting endlessly in exact detail all the joys and pains attending the original experience. Kundera's emphasis is not on the life-affirmation implicit in acceptance of eternal return, but on the "terrifying prospect" of the heavy burden of responsibility that would weigh on a person who knew that her or his decisions were bound to be repeated forever. Awareness that one's choice is irrevocable, that it is for once and for all and can never be corrected nor have its consequences reversed in favor of a more promising alternative, makes it terrifying and a burden. Kundera characterizes such once-and-for-all choices as "unbearable." His primary emphasis is less on the burden posed by the irreversibility of such choices than on the "unbearable" awareness of their "lightness" under nonrecurrent conditions that make it probable they will be totally forgotten as opposed to the heaviness of a choice eternally repeated.

The positions of both writers can readily be characterized as "existentialist." Murdoch had written a book on Sartre before turning to fiction. Nietzsche, the source of Kundera's idea, is widely regarded as one of the first existentialists. The emphasis of both writers on the sheer intractability of real life problems to theory, generalization, and reason itself points to the "absurdity" of life, to the world's blind massive "facticity," to the absence of any knowable "essence" that precedes sheer existence, as well as to the freedom of individuals to take unprecedented actions that are bold plunges into the unknown, a freedom that they may nevertheless conceal from themselves by "inauthentically" conforming to a standardized preconceived pattern of action derived from a "theory" which becomes an externally imposed "role" in the theatrical sense.

Kundera does not confine his thesis of the lightness of being to events in individual biographies but extends it to historical events, including famous ones:

> If the French Revolution were to recur eternally, French historians would be less proud of Robespierre. But because they deal with something that will not return, the bloody years of the Revolution have turned into mere words, theories, and discussions, have become lighter than feathers, frightening to no one. There is an infinite difference between a Robespierre who occurs only once in history and a Robespierre who eternally returns, chopping off French heads...*Einmal ist keinmal*.... History is as light as individual human life, unbearably light, light as a feather, as dust swirling into the air, as whatever will no longer exist tomorrow. [4]

Historical events involve collectivities. Whatever the contribution of particular individuals to setting them in motion, they are classified as "historical" rather than merely "biographical" because they significantly affect many individual human beings. But such collective events are also unique and irreducibly particular, the product of circumstances that will never be exactly repeated. Both the "individual" and the "group" act and are acted upon in ways and under conditions that will never recur. History is a story, a narrative sequence of nonrepeatable events. Like the events of individual lives, historical events may sink into the past without leaving any trace in anyone's memory. Kundera mentions a possible war between two African kingdoms in the fourteenth century as an example and his central character is fearful after the Communist invasion of 1968 put an end to the "Prague Spring" that the same fate may befall Czech history as a result of continued Soviet dominance.[5] Far from being forgotten, however, some historical events are more likely than the events of individual lives, or even individual lives themselves *in toto,* to be only too well remembered yet at the same time to be retrospectively distorted and falsified, as in the case of the French Revolution. Their "lightness" consists in the fact that their uniquely singular occurrence makes possible their fictive revision, reconstruction, and reification enabling them to become raw material for celebratory myths and heroic legends.

There is nothing very startling in the view that both biography and history are full of uncertainties, accidents, coincidences, and unanticipated consequences that are altogether contingent. What is suggestive about the statements of Murdoch and Kundera is their linkage to "theory" and the insistence on the inadequacies of theory, its inability to help us cope with "reality" affirmed by both writers. For Kundera this awareness is painful to the point of being unbearable. For Murdoch's character (a male), on the other hand, it provides an opportunity for creativity, for the full realization of "manhood," for the freedom of choice of which existentialists have made so much, for what contemporary sociological theorists might describe as the reality of "agency." Both writers see theory, consisting of generalizations, as helpless to tell us *what we most urgently and intensely want to know,* which is always particular. This admission has strong implications for social theory and the controversies both epistemological and substantive to which it continues to give rise several centuries after it was first advanced as a hopeful project, most fully in programmatic form by Thomas Hobbes.[6] At issue is what we unavoidably want to know, not in some reflective, purely cognitive sense, but practically in coping with the context-bound personal and historical situations in which we are caught up in living our lives, the existential realities that inexorably press upon us and force us to take them into account.

The extreme nominalism expressed by Murdoch and Kundera has been less imaginatively but more systematically asserted, or at least implied, by the various brands of hermeneutics, poststructuralism, postmodernism, and epistemological relativism which have supplanted the positivist or science-building ambition that dominated social theory and social science in general just a few decades ago. The renewed interest in history by social scientists whose education had not been in that academic discipline is also noteworthy, especially when historical comparisons are made for the purpose of highlighting the differences rather than the similarities among the cases compared. Sometimes these perspectives reflect disappointment in the failures of the science-building project, sometimes they suggest pleasure, at least *Schadenfreude,* in the *hubris* of the social sciences, often they seem to express a sense of liberation from the constraints of disciplined thinking both logical and empirical, or of the refinement of aesthetic taste in the humanities, while for some they perpetuate an adversarial attitude, cynical rather than idealistic or idealizing, towards contemporary dominant ideologies and institutional legitimations. This latter attitude is clearly a response to the loss of credibility of earlier adversarial doctrines from Marxism-Leninism to other versions of socialism, counter-cultural utopias, "participatory democracy," and ever-more comprehensive welfare states, loss of belief, in short, in a host of secular "gods that failed." It is certainly "no accident," as Marxists used to say, that so many of the leading postmodernist thinkers are former Marxists of one or another persuasion.

"Theory" has often been popularly viewed with suspicion as consisting of general and abstract mental constructions in contrast to a hard, "concrete" realm of "fact" consisting of particular objects external to the perceiving mind. Facts are seen as the ultimate reality, the "really real." Popular opinion often tends to see all theories as dubious, airy-fairy mental constructions only doubtfully reflecting the world of facts and prone to fanciful misconceptions. As has often been pointed out, this view implies an entire metaphysics and epistemology in which only the obdurate, saliently material world of facts is real, if inherently vulnerable to distortion and misrepresentation by the human mind. Dr. Johnson's kicking of a stone in declared refutation of Hume's subjective idealism is the classic case. Such a view differs from Kundera's insistence on the "lightness," the "feathery" substance, of the factual particularities that shape people's lives. It also differs from the skepticism at least implied by some postpositivist doctrines as to whether there is a world of indubitably existing objects external to us that we can apprehend mentally with any accuracy.

Theories are efforts of the mind to understand the world by abstracting from what is immediately present, which always has unique aspects, in order to envisage a broader realm or class of objects or events under which those present can be subsumed. Theory is an attempt to transcend the immediate present for the purpose of understanding and ultimately coping with in action a wider temporal and spatial realm. It therefore presupposes a mind capable of orientation to spatial distance and towards the past and future as well as the present, a mind capable of time-space distanciation in Anthony Giddens's useful phrase. The sciences reverse the fact/theory valuation of the popular view in regarding theory as their goal and crowning achievement. If "facts" are seen as "hard," even "brute" in the popular view, they are typically seen as "mere" facts, givens or *"data,"* in the scientist's conception, raw material for the construction of theories that is the scientist's task. The establishing of links, the building of bridges from one set of particular facts to another, is the goal of science and this inevitably involves ignoring what is unique about particular sets. The general propositions that purport to do this amount to "theory" in the broadest sense, even at the primitive inductive level of sheer taxonomy holding that the properties of one set of particular facts will be duplicated in another set that initially resembles them.

The scientific view, though it may regard direct observation of facts as foundational for all knowledge, finds its *raison d'être* in the transcendence of particularity through generalization, which if indifferent to specific human wishes may serve human needs and goals by making prediction possible. Although holding opposed valuations of fact and theory, the popular and the scientific views are in agreement on the foundational importance of a world of objective fact. For the scientist it may merely constitute raw material for the building of theories that are the proudest constructions of the human mind whereas popularly it is seen as ultimate reality itself and mental efforts to go beyond it are viewed with suspicion. Both nevertheless consider a world of preexisting nonmental facts to be the starting-point of all efforts to understand reality.

Newer views in the philosophy of science challenge this consensus in arguing that there are no such things as perceived facts independent of and undetermined by theories. Since thinking involves the manipulation of concepts and all concepts are generalizations, thought itself departs from the sheer particularity of the phenomena its concepts purport to represent. These concepts take the form of linguistic symbols or signifiers, part of a language that constitutes a self-contained system whether or not it reflects any nonlinguistic reality outside of itself. The view that concepts are "nothing but" linguistic signifiers of a signified representation that is also linguistic, neither of them possessing any necessary relationship to external reality, is the centerpiece of contemporary poststructuralist and postmodernist thought, questioning, in effect, all generalizations. Particular objects and events external to the human mind are either seen as ultimately unknowable or their very existence is implicitly doubted in a linguistic version of subjective idealism that matches or surpasses that of Hume.

Murdoch and Kundera do not deny that many of the routine everyday actions of human beings are themselves predictable; only the significant, formative events in the lives of individuals and societies requiring "moments of decision" resist prediction by any conceivable theory and carry therefore the potentiality for Murdoch's creative action and the burden of Kundera's unbearable lightness. Ordinary everyday human actions and interactions are thoroughly predictable. Indeed, in the absence of such predictability human society would hardly be possible. As a stable, recurrent, regularly "reproduced" order, society can be said to consist of the habitually warranted expectations its members hold about one another's actions. A major legitimation of the science-building project in the social sciences used to be to insist on the predictability of human behavior in opposition to an alleged belief in "free will" that saw it as capricious, incalculable, prone to take utterly unexpected and surprising directions. It was pointed out triumphantly that people wear similar clothes, eat at specific times of the day, observe common rules of grammar in speaking, drive on the same side of the road and stop at red lights, reliably count on trains and buses running more or less on time. Yet it was overlooked that the successful "prediction" of none of these regularities depends on systematic inquiry by a group of specialists claiming to apply methods to the study of human life in society that have proven astoundingly successful in the natural sciences.[7]

The more recent assaults upon positivist social science have reversed the argument from predictability in contending that social scientists tacitly presuppose many rules and assumptions they share with the subjects they study. They are quite unable, it is held, to disentangle themselves from the human subject matter of their research and theorizing. Ranging from elaborate epistemological critiques of positivism to "strong" sociology of knowledge claims that the social scientist never escapes the influence of his own cultural world view or social position, the social scientist's claim of privileged access to a realm of "objective" social facts is denied. The social scientist is fated in the language of ethnomethodology to use as a methodological "resource" what should be a "topic" subject to investigation in its own right. He or she is inescapably tainted or biased by prior involvement with the object domain under study.

That object domain consists, of course, of particular phenomena. Nominalism, the insistence that truth resides only in the particularity of objects, is, however, a matter of degree, or of different "levels," as sociologists like to say. Iris Murdoch's Hugo is a total nominalist: "Hugo only noticed details. He never classified. It was as if his vision were sharpened to the point where even classification was impossible, for each thing was seen as absolutely unique."[8] In referring to the misrepresentation of reality inherent in words, Hugo-Murdoch even brilliantly anticipates *avant la lettre* the insistence on the unbridgeable hiatus between signs and their referents that later became identified with linguistic deconstructionism. Doubtless this reflects Murdoch's familiarity with Oxford "ordinary language" philosophy, a major contributor reflecting the influence of Wittgenstein and Austin to the vaunted "linguistic turn" in philosophy and social thought.

Logically, such extreme nominalism makes no exception for cultural nominalism—more often called "cultural relativism"—or a historicism that insists on the absolute specificity of each and every historical situation. A version of the latter is the dictum that "we learn from history only that we learn nothing from history," favored by historians intent on debunking popular beliefs in the putative "lessons" of history. However, the very concepts of culture and history presuppose commonalties among the individual human beings subsumed under them. Why should nominalism stop at the level of groups? Since individuals have identities and personalities that have been shaped by unique experiences, why classify them under general cultural-historical conceptual labels while arguing at the same time that cultures are so unique as to be "incommensurable?" Why not go whole hog and affirm a total nominalism resembling that of Murdoch's Hugo? Even individual selves can be held to have no unity or continuity, but to consist simply of strings of isolated experiences succeeding one another in time, a position amounting to the total solipsism first advanced by Hume and upheld by some later philosophers. The extreme deconstructionism of a Derrida, holding that consciousness is nothing but "a play of signifiers," is a linguistic version.

Insofar as cultural nominalism, the assumption underlying what has come to be known as "identity politics," treats the individuality of persons as nonexistent or as utterly insignificant, it is guilty of an extreme version of what sociologists have criticized as an "oversocialized" conception of human nature.[9] Individuals are seen as mirrors of the culture that has shaped them, as "cultural dopes" who are mere "carriers" of their culture, or as "role-players" reading from ready-made cultural scripts. Negation of personal identity and individuality is implicit in the claim that individual identity is primarily, even exclusively, formed by groups within larger societies just as much as it was by earlier assumptions that it reflected a common culture of the larger society, usually equated in the contemporary world with the nation-state.[10]

Murdoch and Kundera are not, of course, social theorists or preoccupied at all with social theory as such. Existentialism, to be sure, originated as an assertion of the concrete, the contingent, and the particular against the arrogant abstractions of theory. Kierkegaard, the "first existentialist," was reacting against the all-embracing pretensions of Hegelian theory. Nietzsche questioned the universality of the claims of any and all philosophers. For contending that all statements were "interpretations," he has been hailed as an ancestor by contemporary postmodernists eager to deny the possibility of objectivity and universality. But as novelists, Murdoch and Kundera are not engaged in these battles over theory, which postdate

Murdoch's novel in any case. They succeed in articulating vividly and concretely central features of biography and history that evoke a shock of recognition independently of elaborated epistemological or ontological arguments. I cite them because I believe they have identified precisely the circumstances of human life and history that have proved resistant to social theory. This resistance has by now been openly or tacitly widely recognized and accounts for the postpositivist outlooks that have produced so many brands of subjectivist epistemologies and debunking sociologies of knowledge. A mood of disappointment over the manifest failure of the ambitious hopes and aspirations of science-building social science sometimes underlies this outlook. Yet this failure also gives rise to a spirit of jaunty polemical dismissal of the remnants of positivism and of the inevitably surviving theories and ideologies that continue to make universalist claims.

What do we most urgently want to know about human life and history? What questions do we hope and sometimes expect social theory to answer? I do not have in mind primarily the questions and problems directly guiding historians and social scientists in their scholarly investigations, those they see themselves as trying to resolve or explain. (Regrettably, they are often less than forthright and even confused about this starting-point of disciplined inquiry, "the context of discovery" as it has been called.) I am thinking rather of the existential concerns arising out of human life in its historical context antedating systematic inquiry. It is, after all, the existence of such concerns that legitimates the scholarly enterprise itself as more than a mere idle or antiquarian pursuit, a time-killing leisure activity that some persons are permitted to pursue in a relatively prosperous society. The questions, hypotheses, and conjectures that historians and social scientists see as directing their inquiries are not, of course, unrelated to these contextual concerns. The distinction between the purely cognitive and the existential is by no means an absolute one. I have in mind here the kinds of questions, hopes, fears, and expectations that both antedate and legitimate historical and social science scholarship.

The current disillusion with social science is a reaction to the extravagant claims made for it in the past. It directly or tacitly recognizes the limits to which social science can reasonably aspire, limits that Murdoch and Kundera have dramatized in their fictions. But this disillusion is but a part, and a small part, of the larger disillusion with human progress that has been expressed so often and so forcefully in the twentieth century. Postmodernists who declare that only in the past few decades has belief in the inevitability of progress waned show a lamentable lack of historical perspective, ignoring the experiences of several generations immediately preceding their own. Every intellectual generation since the "lost generation" of the 1920s reacting to the Great War has rejected belief in progress as a Victorian shibboleth, or as an even earlier delusion of the faith in science and reason of the eighteenth-century Enlightenment and has usually identified its rejection with such particular historical disasters as the Somme, Hiroshima, Auschwitz, and/or the Gulag. The debunking of progress has been a regular preoccupation of intellectuals throughout the 20th century. Belief that application of the methods of science would point the way to the solution of social problems large and small, from ending war to reducing poverty and inequality, is but one case in point.

Such belief has hardly been a world-historical force comparable to Marxism, although both are products of the Enlightenment. Loss of belief in the potential of the social sciences, particularly in its current postmodernist manifestations, has certainly been influenced by the failures of Marxism, but it has also had independent roots. Faith in social science, or the "behavioral sciences" as they were often then called, was probably at a peak in the United States in the decades right after the Second World War. Much social research was funded by government and private foundations, research institutes attached to major universities were created and provided new career possibilities for research entrepreneurs shuttling between campuses, foundation headquarters, and Washington bureaucracies. The imminence of intellectual breakthroughs equivalent to those that had occurred in the past in physics and biology was often proclaimed; what has been more recently derided as the "waiting for Newton syndrome" was widespread. Perhaps this mood was fated to dissipate when the social problems social scientists claimed to be able to resolve stubbornly persisted, no social scientific equivalent of splitting the atom emerged, and research funds became less available with the end of the postwar boom. In any case, critics of positivist social science began to win a hearing and soon a hundred theoretical and epistemological flowers bloomed, fragmenting the unity of the social sciences which now seemed to resemble more closely the succession of transitory fashions that had always prevailed in the arts rather than the cumulative progress exhibited by the natural sciences. Momentous unforeseen events of which the sudden collapse of Communism was the most recent and dramatic contributed to realization that social scientists had not succeeded in charting the future or even in immunizing us from the surprises history always has had in store for us.

Social research actuated by positivist aspirations has real if modest achievements to its credit, but it has hardly reduced the raw contingencies and uncontrollable outcomes to which human life is subject so vividly stressed by Murdoch and Kundera. As has been pointed out many times in debates over postmodernism, cultural relativism, and the so-called "strong program" in the sociology of knowledge, the claims made by these doctrines are subject to the Cretan paradox that if universally true they must be self-referential thus casting doubt on their own claims to universal truth. But what of the assertion made by Tamarus, Annandine's antagonist in Murdoch's dialogue, that "we are rational animals in the sense of theory-making animals?" Even if it is acknowledged that all theories occlude or ignore important aspects of the particularity of experience and therefore partly falsify that experience, are they all equally useless with nothing to choose between them? Does not theory-making, as Tamarus suggests, fulfill a real human need ? And does not this need also require discrimination among theories and their evaluation by standards of relative truth based on some notion—dare one say it?—of at least partial correspondence to an independently existing reality? Theories may be inadequate in enabling us to cope with the most problematic situations we encounter in practical, decisional contexts yet still answer to cognitive and even emotional needs that are part of our nature and that are not satisfied by just any theory at all.

Notes

1. Iris Murdoch, *Under the Net* (Harmondsworth, Middlesex, UK: Penguin Books, 1954), pp. 80-81.
2. Milan Kundera, *The Unbearable Lightness of Being,* (New York: Harper & Row, 1985), p. 8.
3. Quoted by William Grimes, "Anthony Powell, 94, Chronicler of the Changing Fortunes of Britain's Upper Class, Dies," *New York Times*, March 30, 2000, p. B15.
4. Kundera, *The Unbearable Lightness of Being*, pp. 4, 223.
5. Kundera, *The Unbearable Lightness of Being*, pp. 3, 222-223.
6. There are, of course, other candidates for pioneer visionary of social science.
7. This paragraph summarizes my discussion of the grounding of shared expectations and social norms in the regularities of routine social interactions in chapter 3 of *The*

Problem of Order: What Unites and Divides Societies (Cambridge, MA: Harvard University Press, 1995), pp. 37-69.

8. Murdoch, *Under the Net*, p. 61.
9. Dennis H. Wrong, "The Oversocialized Conception of Man in Modern Sociology," *American Sociological Review, 26* (April 1961), pp. 83-93, most recently reprinted in Wrong, *The Oversocialized Conception of Man* (New Brunswick, NJ: Transaction Publishers, 1999).
10. See Dennis Wrong, "Adversarial Identities and Multiculturalism," *Society,* 37 (January/February 2000), pp. 10-14.

13

The Postmodernist Shuffle

Charles Lemert regards his book as a successor to C. Wright Mills's *The Sociological Imagination* and Alvin Gouldner's *The Coming Crisis of Western Sociology*. His title implies that Gouldner's crisis has come and gone. However, he argues that Western culture is in permanent crisis, which contradicts both the medical and the broader metaphorical uses of the term. Lemert's uncertainty results from the dual nature of the alleged crisis: it is a crisis within sociology reflecting, or rather failing adequately to reflect, crisis in the larger society. This is consistent with Mills and Gouldner, both of whom accused sociology of "lecturing on navigation while the ship is going down" (Auden). Mills thought sociologists were fiddling when Rome was at risk of burning in a nuclear conflagration caused by the "crackpot realism" of "the power elite." Gouldner opened his preface with the declaration that "we theorize today within the sound of guns," meaning the campus rebellions of the late 1960s.

Both of them, Lemert concedes, were far from prescient. Nuclear deterrence "worked," and a Third World War never came. I remember insisting to Mills in 1956 in my Toronto living room that every time the United States had been faced with Soviet or Chinese actions threatening war it had drawn back from the brink—I had in mind the Berlin blockade, the limited war in Korea, and President Eisenhower's refusal to support the French at Dienbienphu against the recommendation of his chief advisers. (Would that his successors had displayed such wisdom in that part of the world a few years later!) Mills's reply was "I think there's a war party in the Pentagon." Indeed there was, as Morris Janowitz was shortly to show in detail in *The Professional Soldier,* but it prevailed only on secondary issues. As for Gouldner's crisis, the student ferment was unmistakably abating by the time his book appeared.

Review of Charles Lemert, *Sociology after the Crisis* (Boulder, CO: Westview Press).

In light of these cautionary examples, Lemert is cagey about the present crisis. He defines it essentially as a crisis of belief rather than of menacing historical events. In his introduction, however, he comes on like Newt Gingrich in quoting a Los Angeles gang member's account of a life of crime, violence, and the fathering of illegitimate children. Or perhaps I should put this the other way around: after Gingrich had blamed some particularly gruesome murders on the welfare state, the White House press secretary said, "It sounded like a college sociology course." One also recalls that Lemert's mentor, Gouldner, attacked sociologists for being custodians of the welfare state, the same charge Gingrich, in another notorious remark, leveled at Bob Dole. A few pages later Lemert invokes Russell Jacoby's much abused label to deplore the absence of "public intellectuals" among today's sociologists. But he doesn't dwell on this for long, perhaps because it is so inherently implausible when one can instantly come up with the names of Amitai Etzioni, Christopher Jencks, William Julius Wilson, the late James Coleman, and Paul Starr, none of them so much as mentioned by Lemert (apart from a short discussion of Coleman as a theorist), although three of them have been presidents of the American Sociological Association in the 1990s.

Lemert's polemic occasionally recalls New Left assaults on "corporate liberalism" that were echoed by Gouldner. Some thinkers are described as "naively" or "hopelessly" liberal, while he fails even to acknowledge the existence of the conservative publicists and intellectuals who have dominated political debate for the past two decades. Like Jacoby, he evidently regards "conservative intellectual" as an oxymoron. He says he initially "hated" Jacoby's *The Last Intellectuals* for criticizing professors for writing badly. Doubtless he is not pleased by Jacoby's more recent complaint in *Lingua Franca* that Gayatri Spivak, whom Lemert urges sociologists to take seriously, "like most postcolonial theorists, cannot write a sentence."[1] Yet Mills, Jacoby's most praised example of his endangered species of "public intellectual," famously mocked sociologists, especially Talcott Parsons, for their bad prose.

Lemert himself is by no means a clumsy or jargon-ridden writer, despite his occasional resort to such non-words as 'liberatory" and "agential" and his habitual use, like other sociologists, of "structure" as both a noun and a verb. But it is sometimes hard to see just what he is getting at because he writes in a mannered style at a high level of abstraction, never venturing into the middle ground between that level and lurid journalistic examples of individual lives of which the L.A. gang member is only the first of several. Essentially, he buys into the whole shebang of what is variously called by friends and foes "postmodernism," "identity politics," "multiculturalism," or "political correctness." Lemert avoids these tendentious labels except for the first, invoked early in the book to dissociate himself from what he sees as the vanished world of Parsons, Mills, and Gouldner, although he later argues that "postmodern" is perhaps "poorly named" since most people don't yet recognize that the world has profoundly changed. But if so, where's the crisis, since to postmodernists everything is a matter of "socially constructed" perspectives? Nietzsche declared that God is dead, but went on to observe that "this tremendous event has yet to reach the ears of men." Might this not also be true of the *Twilight of Man,* the title of an earlier book by Lemert borrowed from his oracle Foucault?

What Lemert thinks has died in the last twenty-five years is "modernity," which in postmodernist fashion he defines as a theory, not a condition. Modernity is equated with belief in progress, with "the story of one world progressing toward a better day when all men will be free and good." Like the neoconservatives, Lemert sees the 1960s as a crucial decade of transition. He today finds the Port Huron Statement and other "early texts of the New Left" to be "quaint, almost old-fashioned." (Some of us thought so at the time.) He is right to see that the New Left was the end of something rather than a new beginning. The sixties agitation was a histrionic attempt to revive a political and ideological subculture going back to the nineteenth century that had first emerged in the United States just before the First World War as what John Patrick Diggins has called "the Lyrical Left."[2] It seems a mite parochial to proclaim that the New Left's failure initiated the end of modernity and the final exposure of the "dark secrets of Western culture." Like most sociologists, most Americans for that matter, Lemert is vague and often inaccurate about anything that happened more than twenty or thirty years ago.

He thinks the Weimar Republic existed in the nineteenth century, a mistake he makes twice so it is not just a blip of the word processor. His view even of recent events, such as the Cold War, is decidedly skewed. He quotes George Kennan, in his "long telegram" of 1946, as saying that the reception of Marxism in Russia was influenced by the insecurities of Russian history and interprets this unexceptionable observation as claiming that "Russians by their nature are afflicted with a truculent and intolerant national character; by inference, Americans are peaceable, hence moral, by nature." He sees this as the foundation of "the global ideology of containment." No one who had read Kennan carefully, let alone knew him, could possibly attribute such views to him. Kennan has habitually criticized what he has called the "legalistic-moralistic" outlook that leads Americans to define wars as all-out crusades and to assume self-righteous postures of moral rectitude in judging other nations. When I worked for him as a research assistant in Princeton a few years after the long telegram and the "Mr. X' article that grew out of it, he was already arguing passionately against making containment into a global policy. I saw him just after the break-up of the Soviet Union and said to him that he must feel proud of how events had vindicated the policy he had first named and advocated. He replied: "I feel so sorry for the Russian people. They didn't deserve all the disasters that have happened to them." No trace of any belief in an eternally aggressive Russian national character there!

Lemert's chapter "The End of Ideology, Really!" requires him to confront the earlier end of ideology theorists. He claims that their view was actually an ideology of the Cold War rejecting Marxism as disproved by the American standard of living. This recycles one of the five erroneous criticisms of the end of ideology listed by Daniel Bell in his 1988 "Afterword" to the reissue of his 1960 book *The End of Ideology*. It quite escapes Lemert that the sociologists of the 1950s—Shils, Bell, Aron, and Lipset—meant by ideology "secular religions" (Aron's term), specifically fascism and communism, aspiring to mobilize masses for political action, although he concedes that their outlook may have been a "purgative necessary after Senator McCarthy's reign of terror." But they were reacting to the *real* terrors of the Final Solution and Stalinism with genuine relief that such ideologies had lost their appeal, rather than expressing a complacent conservatism or Cold War militancy as charged by the radicals of the 1960s whom Lemert echoes. Lemert also overlooks that the end of ideology was proclaimed after the death of Stalin during the first interlude of detente with the Soviet Union; far from being an ideological weapon of the Cold War, it was a recognition (especially by Aron) of the "peaceful coexistence" affirmed at the time by both Soviet and American leaders. Shils later observed that critics were completely mistaken in interpreting the end of ideology "to mean that ideals, ethical standards, general or comprehensive social views and policies, were no longer either relevant or possible in human society."[3] This does, ironically, seem to describe the later postmodernists who, in Lemert's words, "tell the truth of social change—that there is no singular truth behind which to hide the corrupting force of power."

As for the much-touted postmodernist disbelief in progress, I am moved to ask, "So what else is new?" In the first undergraduate course I took in sociology over half a century ago we were assigned "the idea of progress" as an essay topic and expected to brand it a self-congratulatory ethnocentric myth. In the greatest anti-war poem by the greatest of the anti-war poets, Wilfred Owen wrote, in 1917: "None will break ranks, though nations trek from progress." A few years later Yeats wrote "The Second Coming" and Eliot wrote "The Waste Land," the century's two most famous poems and hardly paeans to the modern West. Oswald Spengler's *The Decline of the West* was a best-seller in the 1920s. The years of *entre deux guerres* were dominated by the mood plangently expressed in Cyril Connolly's bon mot "It is closing time in the gardens of the West." Ah well, it's not the fault of the postmodernists that they were born only yesterday! Yet the revived late 1960s' "dream of the golden mountains" (Malcolm Cowley's phrase) having come to nothing, they want to hang onto a few shards of it in the form of identity politics while making a *Weltanschauung* out of their disappointment.

Lemert might respond that his subject is the narrower one of academic sociology, criticized for affirming modernity while ignoring its dark side. Even Bourdieu and Giddens, of whom he writes fairly appreciatively, are charged with being too rational and universalistic and with paying insufficient attention to "the Other." Lemert's primary target is the "classical" thinkers, whom he sees as having laid the rails on which sociology has been traveling ever since, namely, Marx, Durkheim, and Weber. He includes Freud in this company, although he remarks perceptively that "Freud has largely been ignored by sociologists surely because they recognized in what he said that which would threaten the artificially pure space of the social." Lemert occasionally deploys Freud on the unconscious against sociologists who have failed to plumb the full depths of otherness. The classical thinkers, he argues, mourned "lost worlds," but believed that they could be recovered in all their unity and moral purity under modern conditions. Their sociologies amounted to efforts to show how this might be achieved.

This description perfectly fits Marx's theory that the dialectic of history will reinstate "primitive communism" at a level of material abundance. Marx has accurately been called the last great thinker of the Enlightenment before, as Weber put it, "its rosy blush irretrievably faded." Lemert recognizes as much but thinks "it would be wrong to treat Marx too harshly for his failure, if only because his purposes were decent, even noble." Marx's racism and support for European imperialism, seen by Lemert as indelible sins of the West, are not mentioned, although Durkheim's conventionally "patriarchal" view of women receives a lot of attention. Durkheim was, to be sure, the thinker who had the greatest influence on academic sociology and thus is treated at greatest length. Lemert's criticisms are often sound and even acute, although in stressing Durkheim's positive evaluation of modern over traditional society he fails to note that the contrast itself was commonplace even when the valuations were reversed, as in the case of Toennies. Lemert never so much as mentions the Romantic movement that Gouldner thought was a major influence on sociology, or the anti-Enlightenment thinkers, seen as important influences by Robert Nisbet. Obviously, those intellectual traditions do not fit his conception of sociology as totally committed to modernity as moral progress.

Weber, he can't ignore. Lemert's depiction of him as a disillusioned believer in progress and the moral superiority of the West is bizarre. He considers only one work, *The Protestant Ethic and the Spirit of Capitalism,* except for a single sentence from the opening paragraphs of "Politics as a Vocation." His argument depends almost entirely on the first sentence of the "Author's Introduction" to Parsons's translation of *The Protestant Ethic* where Weber maintained that "in Western civilization only, cultural phenomena have appeared which (as we like to think) lie in a line of development having universal significance and value" (Weber's emphasis). Lemert seems unaware that this was not Weber's introduction to The Protestant Ethic but was written fifteen years later to introduce a collection of his essays on the sociology of religion. Parsons chose it to precede his 1930 translation of the earlier essay. Since *The Protestant Ethic* was written *before* Weber's studies of India and China and the "Author's Introduction" long *after*, in the last year of his life, the claim that Weber implicitly was unfavorably contrasting the East with the progressive West is not convincing. Lemert insists that Weber is defining an "ethical disposition" that shows the West to be "measurably superior to the East." Now Weber specified fully and concretely what "cultural phenomena" he had in mind: natural science, mathematics, historical scholarship, jurisprudence, music, architecture, bureaucratic organization, and capitalist enterprise. The West made *technical* advances, even "breakthroughs," in all these areas, which also were present in Eastern civilizations, but in addition to the parenthetical caveat "as we like to think," Weber went on plainly to state: "The question of the relative value of the cultures which are compared here will not receive a single word." So much for the view on which Lemert places immeasurable weight: that "universal significance" meant moral as well as technical or instrumental significance.

As for the famous closing peroration on the "iron cage," Lemert thinks, "The reader of *The Protestant Ethic* would be fully justified to wonder if its concluding pages had been written by some other person," as if the preceding pages were a eulogy of Puritan asceticism and capitalist acquisitiveness. The closing passages are usually cited to show what a pessimist Weber was. But Lemert thinks he was simply "baffled" by the failure of "modern political and economic life actually [to] spread the benefits of rational democracy and capitalist enterprise across, if not the globe, the whole of the West." This failure supposedly led him in "Politics as a Vocation" to ask, "When and why do men obey?" What are their "inner justifications?" But Weber's magisterial essay displays in full his immense historical erudition as he ranges across Medieval Europe, Antiquity, the Middle East, India, China, Mongolia, and Japan as well as the contemporary West to delineate his three types of legitimation and their social contexts. Moreover, the question itself was raised long before the modern era in the Vedic texts, the debate between Socrates and Thrasymachus in Plato's *Republic*, and most saliently by Machiavelli in *Il Principe*. Not for nothing has Wolfgang Mommsen called Weber "the Machiavelli of Heidelberg."

Lemert suggests that even Freud believed he had solved "modernity's riddle" by inventing a science that "could cure the moral ills of modern man." Freud thought that relieving patients of their neuroses would merely restore them to the ordinary unhappiness that was the human lot. Moreover, he maintained that the progress of modern civilization was necessarily purchased at the price of greater repression and neurosis. Why doesn't Lemert simply label Weber and Freud as postmodernists *avant la lettre?* Presumably because, at least in Weber's case, doing so would undermine Lemert's indictment of sociology for clinging to modernist illusions.

In discussing Durkheim, Lemert first makes a statement in the form of a question that he repeats, always in italics, no less than twelve times throughout the book. With occasional slight variations, it reads: *Who am I if things social are different?* Since this gnomic query serves as a veritable mantra condensing the book's thesis, it is worth asking exactly what it means. Most obviously, it connotes the "quest for identity," the title of a 1950s book by Allen Wheelis, a San Francisco psychoanalyst who had as patients several of the beatnik writers. Identity was first used as a psychoanalytic concept by Erik Erikson. "Things social" echoes Durkheim, although since Lemert has a bad case of what Arthur Koestler once called "the French flu" one wonders why he ignores the counter-statement *"les faits sociaux ne sont pas des choses,"* the title of a book by the sociologist Jules Monnerot. His interrogatory mantra seems to be a recognition of the fact that the modern world confronts the individual with a wide range of choices, or at least the illusion of such a range, which imposes a burden of self-definition that is rarely satisfactorily resolved without psychic confusion and conflict. Even after irreversible choices have been made "footfalls echo in the memory / down the passage which we did not take / towards the door we never opened" (Eliot). Erikson and Wheelis were concerned with problems of individual identity rooted in personal experience but in light of the change and diversity of modern life necessarily encountered in some form by everyone.

However, this is *not* what Lemert means. He is interested only in social or group identities and a limited range of them at that: namely, those that "modernity" has denigrated or neglected in its dream, which sociology has always shared, of a better world. He has in mind, surely to no one's surprise, the ascribed identities of race; sex; sexual orientation (assuming it is hereditary); and former colonial subjection, imperialism having been, according to him, the formative experience of the modern West, the precondition for its achievements, and the basis of its exclusions. The radicals of the 1960s unmasked "the West's grand denial of the reality of its own evil and aggression" with the result that individuals today "are thrust alone into a social world so poorly structured as to frustrate their need to know who they are by identification with some larger social whole." (Is such a need really universal?) Lemert later asserts that, compared to earlier generations, "today's youth grew up with an experience much closer to that of those who suffered the Holocaust and the Gulag." I am outraged by this comparison, which is reminiscent of the "student as nigger" slogan of the sixties. Nor am I mollified by the instant qualification that "this does not diminish the far greater horror the latter faced," for Lemert nervously qualifies nearly all of his extreme generalizations. In any case, this loss of faith in the West is the crisis we face.

In direct opposition to Irving Louis Horowitz, who in *The Decomposition of Sociology* attacks sociology for having totally embraced "political correctness," Lemert deplores that "among the human sciences, few other fields so resist as does sociology" the writings of feminists, blacks, postcolonial studies, and "queer theory." This is an exaggeration—does he really think economics, political science, and psychology have imbibed deeply from those wells?—but he is right as against Horowitz. Yet, it never seems to occur to him that sociologists may have reservations because they have long been familiar with and have learned the limits of such doctrines as cultural relativism and the sociology of knowledge, as well as having tried to understand "deviant behavior" from the point of view of those labeled deviant. In addition, among the very first books I was assigned in sociology were studies in the 1930s and early 1940s of the "black experience" authored or co-authored by such black sociologists as Allison Davis, Charles Johnson, St. Clair Drake, and E. Franklin Frazier.

Lemert asks: "Can any social world generate the principle of its own critique? Can modernity generate any truth, any norm, sufficiently powerful to criticize itself ?" The question answers itself: the post-Enlightenment West, surely. New World slavery, segregation in the American South, and all legal racial discrimination were not and could not have been abolished by the efforts of their victims alone. Feminism was not imported from non-Western sources, indeed, even in the bad old days of rampant patriarchy the lesser subordination of women compared to that of other major civilizations contributed to the Western demographic transition, as my teacher Kingsley Davis maintained. As for colonialism, the major colonial power voluntarily surrendered its global empire, the leaders of colonial liberation movements like Gandhi, Nehru, Nkrumah, Bourguiba, Houphouët-Boigny, and Nyerere were educated at the London School of Economics, the Sorbonne, or other Western universities. Most of this long antedated the 1960s.

Lemert is right that Marx, Durkheim, and Weber have little to tell us about the world of the late twentieth century, though I have some reservations in the case of Weber. But our needed new understanding is not likely to be enhanced by the professorial cultivation of old grievances behind the walls of the university, that last sanctuary for causes that have had their day, whether because of partial successes or outright failure.

Notes

1. "Marginal Returns: The Trouble with Post-Colonial Theory," *Lingua Franca,* 5 (Sept./Oct. 1995), p. 36.
2. *The Rise and Fall of the American Left* (New York: W.W. Norton, 1992).
3. Edward A. Shils, *The Constitution of Society* (Chicago: University of Chicago Press, 1982), p. 221.

14

Raymond Aron

Nicolas Baverez has produced a full-length, thoroughly researched biography of Raymond Aron—517 pages of text plus another twenty-four of appendices and index. It is a conventional biography tracing Aron's life from birth, or, rather, from prenatal family history, to death, with concluding reflections on its significance. This particular kind of effort will not have to be undertaken again.

Inevitably, Baverez draws on and often duplicates, citing probably more often than any other source, Aron's own two-volume *Memoires* published in English translation by Holmes and Meier several years ago. Baverez also considerably duplicates Robert Colquhoun's two-volume intellectual biography, originally a dissertation at the London School of Economics, published nine years ago by Sage. Colquhoun interviewed Aron himself and compiled an extraordinarily comprehensive bibliography of Aron's writings in French and in English translation as well as of French and selected Anglo-American reviews and commentaries on them, omitting only Aron's regular weekly newspaper columns.

While Baverez's biography is hardly "personal" in any revelatory, let alone scandalous, sense, it does include a good deal more than both Aron himself and Colquhoun on Aron's sentiments, choices, deeper attitudes, and his personal, political, academic, and journalistic associations. Baverez also provides much more information on Aron's family history, including the interesting fact that he was related to Durkheim, both of them coming from what were originally Alsatian Jewish families. A genealogical chart showing the exact relationship is even provided. He also tells us much more than Aron himself about the personal tragedy of the death at the age of six of one of Aron's children and the mental retardation of another. Aron's

Review of Nicolas Baverez, *Raymond Aron: Un Moraliste au Temps des Ideologues* (Paris: Flammarion, 1993).

memoirs, as Stanley Hoffman pointed out in his obituary tribute in the *New York Review of Books* at the time of Aron's death in 1983, consisted largely of summaries of his writings, including his journalism, the reviews they received, and his responses to criticisms. This is also true of Colquhoun's massive effort. Baverez covers the voluminous writings more briefly with a much more complete filling in of the context of Aron's relation to critics both before and after their commentaries on his work.

Since I reviewed *The Century of Total War* (1954), Aron's first book to be translated into English, he has been an intellectual hero of mine, indeed to me the voice of Reason and Truth itself, as Karl Jaspers once described Max Weber, then and still also a hero. Knowing that Aron had introduced Weber into France though not yet aware of the full extent of his filiation from Weber, I saw Aron as Weber *redivivus* over a generation later. Aron's friend Golo Mann, historian and son of the great novelist, claimed gallantly that "Aron would have arrived at all his political insights without any help from Max Weber." One may doubt that while continuing to regard Aron as the supreme interpreter of the terrible events of the "short" (1914–1990) twentieth century. Despite the frequent complaint that Aron was a "cold pessimist," icy and cerebral in his rationalism, I recognized forty years ago that he shared with Max Weber, a disciplined and relentless realist if there ever was one, an underlying passion and tragic sense of life and history.

The formative period of Aron's intellectual and political outlook was the three years he spent as a student and teacher in Cologne and Berlin where he witnessed Hitler's coming to power. He discovered German philosophy, notably Husserl and Heidegger, and neo-Kantian historicism, introducing, as we had learned previously from Simone de Beauvoir, his old *normalien* classmate Jean-Paul Sartre to phenomenology and helping arrange a sojourn in Germany for Sartre in turn. The Nazi revolution frightened him to the point of abandoning the pacifism in which he had been schooled in the wake of 1914–18 and the comfortable progressivism of his lycée and university teachers. Again resembling Weber, he remained for the rest of his life divided between the summons to political action, or at least influence, and the attractions of theory and scholarship, like Weber serving as a sometime adviser to princes.

Although his two academic chairs at the Sorbonne and the Collège de France were in sociology, I have the impression that Aron is not widely recognized as a sociologist, specifically as a theorist, by American sociologists. This probably results in part from his abandonment of several sociological projects in the 1960s and his return to major work in international relations and the philosophy of history after a conflict with Pierre Bourdieu over the direction of a sociological research institute, an episode recounted in detail by Baverez. Aron was neither a positivist nor a believer in abstract, totalistic theories. Colquhoun reports that when Aron in an informal discussion with Talcott Parsons politely but firmly doubted that a concept of "social action"—was the necessary foundation for sociological theory, Parsons abruptly left the table without a word. Aron also challenged Paul Lazarsfeld's claims for empirical research on a panel at which, as Baverez quotes an observer, Lazarsfeld lost the argument but smoked bigger cigars.

Aron's major sociological subject was the distinctiveness of "industrial society," which, like so many others, he saw as marking a break with the past. Yet he never ceased to insist on the continuing relevance of premodern and presociological thinkers who had reflected on politics and history, such as Thucydides, Machiavelli, Hobbes, Montesquieu, Clausewitz, and Tocqueville. The coming of industrial society did not mean the transcendence of inequality and the internal struggles arising from it, wars and conflicts between nations, or even despotism in the more intensive form of totalitarianism. Indeed, more than any other sociologist, including Weber, Aron was a wide-ranging and profound theorist of war and interstate relations. Industrial society, born in the late eighteenth and early nineteenth century, marked a new and unfathomable beginning, but it did not efface the passions, hierarchies of power, and conflicts that had always marked human history. No more than Weber was Aron a believer in a necessarily progressive direction in history. Yet with his acute sense of the corruptibility of attempts at final judgment he wrote, comparing Machiavelli and Marx:

> But let us not forget that pessimists also resign themselves to the unjustifiable, that they sometimes protect societies against the transports of futile passion but rarely restrain the privileged from the temptations of conservatism. It is dangerous to give men too high a conception of their possible goal; it is scarcely less dangerous to convince them of their indignity and impotence. Between Machiavelli, the observer without illusions, and Marx, the prophet, it is better not to choose but rather to let them pursue, in our own minds and beyond, an inexhaustible and unlimited dialogue (*Politics and History,* Transaction Publishers, 1984, 101).

Then there is politics. Aron's firm anti-Communist and his support for the justice and strategic rationality of the NATO alliance against the Soviet Union did not commend themselves to American sociologists, who have been disproportionately inclined to the sentimental left. Most of them never overcame their inveterate anti-anti-Communism and their ambivalence towards the Cold War, shying away not only from Aron's leading themes but also from the major events of contemporary history. French intellectuals with a more adversarial stance towards modern society, from Sartre to Foucault, have, unsurprisingly, had a greater impact. Nor, unlike the latter pair, was Aron's mode of life flamboyantly deviant. When I mentioned recently to two colleagues that I regarded Aron as a great man, each responded with a variant of the old saw of the Parisian left intellectuals, "C'est mieux de se tromper avec Sartre que d'avoir raison avec Aron." To me, as to Weber, this is an indefensible position for a teacher, whose primary obligation is to get it right, "to tell it like it is" in the once-famous sixties idiom, rather than to voice noble political sentiments or project visions of unrealizable ideals. For Aron, getting it right and persuading others of its rightness was his primary task.

Aron would have had little to learn from the postmodernists for whom historical and cultural relativism is the ultimate wisdom. But he would have seen them as self-indulgent cop-outs for thinking that this meant that anything goes, that all assertions are permissible. What Baverez writes in his final chapter makes this plain and is an appropriate note on which to close:

> The profound originality of Aron is located in the conflicting coexistence of a radical doubt about consciousness and an obstinate pursuit of truth, of the anchorage of man in a contingent history and an aspiration to the universal. Contrary to ideologies which claim to overcome the quest of a transcendence of human history in sanctifying a race or a class, contrary to idealist philosophy which denies the reality of the world, Aron is profoundly modern in that he integrates in one theory of existence and consciousness the necessary failure of his enterprise. The hope of a humanity reconciled with reason in the Kantian sense of the term could not take a historical form. It is a working hypothesis which permits the apprehension of the world in the absence of the power to penetrate the ultimate mystery.

15

C. Wright Mills Recalled

There seems to be something of a revival of interest at the turn of the century in the work of C. Wright Mills, who died nearly forty years ago at the early age of forty-five. His two daughters have now published with a major university press a large collection of their father's correspondence and unpublished autobiographical writings, including their own remembrances of him. The book was launched last fall at the auditorium of the New York Public Library with a panel of readings and speeches followed by a reception. Earlier in the year *The Sociological Imagination* was reprinted with an afterword by Todd Gitlin. The book by Guy Oakes and Arthur Vidich was published in 1999 and reviewed last July in the *Times Literary Supplement* by the well-known sociological theorist Zygmunt Bauman under the title "The Man from Waco." Bauman's review displayed the hagiography common to most latter-day writing on Mills while minimizing that the Oakes-Vidich book was a scarcely veiled attack to the effect that much of the early work responsible for Mills's budding reputation was actually that of his teacher and collaborator the late Hans Gerth. Vidich, like Mills, was a student of Gerth's at the University of Wisconsin in the 1940's and had along with his own former collaborator and fellow-Gerth student the late Joseph Bensman been maintaining this for years. In a review in *New Left Review,* Russell Jacoby, a student of Gerth's in the 1960s, observed that "the tendentious facts and sham indignation of the book are coupled with silence about its own genesis," concluding that in contrast to what it purports to be it "is less a study of professional norms in mid-cen-

Review of Kathryn Mills with Pamela Mills, eds. *C. Wright Mills: Letters and Autobiographical Writings* (Berkeley, Los Angeles and London: University of California Press, 2000) and Guy Oakes and Arthur J. Vidich, *Collaboration, Reputation, and Ethics in American Academic Life: Hans H. Gerth and C. Wright Mills* (Urbana and Chicago: University of Illinois Press, 1999).

tury America than a grudge masquerading as erudition." I wrote a letter to the *Times Literary Supplement* citing Jacoby's review and calling attention to Bauman's numerous errors of fact and interpretation, but delay caused by e-mail malfunction resulted in the journal's printing instead a shorter letter by someone else pointing out many of the same errors.

I was a graduate student of Mills at Columbia in the late 1940s, briefly worked on an abortive dissertation under his supervision, and reviewed and commented on his major books—appreciatively but not uncritically—more frequently than anyone else during his lifetime according to a list of secondary writings on Mills compiled by Irving Louis Horowitz in his edited collection of Mills's articles (also reviewed by me at some length). Kathryn and Pamela Mills asked to see the few letters from Mills I had received, but chose not to include any of them. Horowitz's 1983 book-length intellectual biography is mentioned by Oakes and Vidich only in a critical footnote and Horowitz is no more than listed in the daughters' collection as the editor of two posthumously published works by Mills, although Horowitz's biography was praised for its accuracy and fairness by such luminaries of diverse ideological persuasions as Daniel Bell, Walter Laqueur, Victor Navasky, and Andrew Greeley. Although Horowitz had corresponded voluminously with Mills, no letters to him are included in the daughters' selections. This double exclusion is, one surmises, for exactly opposite reasons: Oakes and Vidich regard Horowitz, whom they report Gerth "twitted as Mills's posthumous legate," as insufficiently critical of Mills whereas despite the judiciousness of Horowitz's occasional criticisms the daughters and wives were evidently unwilling to accept *any* criticism at all of their famous family connection. Mills's widow, a former wife, and his daughters wrote a joint letter to the *New York Times Book Review* protesting a favorable review of the Horowitz biography by Steven Lukes; Horowitz responded, differing with them on several fairly minor issues. I had suggested Lukes as a reviewer after turning down the assignment myself because my own writings on Mills were discussed by Horowitz. Mills's former wife Freya whom I had known slightly long after their divorce also wrote to me objecting to the Horowitz biography under the misapprehension that I still edited the American Sociological Association's review journal.

Oakes and Vidich cite the translated essays of Max Weber jointly edited in 1946 by Gerth and Mills and their coauthored 1954 book

Character and Social Structure as works for which they claim Gerth was largely responsible. Since Mills's German was limited, the charge is highly plausible with respect to the Weber essays. Bauman, however, is right to maintain that without Mills's "Englishing" of Gerth's translations and the stylistic vigor and elegance he contributed to the long introduction, the book would have been much less readable and had much less of an impact. Yet he is utterly wrong to claim that the translated essays introduced American sociologists to Weber: Talcott Parsons deserved credit for that many years earlier. Jacoby's review of the Oakes-Vidich book quotes at length from the fulsome tribute delivered by Gerth at a memorial meeting for Mills shortly after his death. Unlike Jacoby or Vidich, I was present at that meeting and recall an incident that suggests even more strongly that Gerth was at the very least highly ambivalent in his attitude towards Mills. After one of Mills's Columbia colleagues noted for his blunt often tactless honesty made a surprisingly harsh critical personal remark about him in his address to the gathering, Gerth uttered a loud protesting roar and barely restrained himself, or was restrained, from rushing to the podium.

In 1947 I took a course from Mills with the same title as the 1954 coauthored book. Some of the lectures were also based on Mills's first book on labor leaders published the following year as well as on his second 1951 book, *White Collar.* If *Character and Social Structure* was indeed based primarily on Gerth's notes as Oakes and Vidich allege, Mills must have memorized them, for he lectured without notes and was a commanding and responsive classroom presence. He listed such an exciting array of topics for student essays to meet course requirements that when the rest of the class chose to write essays rather than an exam, I did too although I had taken exams for all my other graduate course credits because of my affliction with what I thought was "writers' block," really no more than lack of self-confidence. Eventually, I wrote a paper for Mills on "The Concept of Bureaucracy in Franz Kafka" which Mills graded A+ and recommended I submit to Dwight Macdonald's journal *politics.* This was the period when "Kafka was the rage" (the title of Anatole Broyard's Greenwich Village memoir), so Macdonald rejected my article on grounds of a surfeit of material on Kafka. It was then accepted in a shorter version by a projected new literary journal that never saw the light of day, as neither did my essay that would have been my first published article. I apologize for this self-centered digression. Of Mills's other possible topics for essays, I recall "the mendicant monk as a social type" and "the self-image of the professional salesman," but all of them sounded fascinating at the time.

I also remember that in the same year we were assigned in Paul Lazarsfeld's required course on research methods the task of interviewing in depth an individual white-collar worker. Our interviews were intended to provide material for Mills's study that was sponsored by the Bureau of Applied Social Research directed by Lazarsfeld. Oakes and Vidich show in detail that Mills thinly paraphrased and only broadly acknowledged a student paper for an earlier course of his. Joseph Bensman and my old friend E. Digby Baltzell, both now deceased, also claimed that Mills drew in *White Collar* on papers of theirs without crediting them. My guess is that Mills considered their papers, whether written for Lazarsfeld's courses or for his own, as "data" for his study, although he was perhaps less than scrupulous in crediting others

Oakes and Vidich report that Edward Shils was bitterly convinced that Gerth and Mills had included in their Weber book essays that he, Shils, had translated. Shils later wrote a famous—or infamous—dismissive review of *The Power Elite* for *Encounter.* I surmise it is this review that leads Bauman to exaggerate grossly the alleged rejection of Mills by "the sociological establishment," asserting that Mills was the victim of academic "ostracism" and a "merciless campaign of defamation" throughout his career. Bauman is echoing the legends fostered by New Left student radicals who made a hero and icon of Mills after his premature death, some even suggesting that he had been murdered in the 116th Street subway station at Columbia at the instigation of his colleagues Lazarsfeld and Robert Merton. Bauman doesn't go that far, although he speculates that the rejections may have brought on Mills's early death by heart attack. The major targets of Mills's polemic in *The Sociological Imagination*, notably Parsons, Lazarsfeld and their followers, certainly didn't like it: I debated the book with Lazarsfeld who complained that it was "cocktail party gossip" to which I replied "*in vino veritas.*" But *The Sociological Imagination* was favorably reviewed by Everett Hughes who later included its title in his presidential address to the American Sociological Association and it was received largely with approval by sociologists in the Chicago tradition who tended to be hostile to the Harvard-Columbia ambience that Mills assailed. Bauman describes Shils as "one of the great princes of American sociology," but in actuality Shils, like Mills a cantankerous and acerbic personality, was more distant and alienated from most American sociologists than Mills ever was because he was perceived as a "conservative" and American sociologists have always been disproportionately on the left. Shils did not belong to the ASA and didn't even show up in the late 1980s to receive its highest award for a "career of distinguished scholarship." He won this by a single vote of the selection committee owing largely to my own initiative in nominating him. A well-known past president of the ASA and former colleague of Mills then wrote a letter to the committee arguing that our choice should be rescinded because it was made under untested new procedures, adding sarcastically that as a conservative Shils himself would doubtless prefer sticking to the old rules.

Both his admirers and critics like Shils made much of Mills's Texas background dwelling on his burly physical proportions and his "cowboy" style of aggressiveness, although his father was an insurance agent and he objected that he had never so much as mounted a horse. Certainly, his house building, motorcycle riding, and fascination with machinery were uncommon among New York intellectuals, most of them sedentary technological "klutzes." John Judis's excellent review of the daughters' collection in the *New York Times Book Review* was predictably adorned with a photo of Mills riding his motorcycle. I remember being unduly impressed myself when he drove a VW bug, newly imported into the U.S. in 1956, up the New York State Thruway to speak at my invitation at the University of Toronto, although a few years later I myself drove one across the continent. When driving to my home for drinks, Mills detected a knock in the engine of my second-hand Austin and I had to dissuade him from getting under the car to investigate it while wearing a suit for the banquet in his honor that evening. Yet one of the things one learns from his autobiographical musings in the daughters' collection is how much he was like other intellectuals in his youth, deviant from his fellows after discovering books in high school, bespectacled, and unathletic. His father sent him to Texas A. and M., then a military school, "to make a man of him" and his rebellion against the school foreshadowed his later onslaughts on any and all established authorities.

Mills's political radicalism had less to do with utopian visions—despite Horowitz's subtitle "An American Utopian"—than with mocking and flouting any and all status quos. He described himself as "a born troublemaker." Oakes and Vidich to the contrary notwithstanding, it was not an opportunistic career choice during the last years of the war to associate himself with New York journals of the anti-Stalinist left, then a beleaguered minority though often falsely viewed in retrospect as an entrenched establishment. Mills, of course, had been quick to grasp the superior quality of these journals to the political and cultural alternatives available to a youthful intellectual. But Mills ultimately broke with just about all his friends among intellectuals biting quite a few hands that had fed him; after a trip to Poland and the Soviet Union, he wrote a letter opposing the editors of *Dissent,* to which he had been a contributor, calling them—us—"old futilitarians of the left" because of our qualified support of American foreign policy. He remained an eternal Trotskyist opposing both the Second World War and the Cold War, coming close to affirming in the case of the latter what was later called the "moral equivalence" of the U.S. and the USSR. When Daniel Bell who had first introduced him to New York and its intellectual journals was proposed as a colleague at Columbia, Mills avowed that it would be "over his dead body" though he did not prevail. Despite being hailed as one of its founders, I very much doubt that Mills would have remained a supporter of the student New Left had he lived after 1962.

Todd Gitlin rightly calls *The Sociological Imagination* Mills's "most enduring book." There is a certain irony here: when I sent Mills who was in Europe on sabbatical leave my own long, mostly positive review, he wrote back "I'm glad you liked my little book. I would rather do the stuff [meaning sociology] than write about it." Bauman regrets that Mills's books have not been widely reprinted, but the reason is that they are clearly outdated. *White Collar*, Mills's own favorite, pioneered a multitude of later studies of the "New Class" of nonmanual employees of large bureaucracies. My own review of *The Power Elite* criticized it for overgeneralizing from the Eisenhower administration. Actually, despite the claims of latter-day revivalists, *The Sociological Imagination* also hardly describes the present condition of sociology, although with the field's fragmentation into a host of different approaches and specialties it has lost the postwar aura of excitement it projected when it was smaller and more innovative. "Grand theory" in the Parsonsian mode still exists: there will always be a few people drawn to elaborating highly abstract concepts such as, despite his different origins in neo-Marxism, Jürgen Habermas, perhaps the best contemporary instance. Survey research, attacked by Mills as "abstracted empiricism," is today securely institutionalized outside of academic sociology as well as within it. But neither approach comes close to dominating the field as they did in the 1950s. Moreover, partly as a result of his book's influence, there have been large-scale prize-winning comparative-historical studies that more than satisfy Mills's demand for sensitivity to historical context, as the names of Randall Collins, Barrington Moore, Jr., Theda Skocpol, Charles Tilly, Jack Goldstone, and Jeffrey Paige attest.

If Mills was better at attacking existing establishments than in proposing alternatives to them, his version of what sociology should and might be nevertheless remains powerfully attractive. In the more limited sphere of "knowledge" if not in the realms of "power, politics, and people," the three other headings under which Horowitz grouped his essays, Mills's writing continues to possess a genuinely visionary quality still capable of inspiring youthful would-be social scientists. This is surely no mean achievement.

16

Digby Baltzell

Digby Baltzell was an unusual kind of sociologist. For the first academic term immediately following the end of the Second World War, he, the late Robert Bower, and I were the only new Columbia graduate students in sociology of "preppy" WASP upper-middle class origins, although I was an outlander from Canada. This inevitably drew us together, but Digby alone chose his own background as a subject for study in his sociological work. I don't believe, by the way, that Digby coined the pleonasm "WASP," as is often claimed, though he regrettably used it a lot in *The Protestant Establishment* (1964) which did a good deal to popularize it. It is as a historical sociologist of the American upper class that Digby is likely to be remembered, a chronicler of its rise and decline who used sociological theory to give a sympathetic account of its erstwhile social and political role.

I do not agree with Samuel Klausner that Digby was consciously, or for that matter unconsciously, applying methodological individualism or any other kind of meta-theory or social epistemology he had learned from his teachers at Columbia. Klausner reports that both Robert Lynd and C. Wright Mills were influences on Digby, but he weirdly classifies Lynd as a "subjectivist" on stratification and social class in contrast to Mills's alleged view of society as "objectively stratified."[1] Howard Schneiderman in his introduction to the 1991 collection of Digby's essays describes Lynd's influence on Digby and correctly notes Lynd's "emphasis on the *objective* economic aspects of class" (xiv, his italics). But Klausner's term "inspired" is too strong to describe the influence of Mills whom Digby was far from admiring; he complained, as reported by Schneiderman (xv), that Mills had in *White Collar* included without acknowledging part of a paper that Digby had written for a course. Lynd and Mills were both outspoken leftists hostile in principle to class inequality and social hierarchy. As Digby remarked to me just a few years ago, he never "went through a left-wing phase," and he was not involved at all in the postwar political ferment among intellectuals in the sociology department, on the Columbia campus, and in New York City. This did not involve conflict between left and right, but within the left between communists and their sympathizers against anti-communists, or, as we preferred to call ourselves, anti-Stalinists. Lynd and Mills, incidentally, were on opposite sides of this conflict. Merton was Digby's mentor and inspiration insofar as anyone was.

Nor do I agree with James Abbott's claim that recoil from Nazi Germany after a visit there in his youth was a major force animating Digby's later sociology. It is far-fetched to present him as a defender of Groton and St. Paul's, exclusive elite suburbs, and affluent men's clubs because he thought they were indispensable bulwarks of freedom against a potential American Hitler. Abbott correctly notes that Digby's and my generation were appalled by totalitarianism in both its Nazi and Communist versions. Moreover, Digby was, especially in his earlier work, given to advancing liberal reasons for preserving upper-class institutions of privilege. But it was his attachment to these institutions and his sadness when they failed to live up to their own best ideals that essentially motivated his sociology.

I was not especially aware of Digby's political views when we were students at Columbia. However, his atypical—for sociologists—classical conservatism was evident in *Philadelphia Gentlemen* (1958), his first book, based on his doctoral dissertation. Its very first sentence read "Leadership and some form of stratification are inherent in all human social organization." He then proceeded to label a "classless society" the equivalent of Alice in Wonderland's "unwet water," calling it a "sociological monstrosity" despite its being vainly upheld in "modern social theory" by Marx, Rousseau, and in a more pessimistic vein Michels. He went on to argue that "accountability" to society and "openness" to entry from below were standards by which all necessarily oligarchical "complex societies" should be evaluated. These indeed were the principles that he attacked the WASP upper class for failing to live up to in his next and most popular book, *The Protestant Establishment* (1964). His views were advanced at a time, as he himself later noted, when fierce debate over the famous, or infamous, Davis-Moore theory also justifying inequality was at its peak in sociology.

These ideas, expressed in the three opening paragraphs of Digby's first book, are the *leitmotif* of all of his work, which truly adds up to variations on a common theme. In the somewhat overworked metaphor of the Greek poet revived by Isaiah Berlin, Digby was unmistakably an intellectual hedgehog rather than a fox. I feel sure that he must even have somewhere so described himself—he comes close to doing so in one of the autobiographical essays in the 1991 collection.

Digby and I were drawn together in the 1960s by our common dislike of the radical student movement, although our negative views of it had a somewhat different slant. With Digby's broad historical perspective and indebtedness to Tocqueville, he saw the sound and fury as yet another outbreak of the futilely utopian millenarianism to which Western society had been prone since at least the late Middle Ages. I saw it more narrowly not as a new beginning but as the last expression, the final flare-up before extinction, of a left subculture that had flourished among American intellectuals at least since what Jack Diggins has called "the Lyrical Left" early in the century (1991: 93-143). I shared Digby's admiration for Tocqueville, but not his thoroughly conventional animadversions on Marx. Digby, like the neoconservatives, although it is doubtful whether that label can properly be applied to him, vastly overreacted to the short period we label "the 60s," blaming it for and railing long afterwards against the prevalent crudities of popular culture and political rhetoric while lamenting the decline of America into what he and others misleadingly called "barbarism." Yet as Abbott fails to note he was not so undiscriminating as to identify the vulgarities and moral decline he deplored with the totalitarian threat earlier in the century. What he disdained rather than feared was not a terroristic dictatorship like Hitler's or Stalin's but Tocqueville's "tyranny of the majority" under a tutelary, plebeian and overly "permissive" bureaucratic government. He died too soon in what has turned out to be a long period of prosperity and stability in which most of the negative indices of social pathology rising since the 1960s that he saw as moral decline have turned downwards.

Even before the 1960s, Digby documented the decline since 1940 of the WASP upper class from aristocracy into caste, as the subtitle of *The Protestant Establishment* put it. The establishment had ceased, he argued, to recruit new members from below—its "genteel" anti-Semitism was his major evidence of this—and in retreating with self-satisfaction into its own privileged enclaves it had abandoned the tradition of *noblesse oblige* that reflected its sense of accountability to the larger society. Howard Schneiderman, writing since the 1960s, sees Digby as arguing in favor of equality of opportunity against the complete egalitarianism of full equality of condition apparently affirmed by New Left *marxisant* radicals. Both in his earlier and more saliently in his post-60s work, Digby clearly opposed in classical conservative fashion egalitarianism as "leveling down" ("negative leveling," as Mannheim called it), seeing it as favoring an unattainable equality of condition rather than a desirable (and attainable) equality of opportunity. Most American conservatives have taken this line. But Digby's view in *The Protestant Establishment* was more nuanced than Schneiderman suggests in its relationship to the dominant liberalism shared by the majority of American sociologists. Digby and liberal sociologists were in entire agreement on the very American belief in full equality of opportunity with no barriers of "race, color, or creed," as the old slogan ran, limiting the upward social mobility of the ambitious and talented of whatever origin. Also, Digby's politics were at least until the late 1960s those of a liberal Democrat: he praised Wilson, FDR, Kennedy, and the Philadelphia reformers Clark and Dilworth as model patricians embodying his ideal of promoting greater social justice in opposition to the preservation of caste barriers. Where Digby differed from liberals and most sociologists was in his conservative defense of a hereditary upper class with its own solidarity, style of life, and distinctive institutions, assimilating into its ranks capable individuals who were not to the manor born and transmitting to them its own sense of the responsibilities of political leadership. Liberals and left egalitarians opposed not only the caste-like restrictions of race and ethnicity, but also the hereditary advantages and privileges of birth accruing to a fortunate minority. The term "meritocracy," coined by Michael Young in his famous satire (1958), had not come into general use in the early 1960s, but Digby's view, stated more explicitly in his later writings, implied definite reservations about a meritocracy in which everyone competed, as the current phrase has it, on a "level playing-field." In his post-60s essays he frequently invokes the term nearly always critically. This rather than Schneiderman's utopian equality of condition, let alone the mobocracy or the totalitarianism invoked by Klausner and Abbott, was the main and most relevant target of his criticism.

In 1976 Digby wrote, "…when I wrote *The Protestant Establishment* during the administration of President Kennedy, I still had faith in the ability of the WASP establishment to assimilate talented men and women of other ethnic and religious origins into its ranks. I have no such faith today" (1991: 97). His loss of faith, however, was not because the establishment had become ever-more caste-like in its exclusions, but because it had dispersed and dissolved in response to changes in American life by no means limited to the effects of the turmoil of the 1960s. Although caste barriers of race, religion, gender, and ethnicity had fallen and equality of opportunity become much more of a reality, the establishment had disintegrated, though not solely or even primarily for that reason. Digby became too inclined to blame what he didn't like in American life on the end of "the WASP ascendancy," as Joseph Alsop, also born to it, called it. As I once argued in a long review of *The Protestant Establishment* (Wrong 1965: 83-86; reprinted in Wrong 1976: 135-143), there was something quixotic and even utopian about Digby's former belief that a regenerated Northeastern WASP establishment could ever hope at this late date in American history to become a truly responsible national upper class.

Digby objected in a late essay to my old friend Irving Howe's argument that to defend a hierarchy of literary merit in no way entailed a defense of a social hierarchy based on economic inequality (Baltzell 1994: 177-178). Digby suggested a connection between the two that is, to say the least, questionable. It was hardly people of Social Register backgrounds who won recognition for Joyce, Hemingway, or Faulkner as major writers; the taste of the privileged has usually been flaccidly middlebrow at best. Moreover, Digby's exemplars of establishment virtue, the Roosevelts and Harrimans, wanted to limit gross inequalities of income and wealth out of egalitarian principle.

A tone of nostalgia tended to dominate Digby's later work in contrast to his previous chastisement of the establishment for flouting its own best traditions. On what may have been the very last time I saw him, at an afternoon party in an uptown Manhattan art gallery celebrating the publication of his last book, *Sporting Gentlemen* (1995), he said to me a bit ruefully that a departing guest had just complained to him that he had switched from criticizing the WASP establishment to celebrating it. I replied unsupportively, "Well, Digby, maybe that's just telling it like it is!" But this suggests that, apart from the unquestionable richness of its historical scholarship, a rather different case can be made for Digby's later work, distinct from his "functional" argument for leadership by a hereditary upper class.

In the preface to the 1979 reissue of *Philadelphia Gentlemen,* Digby wrote: "Whenever an upper-class way of life becomes an end in itself, rather than a means of consolidating its power and influence, that upper class has outlived its function." I'm not sure, however, that one cannot make precisely the opposite claim, finding value in the human richness and subtlety of a way of life apart from, and even in contradiction to its larger social functions and context. I recall a description of *War and Peace* as an "idyll of the Russian nobility," although Tolstoy was certainly aware of the exploitation and oppression of the peasantry and of non-Russian peoples (e.g., "Hadji Murad") by that nobility. Be it noted, however, that Tolstoy's idyll was located several generations before his own time. Digby by contrast says it was not until his wartime service that he moved outside and could view detachedly his WASP background. I understand his sentiments of regret that time and change have so utterly extinguished the world of his youth. On the rare occasions that I visit that gleaming glass sky-scrapered and thoroughly multi-ethnic city beside Lake Ontario, I feel a real pang of loss over the disappearance of the old Anglophile Toronto of my parents and grandparents and a nostalgia for the shabby post-Depression, wartime, genteel ("Toronto the Good," it was mockingly called), still overwhelmingly WASP city of my high school and undergraduate years. As a born fourth-generation Torontonian, I felt a surge of indignation at the description in a recent novel of Toronto as a city where nobody who lived there had been born there as if the city had no previous history before postwar mass immigration.

Digby used to lecture to meetings of headmasters of private preparatory schools. At one such meeting, he told me, the headmasters complained of the difficulty since the youth rebellions of the 1960s in imposing traditional dress codes on students. One lone headmaster interjected that he had no such problem: he just laid down the law and imposed severe penalties for students who failed to conform. He turned out to be the Principal of Upper Canada College, my own old prep school. This episode certainly lends support to Seymour Martin Lipset's longstanding generalization that Canadians are more respectful of authority than Americans ([1968] 1970: 37-75; 1990). Yet I find it hard to believe it still holds today. Morning prayers, the compulsory cadet corps, caning, the hazing of newboys, and the British public school practice of "fagging" in the boarding houses[2] have all been abolished. This almost amounts to a full list of everything I rebelled against as a boarder at the school. A much-discussed oral history by an old grad (Fitzgerald 1994) recently exposed the reactionary, repressive ways of the school in the past and was described by one reviewer as "a 369-page scream of pain" (Fulford 1994). I was surprised by my own reaction that the book was too selective in its apparent determination to accentuate the negative.[3]

My colleagues Caroline Persell and Peter Cookson in their excellent study of elite boarding schools charge Digby with romanticism in his defense of the schools as bastions of equality of opportunity (1985: 16-17).[4] Doubtless Digby would defend some of the features of UCC that I strenuously rebelled against, especially the exposure to religion. Compelled as a boarder to go to church every Sunday, I used to write in the hymnals and prayer books "Religion is the opium of the people—Marx" and "Religion is the universal obsessional neurosis of mankind—Freud." I still broadly agree with those propositions, which distinguishes me from Digby who was a devout high-church Episcopalian. Yet my own feelings today about the changes in Toronto and UCC remind me of Michael Harrington who, after stating that he had left the Catholic Church thirty years earlier, confessed that "I sometimes took a rather orthodox attitude toward changes in Catholicism after I turned away from it." He then quoted a Catholic friend who said to him "You want us to keep the mausoleum exactly as it was when you left" (1983: 10).

I think I know, therefore, where Digby was coming from, as they say, and his sentiments, if more affirmative of his past associations and allegiances than my own, are not only attractively human but do him honor.

Notes

1. Lynd was a Marxist, or it might be argued a Veblenian, who in his Middletown books identified just two classes, a "business" class and a "working" class. An incident in a seminar arguing over the always contentious issue of how to define stratification and class, which was reported and repeated by students, is illustrative: Lynd burst out, "Aw, Come on you guys! All I know is that there are a few rich people on top and a lot of poor bastards down at the bottom." This is true to Lynd's blunt, colloquial style and clearly is at a far remove from a subjectivist view of class. Mills's view of stratification was Weberian, encompassing both "objective" and "subjective" aspects.

2. Newboys were required to serve virtually as personal servants to the older, more senior boys, cleaning their rooms, shining their shoes, and running various errands at their command.
3. The author interviewed me for the book, but did not include my testimony, which, struck at least a faintly critical note.
4. Persell and Cookson acknowledge Digby and me (though I am given an incorrect first name) on their list of many people who gave them suggestions and both of us provided jacket endorsements for the book. I recall, however, a conversation with Digby in which we both were critical of the book's title, which obviously contradicted his view that the elite establishment no longer possesses the power it once had. The book was a trade book and the publishers, as Persell told me, liked the titular reference to power and its alliterative ring.

References

Baltzell, E. Digby. [1958] 1979. *Philadelphia Gentlemen: The Making of National Upper Class.* Philadelphia: University of Pennsylvania Press.

—. 1964. *The Protestant Establishment: Aristocracy and Caste in America* (New York: Random House).

—. 1991. *The Protestant Establishment Revisited* (New Brunswick, NJ: Transaction Publishers).

—. 1994. *Judgment and Sensibility* (New Brunswick, NJ: Transaction Publishers).

—. 1995. *Sporting Gentlemen: Men's Tennis from the Age of Honor to the Cult of the Superstar* (New York: The Free Press).

Diggins, John Patrick. 1992. *The Rise and Fall of the American Left* (New York: W.W. Norton).

Fitzgerald, James. 1994. *Old Boys: The Powerful Legacy of Upper Canada College* (Toronto: Macfarlane, Walter, & Ross).

Fulford, Robert. 1994. Toronto *Globe and Mail.* Op-ed.

Harrington, Michael. 1983. *The Politics at God's Funeral* (New York: Penguin Books).

Lipset, Seymour Martin. [1968] 1970. *Revolution and Counterrevolution* (New York: Doubleday Anchor).

—. 1990. *Continental Divide: The Values and Institutions of the United States and Canada* (New York: Routledge).

Persell, Caroline and Peter Cookson. 1985. *Preparing for Power: America's Elite Boarding Schools* (New York: Basic Books).

Wrong, Dennis H. 1965. "Jews, Gentiles, and the New Establishment," *Commentary,* 39: 83-86.

—. 1976. *Skeptical Sociology* (New York: Columbia University Press).

Young, Michael. 1958. *The Rise of the Meritocracy 1870-2033* (London: Thames and Hudson).

17

Etzioni, Socio-Economics, and Human Nature

I first encountered sociology as an undergraduate major in the early 1940's at the University of Toronto in a Department of *Political Economy* that included economics, political science, and sociology as subjects in which one could major. My first full-time teaching job was at Princeton in a Department of Economics and *Social Institutions.* Apart from McGill where Everett Hughes had previously introduced sociology, Canadian universities, including Toronto, the leading one, were at this time rather old-fashioned in their departmental structure and offerings, sociology barely existing as an academic subject let alone a departmentally independent one. The term "political economy" is venerable, actually antedating Adam Smith's *The Wealth of Nations* from which economics as a discipline is conventionally held to derive. In the United States, Princeton was the last major university to introduce any teaching of sociology and did so only after the Second World War. It is no accident that both of these belated institutional practices grouped sociology with economics, the first and most highly developed of the academic social sciences.

Etzioni's proposal to create a new discipline of "socio-economics" as an "interstitial" or "bridging" discipline does not strike me as a startling innovation. Why not propose in addition socio-politics, socio-religion, or socio-literature since these fields also have social aspects that can be distinguished from their main intellectual contents? It might be claimed that economic activity is both more habitual and more universally human than political, religious, and literary activities: such a claim has always, at least implicitly, endowed the diverse forms of economic determinism with their aura of empirical credibility. But the reason, presumably Etzioni's, for singling out socio-economics is because classical economics, the original core of the discipline, possessed a clear-cut "paradigm," a model theory of economic activity bearing at least a surface resemblance to model theories in the natural sciences. There is no equivalent in the other fields studying human activities to the supply and demand market-price determination theory of economics, either for scope, survival in at least modified form, or general acceptance. The theory presupposes, or seems to and certainly did so originally, that the economic pursuits of human beings are always primarily motivated by the rational pursuit of their *individual* material self-interest, although this has long been recognized as an heuristic assumption that largely accounts for the "neo" in "neoclassical." Etzioni wishes to focus on the nonrational but inescapably *social* or collectively shared aspects of economic actions and institutions, hence "socio-economics." The title of his book *The Moral Dimension* is intended to stress the contrast between the egoistic and rationalistic assumptions of the classical model and the emphasis of sociologists on "social norms" imposing emotionally rooted obligations that set clear limits to narrowly self-serving conduct.

Economics as a discipline, however, has never been limited to the applications of a single theory or paradigm, classical or otherwise. As a sociology major in a department dominated by economists, I took courses, some of them required, in labor problems and economic history; other substantive subjects such as economic development have since been added to the field. The chair of the Toronto Department was the great economic historian Harold Adams Innis, who had studied with Veblen at Chicago and was the creator of Canadian economic history as a field of scholarship. We sociologists were constantly remarking on how "sociological" Innis was in showing the interdependence of social institutions in his studies of the cod fishery in the Maritimes, the fur trade in central Canada, and the Western wheat economy. We were at that time enthusiasts for the societal holism of functional analysis, but even if functionalism has since become moribund we were surely right about Innis. One of our major teachers in sociology, as a matter of fact, was S.D. Clark, a student of Innis, whose *The Social Development of Canada* (1942) was an effort to complement Innis's central focus on the economy by surveying crime and deviance, religion, the moral order, and ethnic composition in the various frontier communities across Canada that Innis had defined by their economies based on the extraction of raw materials. Clark later became the effective dean of sociology in Canada when the field finally took off in the 1950s. I should in honesty mention that we students tended to be dismissive of Clark, regarding him as a "mere" historian whom we thought was not "really" a sociologist as we conceived of one. His data, composing much of the book, his first, consisted of reproduced documents—letters, extracts from newspapers, official reports—in contrast to what we saw as the true sociological research methods of polling, interviewing, and descriptive ethnography, obviously inapplicable in the study of communities of the past. I nevertheless wrote a senior honors thesis on the social history of Newfoundland, still at the time a British crown colony, modeled on Clark's book, using the same documentary method he had used.

When I look at the economic books on my own shelf, the dominant presences are Schumpeter, Galbraith, Thurow, and W.W. Rostow, none of them doctrinaire neoclassical theorists and all of whom would presumably loom large in an institutionalized field of socio-economics. Etzioni's comparison of socio-economics to the recognized subfields of social psychology and biochemistry is entirely appropriate. But a number of efforts to constitute these as separate disciplines at the university level have for the most part not been successful. I remain all for economic sociology as a specialty within sociology and there is no reason why it should not become more widely recognized through its own existing academic association and new journal, like some of the other specialties in the larger field. Nor have efforts to create separate departments of demography, certainly an "interstitial" or "bridging" discipline, met with success.

If I remember correctly, Etzioni's 1988 book *The Moral Dimension* was the original basis, the platform, as it were, for the foundation of the Society for the Advancement of Socio-Economics (SASE), which I joined at the outset and have often described as having the most distinguished membership of any academic association to which I have belonged. This would doubtless cease to be so if the field were to become, as Etzioni advocates, departmentalized drawing job seekers, another reason for viewing that prospect with some reluctance. A colleague remarked to me that Etzioni's book, like books by Anthony Giddens and Jeffrey Alexander at roughly the same time, was yet another effort to rewrite Talcott Parsons's *The Structure of Social Action*. This is not altogether apposite, I think, for *The Moral Dimension* is much more narrowly focused. Etzioni was not trying to expound an entire system of theory or meta-theory, nor to interpret illustrious earlier social theorists, but rather to test and reject a particular conception of the essence of human action favored by neoclassical economists. His critique of utilitarianism and economic man, and his stress on the normative and its psychological internalization, do bear similarity to Parsons's major theme in his first and most famous book. But Etzioni was much more empirical, perhaps hoping to persuade the economists, although he now in the present paper sees that as a vain aspiration.

He is most successful in showing that most people most of the time simply do not behave "rationally" as economists conceive of rationality. On this he is entirely convincing. I find myself less satisfied with his tendency to set up a polarity between selfish, pleasure-seeking, individualistic economic man and group-centered, duty-bound, "value-oriented," altruistic man. This is an ancient dualism and I don't think Etzioni moves sufficiently beyond the rather familiar terms in which it has customarily been formulated and argued though he certainly cites apt and adequate evidence that people *do* often act out of duty and behave unselfishly in his examples of voters, smokers who do not oppose taxes on tobacco, and people who care for spouses with Alzheimer's. Still, he is a bit too inclined to cast the debate as one between utterly opposed views of human nature without himself developing a full conception of human nature both countering and partially incorporating the oversimplified economic model. It is perhaps no accident that the same man, Auguste Comte, coined the terms "sociology" and "altruism"—which also suggests just how venerable this economist versus sociologist pairing is, despite Etzioni's insistence that the "socio" in socio-economics does not stand for sociology alone. Etzioni is better on the concrete empirical evidence he musters than on the conceptual issues. The notion that people are ready altruists habitually striving to realize collective values that they have internalized doesn't seem quite right either, granting the economists' too simplified version of maximizing, pleasure-seeking behavior. Most human conduct most of the time falls somewhere between the poles of self-interested calculating hedonism and duty-bound conformity to norms or conscious implementation of moral values. I wish Etzioni would pay more attention to Freud. Nor do I think he has fully avoided an oversocialized conception of man at the level of his own argument for socio-economics, although he properly rejects the extreme conformist-consensual view linked to Parsons.

I have no serious objections to Etzioni's propositions about the social system and the market as a sub-system though I dislike the metaphor "social capsule." Certainly as a sociologist I fully agree that "each individual on his or her own, is more socially determined than determining." But "socially determined" should include the variations in family situations and the idiosyncratic characters of parents, siblings and peers that create individual psychological differences and not be solely identified, or even primarily, with being shaped by the culture of shared social norms to which individuals are exposed. "Socialization" should include the non-normative and the particular as well as that which is obligatory and shared with others. This may be "micro" rather than "macro," but it is "micro-social" rather than strictly individualistic. It is doubtless the case nevertheless that economic activities are subject to greater standardization than other areas of culture and one can have no quarrel with the existence of socio-economics as a major substantive field in whatever form it is institutionalized.

Part 5

Autobiographical Reminiscences

18

A Racial Incident Long Ago

In the late summer of 1943 I volunteered for overseas service in the Canadian Army and was rejected for minor medical reasons but accepted for home service. Rather than risk a posting to guard a munitions dump in the wilds of northern Canada, I decided to return to university several weeks after the beginning of the term to complete my third undergraduate year since students in Canada were exempted from military duty. When I stopped by for the first time at the house occupied by the fraternity to which I belonged, Delta Kappa Epsilon, my friend Victor Long took me aside and informed me proudly that he had succeeded in persuading the active brothers to include among their annual pledged new members a "Negro" from one of the smaller islands in the British West Indies. Because of the war many well-off dark-skinned West Indian families had chosen to send their sons and daughters to Canadian universities instead of to England, usually to Oxford or Cambridge, as had been their previous custom.

Victor was the manager of the Deke house and one of the few active members who lived there, most of them living at home in the city of Toronto with their parents. The chapter house was a narrow old three-story Victorian town house containing seven or eight bedrooms just off the campus. Several of the rooms were customarily rented to older single men with jobs downtown who had no connection with the university, although their number occasionally included graduate students and former members of fraternity chapters at other universities. During the summer, Victor had rented a room to a "black" West Indian pre-law student and when pledge week began he succeeded in persuading the active brothers to accept Phil Kerwick unanimously as a prospective new member. The arduous hazing of the initiation that pledges had to undergo which lasted a full week was about to begin a few days after my initial visit.

Victor had been a friend of mine at boarding school. A year ahead of me, he had recruited me to the fraternity when I entered the university. He and I, as well as another member of the fraternity who had since joined the navy, had been a clique of "intellectuals" in our boarding house, holding ourselves somewhat aloof from our low-brow, sports-obsessed fellow-boarders. Victor's late father had been a professor; my outlook had been shaped by two years residence in Europe attending a cosmopolitan school created for the children of international civil servants. On entering the university I had separated myself from my private school classmates by joining a college other than the one most of them chose; with my parents living in another city, I feared a degree of social isolation before I had made new friends, so I swallowed my disapproval of Greek-letter fraternities and let Victor persuade me to join his fraternity. I had lived in the house for a single semester in my freshman year, but disliking the fraternity atmosphere I soon moved out and ever since had lived in rooming-houses in the university neighborhood, although I ate meals quite regularly at the fraternity and attended their dances, chapter meetings, and occasional beer parties. Victor remained my only personal friend in the fraternity. I thought of myself as a radical socialist in rebellion against the smug upper-middle-class, career-minded brothers. I was majoring in the disreputable subject of sociology that attracted many Jews, and most of my friends at the university were Jewish as had been the case at school in Europe earlier in my life.

A few days after the start of initiation week I stopped in at the chapter house and was informed that the night before one of the chapter's senior alumni had come by and asked to see the pledges. On observing a dusky face among them, he reportedly exclaimed "You'll be pledging Jews next!" and stomped out of the house. The current officers immediately stopped Kerwick's participation in the initiation before its completion at the end of the week. Long and I, joined by Bill Robertson, another boarding member from an out-of-town, non-private school background who had been recruited by Long the previous year, declined to attend the banquet honoring the new brothers and instead took a glum Phil Kerwick out to dinner, consoling him and assuring him that we were prepared to fight his exclusion. Phil was tall and good-looking, coffee-colored with a long face and smooth black hair curling only at the edges, given to wearing white V-necked, navy blue-trimmed knit sweaters associated with cricket, which he had played on his native island. He spoke with an accent common to upper-class black West Indians closer to English than to American speech. I was struck that evening by his linking his rejection to persecution of "the South" by "the North" rather than to race.

The alumnus who had made the original complaint was, it so happened, the president of the Toronto Stock Exchange. To me, his reaction, including his anti-Semitism, seemed only too typical of what was to be expected from a big capitalist, confirming my passionately held socialist beliefs. That the active brothers frequently made conventional anti-Semitic remarks accounted considerably for my earlier alienation from the fraternity, a repetition of my previous boarding school experience. The alumnus's reported complaint revealed how out of the question it was for a Jew even to be considered as a possible member of the fraternity, clearly far more so than for a Negro. The city contained a large immigrant Jewish community still somewhat concentrated in "the ghetto"—what sociologists have called the "area of first settlement"—while the second-generation children of the immigrants were enrolling in the university in large numbers. There were, on the other hand, very few nonwhite people living in the city. Another source of my distance from the active brothers was that I had enthusiastically in my freshman year campaigned for the CCF Party (the Canadian socialist party) in a famous federal by-election in which a former Conservative prime minister, Arthur Meighen, was attempting to return to the House of Commons to resume leadership of his party after a long absence from politics. The Liberal government in Ottawa had magnanimously refused to run a candidate against him, but the CCF, very much a minor party, insisted on doing so and their obscure candidate surprised by winning the election, the beginning of the party's rise to political prominence in the next few years in several provinces. Some of my fraternity brothers were active in driving Tory voters to the polls in their parents' cars, so my involvement on the other side hardly improved my relations with them. No one can have been surprised that I opposed the action against Kerwick.

At the next chapter meeting, Long, Robertson, and I insisted that since Kerwick had originally been unanimously accepted and had undergone most of the initiation, he should be welcomed as a full member in accordance with fraternity rules. A majority, including most of the newly initiated members, supported us. The outvoted minority led by the presiding officers claimed that the required unanimous vote for Kerwick was now lacking despite the original vote weeks earlier to pledge him; there was a vote to postpone a final decision. We were joined in our determination to fight for Kerwick's full acceptance by another brother, Jimmy Kelliher, also a boarder in the house though a "legacy" from a conventional private school background. The boarders, including Kerwick, living in close everyday contact, inevitably became friends.

The four of us decided to continue the fight by communicating with the university authorities and with older prominent alumni of the chapter to ask them if they approved of what was clearly a case of flagrant racial discrimination at a time when the nation was at war with a vicious racist enemy. We then hoped be able to confront the active brothers with the support for Kerwick of other important adult authorities leading to a decisive vote to admit him to membership. Telephone calls and in a few cases office visits were made. Victor Long, our informal leader, visited the president of the university. The premier of the province George Drew, later the leader of the federal Conservative Party and High Commissioner to London, happened to be a former member of the fraternity chapter and was telephoned. The president of the university expressed his opposition to racial discrimination, but said he could do nothing since the university neither recognized nor approved of Greek-letter fraternities and hence had no power to regulate them. Premier Drew asked if the rejected candidate was physically Negroid in appearance; told that he was, Drew declared that a good thing since the man could not unexpectedly become the father of "a black baby." He then proclaimed his strong opposition to racial discrimination. I visited, in his downtown office, Clifford Sifton, another former member of the local chapter and the publisher of a chain of prominent newspapers, most of them in Western Canada. He eloquently denounced all forms of racial discrimination and referred to the ideals animating the war against Nazi Germany. I also spoke over the telephone to a distant relative, another alumnus of the chapter and the owner of a local liquor distillery. I have probably forgotten still other alumni to whom we may have appealed, but we encountered none who did not at least in principle support our position and congratulate us on our youthful idealism.

When we reported this at the next chapter meeting we were accused of having violated the oath of secrecy regarding internal fraternity affairs. We responded that we were upholding a much higher principle. The officers had not been inactive: the chapter's alumni association held the mortgage on the house and on learning what had happened threatened to evict the fraternity if Phil Kerwick became a member. An appeal for resolution of the conflict had been made to the fraternity's permanent headquarters in New York City and its director had agreed to address us at the next chapter meeting. Delta Kappa Epsilon, founded in the eighteenth century at Yale, was one of the oldest and largest Greek-letter fraternities in North America, with chapters at most major universities in the United States and Canada. Locally, it was not especially prominent compared to several others that recruited athletes or campus politicians.

There was a good deal of informal discussion and argument over the next few weeks. The threat to the mortgage on the chapter house did not go unmentioned yet was not the main argument for now rejecting Kerwick after having initially accepted him. The brothers opposed to his membership insisted to a man that he was a fine fellow whom they would love to have as a brother but that his membership might discourage other less enlightened students from pledging to the fraternity. We predictably replied that such prejudiced students were in any event undesirable. When asked why this had not been a consideration at the time of their original unanimous vote, Kerwick's opponents waffled and occasionally suggested that the alumni elders must possess greater worldly wisdom to which we ought to defer. The president of the chapter, whom I had known at private school, asked me if I would at least concede that my attitude was rare and unconventional. I told him defiantly that it was his and the senior brothers' attitude that would prove to be rare and unpopular in the new world a'coming after the war.

After a few weeks the international director, a middle-aged man from the fraternity's permanent offices in Manhattan, spoke at our next chapter meeting. He proclaimed that there was a vital, even sacred, bond among the enormous number of fraternity members that endured long after they had graduated and embarked on important careers. If any brother, whether active or not, objected to a proposed new member, his objection should be honored even if there was little likelihood of their ever meeting. The Dekes had many chapters in the South and even during the American Civil War, we were told, brothers on opposite sides had fraternized across the military lines. He pointed out that Southern members would object to a Negro brother and that, whatever our disagreement with that attitude, we should respect and comply with it. Someone must have told him that Kerwick's supporters would resign from the fraternity if Kerwick were not admitted, for we were informed that it was impossible to terminate membership since our names were embossed indelibly on a huge golden scroll at the Manhattan headquarters.

The director may have believed he had some effect on us, but the active brothers certainly knew us well enough to have had little confidence that his words could change our minds. We were hardly likely to be impressed by a man who made a life career out of promoting his college fraternity. The president of the chapter thanked him and then announced, after an affirmative vote, that Phil Kerwick would be invited to continue to live in the house for as long as he wished. As I later argued, this completely invalidated the main reason that had repeatedly been given for rejecting Kerwick: that his membership might discourage future pledges. For, in light of the secrecy oath and the determination to hush-up the present controversy, it would be generally assumed on campus that any undergraduate who lived in the fraternity house must be a member.

Long, Robertson, and I then made short speeches giving our reasons for resigning, ending by unclipping our fraternity pins from our lapels and placing them on the table in front of the dais. I spoke first, invoked the ideals in the name of which we were fighting Nazi Germany, mentioned that I could not face my Jewish friends were I to remain in the fraternity, and sat down feeling a flush of embarrassment at what I thought was my overheated, self-righteous rhetoric. Robertson announced his resignation, then intoned Polonius's words from *Hamlet* : "This above all to thine own self be true and it must follow as the night the day thou canst not then be false to any man," and concluded "that is what I'm doing." The quotation was undoubtedly known to the brothers less out of familiarity with Shakespeare than from a current best-selling novel about the Battle of Britain, *This Above All* by Eric Knight. Long made a soft-spoken, low-key speech that was much more impressive than the others. Finally, Kelliher rambled on emotionally announcing that he intended to remain a member committed to opposing racial prejudice from within.

Nothing at all changed after this denouement. Long, Robertson, Kelliher, and Kerwick himself continued to live in the house, Kelliher eventually replacing Long as house manager after Long finally moved out though just around the block and without ceasing to frequent the frat house. I continued to eat most of my meals there and took a girl to the Christmas dance at which there was a lot of drinking. A keenly disillusioning event for me occurred in the spring. Kelliher, Kerwick, I, and perhaps others, not to my recollection including Long or Robertson, were drinking beer in one of the back bedrooms. Kerwick spoke up bitterly, accusing the four of us who had fought his rejection of having no real personal concern for him, of simply using him "to make a point," treating him in effect as a sacrificial goat on the altar of our own proudly declared high principles, which he now deeply resented. He was not, he insisted, even opposed to racial discrimination as such, for he, his family, and friends at home discriminated against people whose skins were darker than their own. He regarded his rejection as a typical case of "the North" vaunting its superiority over "the South." He declared his ardent support for Juan Peron as a "Southern" leader who refused to accept this humbly and said he would return home and pursue a similar politics. Peron had just come to power in Argentina and was receiving a very negative press in North America for his alleged fascist tendencies and support of Mussolini and Franco, even of Hitler. Neither Kelliher nor I defended ourselves against Kerwick's attack. Indeed, I felt that he was essentially right in thinking that the four of us, most of all myself, had seized upon the occasion to "take a stand" in support of noble but abstract ideals. I was not prepared to concede, however, that we had acted wrongly.

At some later point, my father pointed out that my action in resigning, of which I was inordinately proud, had actually cost me exactly nothing since I placed little value on my fraternity membership in itself and continued to take advantage of the good, inexpensive meals served there and the parties. I resolved to end all contacts with the fraternity. I did so in my senior year and was pleased when, encountering Kelliher one day, he told me that several of the new pledges had embarrassed the older brothers by asking why I never came around, having spotted me on the campus after seeing my photo with that of the current members on the wall of one of the fraternity lounges. After my graduation I did stay at the Deke house on at least two short visits to the city in the summertime when only the nonmembers who rented rooms and the domestic staff of a cook and steward were apt to be present. I now regret having done this, feeling that it compromised my principled rejection of membership in the fraternity.

I told friends about the affair and may have described it in a paper I presented to the university's elite intellectual discussion club, joined only by invitation, of which I was president in my senior year. I chose to speak on the topic of "prejudice" and reported on studies by sociologists, mostly but not exclusively of communities in the American South, documenting the subordination of Negroes. I had not yet read Gunnar Myrdal's famous *An American Dilemma*, published the previous year, which drew heavily on those studies. That same year a flamboyant American anthropologist whose courses I was taking got himself a local radio show on which he presented a fictional account of a native South Sea Islander encountering the strange ways of contemporary Canadians, especially discrimination against him because of his skin color; as anthropologists had often done before, he was repeating the satiric genre of social criticism invented by Montesquieu in *Lettres Persanes*. It is an illusion that, as the news media often seem to suggest, concern over race relations and the oppression of blacks in the United States did not develop until the civil rights movement of the late 1950s and early 1960s. I never thought I was adopting a strikingly deviant position on the Kerwick affair though I welcomed, overeagerly no doubt, the opportunity for principled action.

The director who had addressed us was evidently right about permanent membership in the fraternity, for I received mail from the New York DKE headquarters for some time afterwards. A few years after the war, liberal groups publicly criticized college Greek-letter fraternities for practicing racial and religious discrimination. Several universities, including, if I remember correctly, Columbia where I was a graduate student, responded by abolishing fraternities on their campuses. Indeed, the issue still crops up occasionally today. I received at this time a printed brochure from DKE headquarters intended to counter these attacks. It opened with the rhetorical question of whether the Communist goal of subverting America would not be most effectively promoted by the selection for attack of Greek-letter fraternities. I thought this was so preposterously typical both of fraternities and of aspects of the prevailing *zeitgeist* in the early years of the Cold War that I saved it for several years.

The University of Toronto in its postwar period of rapid expansion bought the chapter house, tore it down, and constructed an institutional building on the site. I am not sure whether this happened before or after I returned to my alma mater for two years as a faculty member a decade after my graduation. I did not ever visit the house again nor have much contact with anyone who had been directly involved in the Kerwick affair. I may have run into Victor Long at some social or cultural event and I used to see Bill Robertson occasionally on the street where he worked for a social work agency near the campus, but we did no more than nod to each other. To this day I don't know whether the chapter survived in another location or what became of any of the participants I had known.

For a long time I thought of writing a story about the affair in an ironic vein like that of two famous stories by Lionel Trilling of encounters between "the liberal imagination" and the resistance to it offered by complex, stubborn realities. My literary ambitions sadly lapsed when I became an academic social scientist and I never got around to this project. The present account is no more than my straightforward recollection of the affair. Nowadays accusations and denials of racism or anti-Semitism are ubiquitous; politicians frequently bring up against their opponents past membership in discriminatory organizations, including college Greek-letter fraternities. The Bushes both father and son, as a matter of fact, belonged to the original DKE chapter at Yale, although it had certainly ceased to discriminate, if it ever had done so, before their membership after the war.

19

Remembering the Rosenbergs and McCarthyism

A fundamental ambiguity made virtually inevitable the controversies raised by the Rosenberg case and the general penalties imposed on Communists and their sympathizers after the Second World War. The Rosenbergs had spied for a friendly ally in wartime, but the law under which they were prosecuted and the prescribed punishments were originally intended to apply to espionage on behalf of a military enemy. The former ally for which they had spied, the Soviet Union, had nevertheless become a national adversary in the absence of any open military conflict; the limited hot war in Korea that broke out just days after the Rosenbergs' indictment was with a nation controlled only indirectly by the Soviet Union. Obviously, legal technicalities were raised by these facts that were invoked unsurprisingly by Communist sympathizers and some absolute civil libertarians to oppose the legal and other penalties to which suspected Communists were subjected.

Sam Roberts' 500-page book is largely based on interviews with David Greenglass that are much more recent and extensive than any previous ones.[1] Unlike the books by Professors Radosh and Schrecker,[2] Roberts' book is not an academic study, nor is he a lawyer like some earlier authors on the case. As his somewhat sensationalist title suggests, he is a professional journalist, a lively writer who tells the story vividly and with many new descriptive details as well as giving Greenglass's fullest account. However, I do not think that Roberts has added anything substantially new bearing directly on "the guilt or innocence" of the Rosenbergs, nor on larger debates about "U.S. foreign policy after World War II and the role of Communists in American politics," to cite the title of a panel discussion of the book at the New School for Social Research on which I have drawn for this commentary whose members were Roberts, Radosh, Schrecker, and myself. None of us argued that the Rosenbergs were innocent. Indeed, it would be hard since the Venona decrypts to find anyone today who did. All of us, however, evidently believed that the case for Ethel Rosenberg's involvement with her husband's espionage was at the very least slight—this is an issue not much discussed at the time though Roberts quotes doubts about it back then, some by people directly involved in the case. All of us rejected the justice and political wisdom of the death penalty, as did Louis Nizer in his well-known book of nearly thirty years ago *The Implosion Conspiracy*, although he thought the guilty verdict a correct one. Does *anyone* today defend the death penalty for the Rosenbergs now that capital punishment itself is rare, illegal in some states, and was briefly outlawed altogether by the Supreme Court?

I have *not* written a book on the subject nor made it a continuing specialty of mine academically or journalistically. I am, however, older—I think—than Roberts, Radosh, and Schrecker, perhaps the only one of the four of us old enough to have followed fairly closely the relevant events at the time of their occurrence, to have known several principals, and to have written about them close to the time in various periodicals. I have also published reviews of some of the later books containing material about them, including an earlier one of Schrecker's. I was present at a number of the relevant public events now of some historical interest, so I shall recount my memories of them rather than strictly reviewing these three recent books on the period.

But before I do that let me mention two points on which I find myself in disagreement with Radosh and Schrecker though they are fairly minor differences for none of us is a partisan of the former Soviet Union, nor an admirer of Senator McCarthy, nor, as previously stated, a believer in the Rosenbergs' utter innocence, if there are indeed any of these left today. I don't agree with Radosh's suggestion that the anti-communist left intellectuals—the anti-Stalinist Left as we liked to call ourselves—had much if any role in reducing the influence of communism in America at large "by the 50s" as opposed simply to the impact of the Cold War itself, nor did we, a much beleaguered minority on the Left even in New York City, greatly influence American foreign policy. The architects of American policy reacted directly against further Soviet expansion, namely, Truman, Marshall, Harriman, Forrestal, Acheson, Kennan, Bohlen,

Loy Henderson, Llewellyn Thompson, Jack Hickerson and a few others. Much as we may regret the limited role of American intellectuals, the Rutgers historian William O'Neill had it exactly right when he wrote that history would have been much the same if the intellectuals and their political journals had never existed. [3] O'Neill specifically mentioned the *Nation,* the *New Republic, Partisan Review, Commentary,* and the *New Leader* in this connection. I remember George Kennan, whose research assistant I was in Princeton in 1951-52, asking me what the American Congress for Cultural Freedom was when he was invited to join it and he was himself certainly an intellectual. To mention only two major policymakers whom I knew well personally, I doubt that he or Dean Acheson, a friend of my family's since the 1920s, had in the 1940s ever heard of Max Eastman, Sidney Hook, Dwight Macdonald, Lionel Trilling, Philip Rahv, or Irving Howe.

Schrecker maintains that there would have been no McCarthyism without the American Communist Party. This may seem obvious, but I doubt it so long as there were presumptive highly placed Soviet sympathizers in the government and society as possible targets of attack. But that is a minor criticism. The proper formulation is: *There would have been no McCarthyism without the Cold War.* And the Cold War was a response to Soviet power in the world. The domestic role and the specific doctrines of the American Communist Party were of little or no relevance to the American government apart from their support for the Soviet Union. McCarthyism was a relatively late fallout from the Cold War in domestic politics, relatively late because that conflict had been going on for three or four years when McCarthy first emerged as the arch Communist-hunter with his famous Wheeling, West Virginia speech in early 1950. The Rosenberg case was made public when the Rosenbergs were indicted just over four months later and may have contributed something to McCarthy's being taken more seriously after that, although I think the outbreak of the Korean war just over a week after their indictment was more important in lending weight and possible credibility to his charges. And, especially after China's intervention, the war was largely responsible for the inflamed atmosphere in which the Rosenbergs were condemned to death less than a month later.

But the Rosenbergs were not the first people to arouse intense and bitter controversy when accused of espionage and/or Communist allegiances, granting that the charge of having stolen atomic secrets was the most serious one to be made: controversies over the cases of William Remington, Judith Coplon, and Alger Hiss all preceded the Rosenbergs, as did the Smith Act prosecutions of the American communist leaders. I strongly object to Schrecker's extension of the label "McCarthyism" to the period *before* McCarthy's 1950 speech insofar as it suggests that earlier charges of Communism and espionage were as groundless as his wild and far-ranging accusations. Today virtually no one regards McCarthy as anything but a noisome demagogue who recklessly and falsely attacked people for alleged communist associations without ever, as is often pointed out, identifying a single person previously unknown for such associations. The term "McCarthyite" has become a synonym for "smearing" people with false charges even in cases having nothing to do with Communism or even with politics. That is not to say that there were not some groundless accusations resembling McCarthy's made in the late 1940s: Schrecker recounts those of J. B. Matthews, Fulton Sheen, and several other right-wingers. The Cold War was a necessary and virtually a sufficient condition for McCarthyism in her larger sense, especially after the unexpected Republican loss of the 1948 election and, as I have already suggested, the later outbreak of limited hot war in Korea. But other political and legal anti-Communist actions were legitimate, appropriate, and in my view necessary or at least unavoidable. Their number includes the most publicized Hiss and Rosenberg cases, publicized because they were widely claimed to be innocent victims of government "frame-ups," the chief claimant in the Rosenberg case being the American Communist Party and its various "front" groups.

It is necessary to distinguish among attitudes towards communism, anti-Communism, the Cold War, McCarthyism, and particular cases of people charged with Soviet sympathies or espionage. Attitudes towards all of these were independently variable though too often retrospectively lumped together as if they always formed a consistent bundle constituting a single point of view.

I became an anti-Communist leftist in my teens in the early 1940s during the Stalin-Hitler pact, much more firmly so, like many others, after reading Arthur Koestler in the last year of the war. It was entirely credible to me from the outset that Remington, Coplon, Hiss, and others might have spied for the Soviet Union. Partly this was because I was living with my parents just a few blocks from the Soviet embassy in Ottawa in early September, 1945 when Igor

Gouzenko defected with a batch of papers detailing Soviet espionage taken from a locked file; his apartment was even closer to our house. He first took the papers to one of the Ottawa newspapers where he was turned away as a crank by a young woman employee whom I knew. (A week or so later she and several other recent University of Toronto graduates in Ottawa including myself went to New York to enroll as graduate students at Columbia.) Gouzenko's documents two days later reached Norman Robertson, the undersecretary of state for external affairs, who showed them to my father, the associate undersecretary—they became the very first people fully to examine them. Robertson and Prime Minister Mackenzie King then flew to Washington, showed them to Lester Pearson, the Canadian Ambassador, who took them to President Truman. The Gouzenko documents named over twenty spies and agents in Canada, mentioned the existence of Soviet espionage rings in the United States and that a high State Department official later identified as probably Alger Hiss was a Soviet agent. Their contents were not made public until February, 1946. Eleven of the Canadians and the physicist Alan Nunn May in Britain were prosecuted and found guilty of espionage, six were judged not guilty, and five were not indicted because of insufficient corroborating evidence.

I had no reason to think that any of those found guilty had been framed: I had at a party in his honor met one of them, the organizer of the Labour-Progressive Party, the renamed Canadian Communist Party, another one worked for my father's department in Ottawa and was involved in the later case of Herbert Norman, a high diplomat accused of having a Communist past, whom I did know well as a family friend, innocent in my view of all but long ago youthful Communist sympathies though he committed suicide when later accused before the McCarran Committee of the U.S. Senate.

I was in the crowd on the steps of Low Library when Columbia awarded an honorary degree to Winston Churchill just after his famous Fulton, Missouri "Iron Curtain" speech in early 1946 from which many people date the beginning of the Cold War. I attended that day or the next a rally in MacCarter Theater to protest the award—as an observer not as a sympathizer since I was what was later called a "premature anti-Communist," meaning an anti-Communist well *before* the Cold War. For this reason, I deliberately did not sit with my friends and fellow graduate students who supported the rally and cheered the speakers, Corliss Lamont, Howard Fast, and Muriel

Rukeyser. I recall being outraged when Fast called Churchill "this vicious war-mongering old man."

I attended, again as an anti-Communist observer, a rally in the old Madison Square Garden organized in connection with the famous 1949 Waldorf Conference opposing American policy towards the Soviet Union at which Henry Wallace, third party presidential candidate the year before, and the Soviet cultural czar Fadayev, were speakers, and Dmitri Shostakovich was introduced as the high point of the meeting. I was also present, this time as a sympathizer, at a public meeting opposing the conference at Freedom House on 44th Street across from Bryant Park at which Americans for Intellectual Freedom, which later became the American branch of the international Congress for Cultural Freedom was organized. Several histories of "the New York intellectuals" date their organization and self-consciousness as a group from this protest, although my impression is that they should be dated from their opposition to the Wallace campaign the year before. Sidney Hook was a major speaker and organizer on both of these occasions.

I attended in the early 1950s, strictly as an observer, a public meeting at the Nassau Inn in Princeton of the Communist-organized Emergency Civil Rights Congress that had for some years defended the "rights" of Communists under attack, including the Rosenbergs, in opposition to the ACLU, which had declined to do so. I remember sitting with the one full-time employee of the American Committee for Cultural Freedom and our jointly deploring the pro-Communist or neutralist biases of the speakers.

On the afternoon of June 18, 1953, I went with my mother to the public hearing room of the Supreme Court to await the Court's decision on Justice Douglas's stay of the execution of the Rosenbergs scheduled for the following evening. The court had adjourned until October, but had been summoned back into emergency session by Attorney General Herbert Brownell to adjudicate Justice Douglas's stay order. Louis Nizer has reported that huge crowds sought admission to the hearing room—I don't recall that, for my mother had been supplied by Justice Frankfurter, a family friend, with regular tickets of admission. We sat there for several hours—I remember being introduced by another family friend to one of the Rosenbergs' lawyers, John Finerty, after being told by him proudly of Finerty's past role in defending Sacco and Vanzetti and Tom Mooney. I also recall a few rows ahead of us Theodore Roosevelt's daughter, Alice

Roosevelt Longworth, expressing her hopes that the stay would be vacated and the execution duly carried out. My mother eventually left to prepare for dinner that evening and soon afterward the Court was adjourned without a decision.

As I walked out of the Supreme Court building, I encountered a young woman with whom I had gone to school in Geneva, Switzerland before the war. She was half-English and half-French and, perfectly bilingual, had during the war been parachuted by the British Secret Service into occupied France and had written a book about her experiences. I knew that she and her husband, who was the UN correspondent for a Paris newspaper, were strong Communist supporters, "robbing the party of dues " as we used to say. She had come down from New York with the National Committee to Secure Justice for the Rosenbergs. Waving her arms—her gestures were all very French—she went into a tirade about how this was "America's Dreyfus Case—fascism had come to America," and so on. I managed to get out that while I believed the Rosenbergs to be guilty, I was strongly opposed to their being sentenced to death. Over twenty years later when Anne-Marie was no longer a Communist sympathizer, I recall her on a visit to New York laughingly showing me in the Nizer book what she said was a photograph of herself weeping after the execution with her face hidden in her arms on a table in the company of the Rosenbergs' lawyer Emmanuel Bloch.

I then walked down the steps of the Court and Bloch came out just behind me attracting a dozen or so newspaper photographers who rushed up flashing their light-bulb cameras. As I reached the bottom of the steps a big black car drew up on Constitution Avenue and a well-groomed blonde middle-aged lady alighted from the drivers' seat and asked me what was going on, I told her and she expostulated "Those lousy bastards! I hope they fry! The chair is too good for them!" I told her I didn't agree and she screamed, "You're just the kind of person we don't need in this country," and got back into her car. I was shaken by the irrationality of both sides on the case and said so at dinner that evening, but it was dismissed by my father as unimportant with a wave of his hand. He was, I should mention, the Canadian ambassador, working long hours at the time as Canadian representative to the ongoing Korean peace talks and he was already suffering from the high blood pressure from which he died less than a year later.

About thirty years later, not quite twenty years ago, I went with Ron Radosh at his invitation to a Columbia University Seminar at which he presented the findings of his *The Rosenberg File* in the presence of the best friend of one of the Rosenbergs' two sons. Before the seminar we had dinner at Butler Hall sitting at a table for four with Ron, his co-author Joyce Milton, and Victor Navasky, the only time I have ever met the editor then of the *Nation.* I'm afraid I don't recall much of what transpired at the seminar. Not long after this, I attended a panel discussion at Town Hall at which Ron and Joyce debated Walter and Miriam Schneir on the Rosenberg case.[4] Ron telephoned me afterwards to complain that my friend Irving Howe, sitting in a front row, hadn't praised him for his presentation though agreeing with him strongly. I said Irving was just not an effusive person and he had doubtless been shocked by the large audience's support for the Schneirs and the Rosenbergs at this relatively late date, my reaction also up in the balcony after receiving hostile glares from my neighbors when I applauded Ron's speech. I remember Ron walking to the front of the platform and shouting, "You have wasted your lives!" to the booing audience. In his new book, Ron complains that Irving showed little interest in printing him on the case in *Dissent* nor did Michael Harrington give him a forum at the DSOC (Democratic Socialist Organizing Committee); Ron attributes this to a supposed decline in the anti-Communism of such onetime anti-Communist stalwarts, also mentioning disagreements with them over former fellow-travelers in the 1990s when he left the editorial board of *Dissent.* This strikes me as ridiculous: neither Irving nor Mike were academic historians and they just didn't think this once controversial thirty-year-old case worth rehashing yet again when doubters of the Rosenbergs' guilt were scarcely a major political presence, nor *after* the collapse of the Soviet bloc did the issue of previous allegiances of other people and Third World regimes seem terribly vital.

The Rosenbergs were not prosecuted until June, 1950 when the Cold War had been underway for at least three or four years. Their prosecution came a few months after Senator Joseph McCarthy had made his famous Wheeling speech that first won him notoriety for denouncing Communists in the government and it may have added to his eventually being taken seriously though, as previously indicated, I think the Korean War probably played a greater role. Having thought the Rosenbergs guilty at the time, I have not changed my mind since, though the books by Roberts, Radosh, and Schrecker, as well as by earlier writers, have led me to question more fully the verdict against Ethel. As for the larger context, having been from the very beginning what came to be known invidiously—in a label coined originally by one of my own graduate school teachers, C. Wright Mills—as a "Cold War liberal," I have not changed my mind about the case. Though I tended to play it down at the time, I was certainly influenced by having a worms-eye, as it were, "insider's" view of American foreign policy as a result of my father's service as Canadian Ambassador to the United States from 1946 to 1953. He held this post for such an unusually long period because he had been a personal friend of Dean Acheson since first serving in Washington in the 1920s and Acheson was either Undersecretary to George Marshall or Secretary of State during most of this period. The Achesons were old family friends and I several times had the opportunity of hearing Dean discuss foreign policy issues informally over ubiquitous Washington cocktails. Through my father's connections, I obtained in 1951-52 employment as Research Assistant to George Kennan at the Institute for Advanced Study in Princeton, the first year that Kennan was away from the State Department on a Ford Foundation grant before being named Ambassador to the Soviet Union by President Truman in the spring of 1952 which ended our project. Unsurprisingly, I regarded the attacks by Senator McCarthy and his sympathizers on Acheson and to a lesser extent on Kennan as "soft on Communism" as utterly preposterous and was greatly disturbed by them. They were, of course, if any two men were, the major architects of the American postwar policy of resisting the further expansion of the Soviet Union, "present at the creation," as Acheson put it in his memoir, meaning the creation of the Cold War.

Roberts' book together with Radosh's *The Rosenberg File* provides pretty much the full story of the Rosenberg case. Radosh's new book is inevitably slighter, for it is a memoir of what it was like to start out as a "red diaper baby," his own self-description, and undergo eventual disillusion. The book is essentially an *apologia pro vita sua,* informative and often enthralling but too disposed to exaggerate the numbers and influence of past Communist sympathizers and anti-anti-Communists well into the 1980s while criticizing non-historians such as Howe, Harrington, and other *Dissent* writers who doubted the political importance of dwelling on this ancient history so late in the day, the more so after the dissolution of the

Soviet bloc over a decade ago. Despite her insensitivity to the genuine moral indignation felt by past anti-Communists scandalized by the blindness and partisanship of so many prominent intellectuals, Schrecker's book is a fairly complete record of the condemnations and prosecutions of Communists from the 1920s through the 1950s and the effect of the issue on American culture. All three books can be recommended subject to the qualifications I have made.

Notes

1. Sam Roberts, *The Brother: The Untold Story of Atomic Spy David Greenglass and How He Sent His Sister, Ethel Rosenberg, to the Electric Chair* (New York: Random House, 2001), 543 pp.
2. Ronald Radosh, *Commies: A Journey Through the Old Left, the New Left, and the Leftover Left* (San Francisco, CA: Encounter Books, 2001), 216 pp.; Ellen Schrecker, *Many Are The Crimes: McCarthyism in America* (Princeton, NJ: Princeton University Press, 1998), 573 pp.
3. William L. O'Neill, *A Better World—The Great Schism: Stalinism and the American Intellectuals* (New York: Simon & Schuster, 1982), 447 pp.
4. Walter and Miriam Schneir, *Invitation to an Inquest,*

20

Fated to be a Professor?

It hardly seems surprising that I can't remember seriously contemplating attending any university other than the University of Toronto or that I should have gone on to become a professor. My family line includes professors going back four generations, most of the first three associated with the University of Toronto. A great-grandfather on my mother's side was a classicist, a Protestant immigrant from Ireland who became the second president of the university. He even has a Toronto street named after him, although McCaul Street has been in a shabby, deteriorated downtown neighborhood for as long as I can remember. Both of my grandfathers were prominent professors at the University of Toronto. One was a classicist recruited from Oxford by McCaul, who married McCaul's daughter, became Principal of University College, the largest liberal arts college, served briefly as acting president of the university, and has a building, Hutton House on the University College campus, named after him. My paternal grandfather, George Wrong, was the founder of the university's history department and the creator of Canadian history as a scholarly discipline. He wrote the textbooks on Canadian and British history that were used for many years in the Ontario public schools. I remember as a small child tradespeople recalling this, not always fondly, and making the inevitable hackneyed jokes about the Wrong name.

George Wrong's oldest son married one of the four daughters of a famous master of Balliol College, Oxford, and himself became a don at Magdalen College, publishing several books on Canadian history before dying young, when still in his thirties, though not before fathering six children. My father taught history at the University of Toronto for several years before joining the newly created Canadian Department of External Affairs along with his fellow junior member of the University of Toronto history department, Lester

Bowles ("Mike") Pearson, who won the Nobel Peace Prize in 1956 and became Prime Minister of Canada in the 1960s. My father and his siblings produced a total of eleven children. Of the four males, two became history professors, one (me) a sociology professor, and the other a medical doctor and professor who retired recently from the chair in Internal Medicine at the University of London. Of the seven women, one became a history professor in Scotland, one a private school teacher of Latin and Greek in Washington, D.C., and one a teacher with a doctorate in history in women's studies at a Quebec community college. Another of the seven, my sister, is a psychotherapist with a doctorate in psychology, two others are medical doctors, and one is a journalist in Montreal.

All this is rather daunting, not to say humbling, if one fancies that one has struck out on one's own in independent fashion. Perhaps I was fated to become a professor no matter what, but in choosing the identity of "intellectual" when still in high school with no thought of turning it to occupational advantage I had embraced a secular "calling" or "vocation" that was universalistic in reach and aspiration, even though it is now evident that in its combination of left political concerns and literary modernism it was very much a unique product of the fourth, fifth, and sixth decades of the twentieth century.

Identity involves the acceptance of both a label applied to oneself and the cherishing of an aspiration to uphold, affirm, and justify the label. It is not just passive acquiescence in how other people define one, as is sometimes at least implied by "labeling" theorists of deviance, but it is something striven for, a project or *pour-soi* in Sartre's sense that only delusively becomes an *en-soi,* or a closed and fixed result of achievement. Identity in this sense includes what Freud called "ego-ideal," as Erik Erikson has contended in his famous elaboration of the concept.

I decided to become an intellectual in rebellion against and dissociation from the values of the elite preparatory school where my parents sent me as a boarder very much against my will. I don't quite mean that I decided one day I wanted to be an intellectual the way small children want to be firemen, engine-drivers, or professional athletes. I was nevertheless aware of the label as referring to a social and psychological type and it had a positive aura for me. Essentially, I assumed two subordinate identities that together made up pretty much what it meant to be an intellectual in that time and place: political radicalism and the ambition to be a writer. Until quite recently, an intellectual meant someone with literary and left-wing political interests as these were reflected and represented in such journals as the *Nation,* the *New Republic,* the *New Statesman and Nation*, and the *Canadian Forum,* to name only the journals, the so-called "liberal weeklies," that I began to read near my sixteenth birthday. I also made the acquaintance of more specialized periodicals like the *New International,* the *New Directions* annuals, *Penguin New Writing,* and *Partisan Review* (though I did not read this at all regularly until my senior year at college). In Canada, incidentally, one had easy access to British as well as American publications, including books and journals that were not available for sale or distribution in the United States such as many Penguin and Pelican and Left Book Club books and pamphlets which converted me to socialism.

Russell Jacoby is quite right that intellectuals of this sort are no longer around. He is also quite right, I think, in blaming the academicization of all intellectual and non-commercial literary life for this result. I do not agree, however, with his label "public intellectual" for the disappearing breed, a label that seems, unfortunately, to have rather caught on. The intellectuals of yore, their identities forged out of left-wing political and modernist literary interests, did not see themselves as addressing a wide public. They wrote for one another just as contemporary academics write for their colleagues, as Jacoby complains. That yesterday's intellectuals wrote better and reasoned more sharply and less pretentiously than today's professors is in part, but only in part, due to the baleful influence of the academy and its intellectual routines.

In enrolling at the University of Toronto I made a point of separating myself from my Upper Canada College classmates by entering the large nondenominational arts college, a third of whose students were Jewish. I had already acquired a veritable philo-Semitic outlook, for in Geneva (where I lived for two years in my early teens) most of my friends had been American Jews from New York City or German Jews on the first leg of permanent migration from Nazi Germany. There was an awful lot of anti-Semitism of the genteel variety in Toronto at this time, against which I rebelled.

Why did I take up sociology? It used to attract intellectuals of my orientation because of the seeming boundlessness and generality of its subject matter—one recalls Dan Bell as a graduate student announcing to a senior professor that he was a "specialist in generalizations." Then there was the link to social problems, reform, and, thus, the political left. The old association between socialism and sociology going back to the 1830s with Saint-Simon as the father of both still had resonance in the 1940s. One wonders how the death of socialism as a utopian project, a *Weltanschauung*, a total outlook rooted in faith and passionate commitment will affect sociology and the kind of people attracted to it in the future. Of course an interest in solving social problems in a more limited, applied way will continue to sustain some sociology for as long as we have social problems. At the University of Toronto in the 1940s, the majority of students who majored in sociology, most of them women, thought of it as a preparation for a possible career in social work.

Why, since I had not given up wanting to be a writer and edited and contributed to the college literary magazine, did my socialism dictate my choice of major? To want to be a writer back then was quite distinct from wanting to be a literary scholar or critic. Most aspiring writers in those benighted or blessed days before the Yale School and deconstruction had no thought of becoming critics: the leading critics were often also leading novelists and/or poets like T.S. Eliot, Allen Tate, and Robert Penn Warren, who were usually not academics, or were just beginning to enter the universities, particularly if they were not very successful as creative writers.

I had become sufficiently interested in sociology by the end of my senior year to decide—rather unimaginatively, I now think—to do graduate work in it. Sociology was then much more closely associated with anthropology. The director of studies in sociology at Toronto—there was no independent department—was C.W.M. Hart, an Australian student of Radcliffe-Brown. Several of our circle of interested, intellectual students who wanted to continue in graduate work were attracted to anthropology, including Elizabeth Bott and Erving Goffman who both went to Chicago as most aspiring Canadian sociologists did at that time largely thanks to Everett Hughes. I and a couple of others went to Columbia instead. For me, the attractions of New York City, where I had visited friends some years before, were powerful. Also, Robert K. Merton had spoken at Toronto on manifest and latent functions that spring, which was an added incentive for going to Columbia. I had, of course, no notion at the time that leadership in sociology was about to pass from Chicago to Columbia—largely owing to Merton—just at that moment.

Another attraction of New York was that in my senior year I had read *Partisan Review,* Arthur Koestler, and George Orwell, identifying as a result with the small but highly select group of literary highbrows who also affirmed anti-Stalinist left political views. I recall that my very first week in New York I picked up a copy of Dwight Macdonald's *politics* at the newsstand in front of the 116th Street subway station at Columbia, encountering in it the names of people I would later meet: Macdonald himself, Irving Howe, Louis Clair (Lewis Coser), C. Wright Mills, Paul Goodman, and Lionel Abel.

Robert S. Lynd was the left-wing voice in the Columbia sociology department at this time. (Mills had only recently joined the department and was not full time.) Under Lynd's auspices, a graduate student Socialist Club was organized and I became its first, and it turned out, only president. Our very first public meeting in early 1946 was a panel discussion of the proposition that the Soviet Union was a true socialist society and therefore the only hope for peace and progress in the world. Lynd's son Staughton, a precocious high school senior who later was prominent in the New Left of the 1960s, affirmed this statement and I opposed it, insisting that the Soviet Union was a totalitarian and imperialist despotism little if at all better than the just-defeated Nazi Germany. The audience, including Lynd Senior, did not much like my view with one exception who spoke up for me from the floor—Nathan Glazer. Nat later drew me into reviewing for the *New Leader* and *Commentary* where he was an editor. Politically involved graduate students were split between the largest group that upheld the prevailing pro-Soviet views of most American liberals and looked to Lynd on the faculty for support, and a smaller, much more highly intellectual, anti-Stalinist, neo-Trotskyist group that included Glazer, Rose Coser, Monroe Berger, and myself, rather drawn to Mills, who published fairly often in anti-Stalinist left journals like *politics, Commentary,* and *Partisan Review.*

Merton and Paul Lazarsfeld were just beginning in 1945–1947—my years of full-time residency—to establish their ascendancy over the sociology department. The "unity of theory and research" that was the goal of the sociology they promoted, with research meaning survey research in the tradition Lazarsfeld established at the Bureau of Applied Social Research, was not yet as dominant as it became in the 1950s. This was not at all the kind of sociology, needless to say, that appealed to my sort of intellectual. I had little or no interest in becoming a specialized expert or a technician in possession of various certified research skills or even an academic man confined to a limited field of knowledge. I felt, consequently, more and more identified with the political and cultural world of the "New York Intellectuals," as they have now come to be labeled, and alienated from the positivistic or science-building claims of sociology in general and sociology at Columbia in particular.

But I had to earn a living. By this time, I am sorry to say, I had given up my earlier literary aspirations. I wistfully considered the possibility of becoming an editor or an intellectual journalist on one of the general political-cultural journals in the ambience of the New York intellectuals. In the meantime, I held several bottom-level teaching jobs in sociology departments and desperately wrestled with what William James called the "Ph.D. Octopus." I made several abortive attempts to write dissertations on political and literary subjects reflecting my "real" interests, and, or so I thought, succeeded only in convincing in quick succession Merton, Mills, and Leo Lowenthal of my hopeless inadequacy as a prospective scholar or scientist. Finally I turned to a specialized and enclaved field that I had encountered more or less by accident in the course of teaching, namely, demography, and managed to complete a dissertation under the direction of Kingsley Davis and earn the degree a full eleven years after first enrolling as a graduate student in the fall of 1945. I joined a department (Brown) that was trying to develop a graduate program in demography and eventually received tenure there.

I continued to write fairly regularly for journals associated with the New York intellectuals, *Commentary, Dissent, Partisan Review,* and *The New Leader,* through the 1950s and 1960s. Before I had tenure, at least two chairmen urged me to desist from this writing, assuring me it would do my career no good at all and perhaps even prejudice my chances for tenure. I did not follow their advice. My view of the reigning tendencies in sociology, both empirical and theoretical, continued to be highly critical. In common with a few others, I saw the work of Mills and David Riesman in the 1950s as a beacon of what sociology might be, but, alas, was not.

Mills's *The Sociological Imagination,* which I read in manuscript, was a book I would dearly love to have written myself. Barrington Moore, Jr.'s criticisms of functionalism and ahistorical theorizing in sociology also greatly appealed to me. I contributed my own mite to the onslaught on dominant trends in sociology with a much-reprinted 1961 article called "The Oversocialized Conception of Man in Modern Sociology." These critical assessments of the major trends in sociology succeeded, of course, in disestablishing so-called establishment sociology by at least the end of the 1960s. There resulted the pluralism of diverse approaches that survives to the present day. It is difficult to recall today how bold and embattled those of us attacking what is often called "positivistic" but I prefer to call "science-building" sociology felt back in the 1950s—the "humanistic underground" as I once called us, though I no longer much like that label.

Back to the complex and usually misunderstood relation between political ideology and sociology: the critics of sociology in the 1950s attacked from, or their arguments were at least highly congruent with, a broadly left perspective. They raised the old Lynd "Knowledge for What?" question. They called attention to the relative neglect of change, conflict, power, coercion, and inequality in mainstream sociology. Yet, even the most directly political and radical of the critics, such as Mills, were not advocates of violence nor even revolutionary Marxists. Radicalization came only in the late 1960s when the New Left student movement swept over the campuses in opposition to the war in Vietnam and American foreign policy—for that matter, American society—in general.

I had little sympathy with these developments with which "the sixties" tend nowadays to be primarily identified. Why or why not? My politics were by no means shaped solely by my association and identification with the anti-Stalinism of the New York intellectuals. That, to be sure, might have been sufficient to put me in opposition to the New Left and even to turn me into a neoconservative in the 1970s or 1980s, like a number of prominent old anti-Stalinist intellectuals. But, I became neither a New Left supporter nor a neoconservative. The main reason, I think, was because I saw the world at large and foreign policy, especially the Cold War, in particular from a somewhat different angle. My father served as Canadian ambassador to the United States from 1946 to 1953, the formative years of the Cold War. He held this post for so long because he had been a personal friend of Dean Acheson, secretary of state from 1949 to 1953, since the 1920s when he began his diplomatic career with a ten-year stint in Washington, where I, in effect, grew up. So, I had the benefit of a kind of worm's-eye view of history in the making and knew, in addition to Acheson, several of the top foreign policy officials in the Truman administration. I also worked in Princeton for a year in the early 1950s as a research assistant to

George Kennan, the prime creator of the American policy of "containing" the Soviet Union.

A result of these experiences and exposures was that I was from the very beginning of the Cold War, a bona fide example of what Mills with invidious intent labeled a "Cold War liberal." And I remained one until the Cold War ended in 1989-1991. Ultimately, I think my attitude toward the Cold War had roots going back to my two years of early adolescence spent in Geneva on the eve of the Second World War when the Munich crisis became the first historical event that I remember as having an impact on my own life. I recall vividly my mother's outrage over the abandonment of Czechoslovakia—my father almost certainly shared her view, but his official position obliged him to keep his opinions to himself. What I acquired was the firm belief that resistance to aggression by expansionist dictators was right in itself and more likely to avoid all-out war than acquiescing in it. My support of the United States and NATO in the Cold War kept me from joining the New Left radicals in the 1960s and my liberalism kept me from becoming a neoconservative in the 1970s. I did not, to be sure, support the war in Vietnam, but I never regarded it as an inherently immoral enterprise and I was inclined to dislike the anti-war protest movement as much or more than the war itself. I always regarded Soviet power as the adversary, not some noxious ideology of "communism," and I agreed with Kennan's view of the necessary limits to the policy of "containment" that he gave its name.

The New Left struck me from the outset as the end of something rather than as a new beginning, as a pathetic willed and thoroughly histrionic attempt to revive a set of political and ideological impulses going back to the nineteenth century that had no future. I remember seeing a student with a raised red fist stenciled on the back of his canvas jacket wearing a T-shirt with "power to the people" emblazoned on it. I burst out laughing—it seemed to me a species of play-acting that could not possibly be taken seriously. To me, the 1930s were to the 1960s as the first time tragedy, the second time farce, in Marx's famous aphorism. With all the sound and fury between 1968 and 1970, I did come to wonder whether I was not perhaps missing something, whether the huge shadows cast by Hitler, the Second World War, Stalinism, and the early Cold War did not prevent me from seeing some vital historical meaning in the ferment of the 1960s. But, of course, I turned out to be right in my initial reaction.

New York University is in the heart of Greenwich Village where so many innovative cultural and political movements are born and their adherents live. The amorphousness of sociology as a field ensures that it will attract a probably disproportionate number of students attuned to *le dernier cri* in culture and politics, searchers for the true meaning of life, and *engagés* and *enragés* determined to change the world. Inevitably, we had more than our share of these in the New York University sociology department; the waves of the 1960s virtually inundated us. After fighting the battles of the day on the issues of the day in the department during the late 1960s and early 1970s, we had to go through the whole thing all over again roughly a decade later when a group of radical students transferred from the New School—also in the Village—after New York State took away its accreditation to award the Ph.D. degree in sociology. This time, though, the faculty was united and the students got nowhere.

Until just a very few years ago, one heard from the lips of students Marxist clichés that one had, after a brief youthful flirtation with them, rejected, believing one had outgrown them intellectually years before. I first read Marx in high school. As the ferment of the 1960s subsided in the later 1970s, its main effect on sociology was the absorption of Marx into the pantheon of major theorists and the emergence of Marxist schools within the discipline. That previously unknown or neglected Marxist thinkers of the 1930s were now read—Lukàcs, Gramsci, some of the writings of the Frankfurt School—was certainly a good thing. And insofar as Marx had previously suffered neglect, a serious oversight was rectified. But most of the Marxist theorizing and debates within sociology struck me as tortuous, ponderously scholastic echoes of the crisper, more focused and politically relevant discussions that I had read long ago in old Shachtmanite publications and in *politics, Partisan Review,* and the early issues of *Dissent*. This was particularly true of the interminable disquisitions on the role of the state, which have recently been definitively and I hope finally exposed as vacuous and tautological by Axel van den Berg, a young Canadian sociologist of Dutch origin at McGill.

I apologize for repeating a bon mot I've used before: the Western university has always been the graveyard of dead causes, both religious and political. And Marxism cannot be abstracted from its appeal as an ideology, a political faith, and guide to action. It is hard to think of any cases of Marxist thinkers who have happened to be politically conservative or defenders of capitalism. (No, Joseph Schumpeter does not qualify.) The events of 1989-91 probably mean that the process of incorporating Marxism into academic sociology has come to an end. Yes, I know that Marx might not have, even probably would not have, approved of the deeds of Stalin or even of Lenin. But Max Weber wrote in 1919—to Lukàcs—that the Russian Revolution would prove to be a disaster that would discredit socialism for a hundred years—surely the most accurate historical prediction ever made by a major sociologist. Yet, if the October Revolution had not happened, it is likely that Marxism would have long since become primarily of historical interest as the social democratic parties originally inspired by it became the moderate, reformist agencies operating within the confines of capitalism that they have now become. Enough, I sometimes think that I have wasted far too much intellectual energy arguing with Marxists and about Marxism during at least two periods of my life separated by several decades.

But that is because Marxism has been at least one major tendency of the "short" twentieth century that is now over, having begun in historical as distinct from chronological time in 1914 and ended in 1991. Apart from literature, all of my major intellectual interests within and at the margins of sociology have been closely tied to the cataclysmic events, mostly disastrous, of this century. All of the writers and thinkers who have most influenced me at one time or another and even served as what we like to call "role-models," have been deeply implicated in the issues and experiences of the century: Erich Fromm, Edmund Wilson, George Orwell, Arthur Koestler, Max Weber, Hannah Arendt, David Riesman, George Kennan, George Lichtheim, Isaiah Berlin, Raymond Aron, Leszek Kolakowski, and Milan Kundera. An uncle of mine whom I never knew was killed on July 1, 1916, the first day of the Battle of the Somme, perhaps the real date when what Aron called "the century of total war" began. Two weeks later my father, only twenty-two years old, went into action on the Somme as an upgraded junior officer in the British Army and his later choice of a diplomatic career was shaped by the experience. Yes, there is a juncture between biography and history! Total wars, social revolutions aimed at total transformations of the social order, even "the democratic class struggle" as the dominant theme of our politics, are now over, although they continue to loom large in our sociology as the backwash from their last gasp in the 1960s. Who knows just what will replace them?

Index